Purple Haze

PHILOSOPHY OF MIND SERIES

Series Editor
David J. Chalmers, University of Arizona

Purple Haze

The Puzzle of Consciousness

Joseph Levine

OXFORD
UNIVERSITY PRESS

OXFORD
UNIVERSITY PRESS

Oxford   New York
Auckland Bangkok Buenos Aires   Cape Town   Chennai
Dar es Salaam Delhi Hong Kong   Istanbul   Karachi Kolkata
Kuala Lumpur Madrid Melbourne   Mexico City Mumbai   Nairobi
São Paulo   Shanghai   Taipei Tokyo Toronto

Copyright © 2001 by Oxford University Press, Inc.

Published by Oxford University Press, Inc.,
198 Madison Avenue, New York, New York 10016

www.oup.com

First issued as an Oxford University Press paperback, 2004

Oxford is a registered trademark of Oxford University Press.

Library of Congress Cataloging-in-Publication Data
Levine, Joseph, 1952–
Purple haze : the puzzle of consciousness / Joseph Levine.
p. cm. — (Philosophy of mind series)
Includes bibliographical references and index.
ISBN 0-19-513235-1; 0-19-517308-2 (pbk.)
1. Qualia. 2. Consciousness. I. Title. II. Series.
BD418.3 .L48   2000
128'.2—dc21   99-087912

9 8 7 6 5 4 3 2 1

Printed in the United States of America
on acid-free paper

In Memory of
Jack and Ettabelle Levine

Acknowledgments

My biggest debt is to the two philosophers who have been my constant philosophical companions since I began graduate school, and whose influence extends throughout my work: Louise Antony and Georges Rey. (Of course this is not to say they agree with most of what I have to say in this book—quite the contrary.) I also need to give a special thanks to three people who provided me with extensive written comments on an earlier draft of the manuscript: David Chalmers, Janet Levin, and, again, Georges Rey. I received very helpful comments as well from David Auerbach, Katalin Balog, Alex Byrne, John Carroll, W.R. Carter, Doug Jesseph, Barry Loewer, and Daniel Stoljar. In addition, I have benefitted enormously from conversations with the following philosophers on the topics addressed in this book: Ned Block, Owen Flanagan, Jerry Fodor, Güven Güzeldere, C.L. Hardin, David Hilbert, Terry Horgan, Brian Loar, Bill Lycan, Brian McLaughlin, Andrew Melnyk, Martine Nida-Rumelin, Michael Pauen, Michael Ridge, Bob Van Gulick, Stephen Yablo, and, of course, all those mentioned above (again, especially Louise Antony and Georges Rey). An additional special thanks goes to Doug Jesseph for suggesting the title.

Various discussions in the book draw on previously published work, but only in one instance is an entire article reproduced in the text. Sections 5.2 and 5.3 come from Levine (1994), and I thank the publishers of *Philosophical Topics* for permission to use it here.

The bulk of the manuscript was written with the support of a fellowship from the American Council of Learned Societies, for which I am grateful. I also want to acknowledge support for finishing the manuscript from the North Carolina State University College of Humanities and Social Sciences Summer Stipend fund.

I want to thank Louise, Paul, and Rachel for their emotional support and generally for being the people they are and giving me the kind of family I have. Finally, I want to acknowledge a very special debt to Jimi Hendrix: he taught me what it's like to want to kiss the sky.

March, 2000   J. L.
Raleigh, North Carolina

Contents

Purple Haze

Introduction
"Purple Haze"

Why is there a mind-body problem? This book is an attempt to answer that question. It is not my intention to present a solution to the problem. On the contrary, I hope to demonstrate that there really is a problem here, and that we are far short of the conceptual resources required for its solution. In this chapter I will briefly, and without much argument, present my case. In the chapters that follow I will try to convince you of its merit.

When I think of what's distinctive of mental phenomena, of my mental life, three features stand out. First, I am a rational, intelligent creature. I do not merely react to my environment in a reflexive, *mindless* way, but rather I plan, deliberate (at least on occasion), and generally try to act in a way that is rationally connected to the attainment of my goals. We might add, as a part of this feature, the very fact that I have goals. Objects that clearly lack minds, such as tables and chairs, or even plants and sufficiently lower animals, do not, I presume, share this feature. Their behavior, if such it could be called, is totally governed by—is predictable and explicable in terms of—mindless laws of nature. They do not set goals and then deliberate how to achieve them.

The second distinctive feature is actually included in the first, but it deserves special notice. In order to conceive a plan and act on it, one must be able, of course, to conceive in the first place. That is, one must have the capacity to represent the situation one is in, to represent possible courses of action, and then to intelligently manipulate these representations so as to derive a representation of the course of action to be pursued. Rationality thus has two crucial aspects: the ability to represent, and the ability to intelligently manipulate representations in the light of their contents, what it is they represent. There is presumably nothing in a table or chair that *means* anything, that is about anything. It just is. But in me there are states, or entities, that have meaning; they are about the chair, for instance.

The third feature that seems distinctive about mental phenomena is that much of mental life involves conscious experience. I don't just react to the world, nor even do I just act on it; I experience it. When I look about my study as I work I see the green leaves of the avocado plant, the red diskette case next to my computer, I feel the breeze from the heating vent and the hard back of my desk chair. To use Thomas Nagel's (1974) much-worn

3

phrase, "there is something it's like" for me to see and feel what I see and feel. Again, I don't believe there is anything it's like for the chair to have me sitting on it, nor for the diskette case to be red; nor, I also presume, for the avocado plant to have green leaves.

I have identified three features of mentality: rationality, representation (or, to use the standard term, intentionality), and consciousness. In all three ways we, and maybe higher animals, seem to differ from the rest of nature. So immediately the question arises: Do these features that distinguish minds from everything else in nature mark a fundamental division between the natural, or the physical, and the non-natural, or the immaterial? Are we, and the phenomena that constitute our mental lives, an integral part of the natural, physical world, or not? There is a long philosophical tradition, epitomized by Cartesian dualism, according to which minds are distinctly outside the natural order. There is another tradition, materialism, exemplified by Descartes's contemporary Hobbes, and which has since achieved the status of consensus (though with many vocal opponents), according to which mental phenomena are ultimately natural, physical phenomena. They are immensely complicated, of course, and do not arise except in special circumstances, but still they are in the end not fundamentally different in kind from the rest of nature.

What makes the mind-body issue a *problem* is that both positions seem to have excellent considerations in their favor. On the dualist side, one need only point to just how distinctive these three features are, and how difficult it is to see how mere matter and energy could support them. What is it about a physical state, such as a sequence of neural firings in the brain, that could give rise to a representational feature, such as my thinking about the red diskette case on my computer table? That is, what could make something in my brain be *about* the diskette case? Furthermore, what is it about an event in my brain that could give rise to my having an experience of red? The relations between the two sorts of phenomena seem baffling. It therefore seems plausible to adopt the hypothesis that the reason we can't understand how mere matter and energy can support these features is that they can't. Minds are just different kinds of entities; or, at least, mental phenomena are different sorts of phenomena.

On the other side, there are deep reasons for supposing that minds must really be natural, physical things after all, and these three features must really be ultimately natural, physical features. J.J.C. Smart (1959) summarized the case for materialism eloquently in the following passage:

> Why do I wish to resist this suggestion [dualism]? Mainly because of Occam's razor. It seems to me that science is increasingly giving us a viewpoint whereby organisms are able to be seen as physicochemical mechanisms: it seems that even the behavior of man himself will one day be explicable in mechanistic terms. There does seem to be, so far as science is concerned, nothing in the world but increasingly complex arrangements of physical constituents. All except for one place: in consciousness. . . . I

just cannot believe that this can be so. That everything should be explicable in terms of physics . . . except the occurrence of sensations seems to me to be frankly unbelievable. Such sensations would be "nomological danglers." . . . Certainly we are pretty sure in the future to come across new ultimate laws of a novel type, but I expect them to relate simple constituents. . . . I cannot believe that ultimate laws of nature could relate simple constituents to configurations consisting of perhaps billions of neurons. . . . Such ultimate laws would be like nothing so far known in science. They have a queer "smell" to them. (142)

For my part, the materialist case essentially rests on the phenomenon of mental-physical causal interaction. Encounters with light waves that bounce off my red diskette case cause me to have conscious experiences of red expanses. My figuring out what to do in a situation causes my body to move in various ways. My thinking about materialism causes my fingers to type on the computer keys. It seems overwhelmingly obvious that mental phenomena are both causes and effects of non-mental, physical phenomena. What's more, within the realm of non-mental physical phenomena, the hypothesis that what determines the distribution of matter and energy is exclusively determined (to the extent there is determination) by non-mental, physical forces, seems very well confirmed. But the motions of my fingers, speech articulatory systems, arms, and legs all involve changes in the distribution of matter and energy. Thus only if mental phenomena are somehow constructible from, or constituted by, the physical phenomena that serve as the ultimate causal basis for all changes in the distribution of matter and energy does it seem possible to make sense out of mental-physical causal interaction.

The attempt to show how mental phenomena can be accounted for in non-mental, physical terms is often called the project of "naturalizing the mind."[1] Now, with respect to the first two features of mentality, rationality and intentionality, I think some significant progress has been made on this project. With the advent of formal logic, and with it computer science, we see how rules defined purely by reference to formal (or syntactic) features of representations can be formulated so as to respect rules of logical entailment or rational inference. Formal, syntactic properties, like the shapes of letters and numerals, are clearly the sorts of properties that can be explained by reference to their physical embodiments. There is no mystery about how mere matter and energy can give rise to these formally defined processes. So long as rational mental processes can be explained in terms of formal processes, at least this feature of mental life will have been naturalized.

This is not to say that rationality has in fact been fully explained in terms of formal processes. We know how to capture deductive, and certain forms of inductive reasoning in formal terms, but we are a far cry from showing that the entire range of rational processes that constitute standard common sense can be so explained. Fodor (1987), one of the chief champions of the computational theory of mind, is in fact quite pessimistic about the prospects for substantial success in this regard. Still, others are not so pessimistic, and the point is that if rationality can be adequately treated as a formal process, then materialism has nothing to fear from that quarter.

Of course formal processes defined over meaningless symbols won't suffice, which is why we need an account of intentionality as well. How do the objects over which rational processes are defined get their meanings, their representational contents? Though here too the picture is not by any means complete, it seems to me that substantial progress has been made. There seem to be two natural, materialistically respectable, sources for generating meaning: causal/inferential relations among representations, and causal/informational relations between representations and their referents. Roughly, they work like this. One source for attaching a content to a representation is the nomic or causal relation that obtains between that representation and what it is about. So, if something in my head, my symbol <horse>, is normally caused to "light up" in the presence of horses, it will, subject to various conditions, carry the information that there is a horse in the vicinity when it lights up. This fact about the information it carries when lit up, subject to further, very complicated conditions, can then serve as the basis for interpreting the symbol as expressing the content HORSE.[2] There are many variations on this theme extant in the literature, but this basic idea should suffice for now.[3]

The second source for representational content is the set of inferential relations that a representation maintains with other representations. It is plausible to think that among the determinants of the fact that my thinking <it's a horse> means IT'S A HORSE is the fact that I am disposed to infer <it's an animal> from <it's a horse>. It is in fact a matter of considerable controversy whether a symbol's inferential relations contribute to its content.[4] But for my purposes here all that matters is this. If conceptual role is a determinant of content, it can be explained naturalistically to the extent that rational inference can be.

If mentality were exhausted by the first two features, I don't think the mind-body problem would be so pressing. Sure, we don't completely understand how either rational inference or intentionality arises in nature, and it may turn out that we never will. But at the moment there is no reason for deep-seated pessimism. The explanatory mechanisms we have available—formal processes with nomic/informational relations—might do the job. We have at least a clue how something made out of what we're made out of could possibly support these features of mental life. But when it comes to consciousness, I maintain, we are clueless.

Let's take my current visual experience as I gaze upon my red diskette case, lying by my side on the computer table. I am having an experience with a complex qualitative character, one component of which is the color I perceive. Let's dub this aspect of my experience its "reddish" character.[5] There are two important dimensions to my having this reddish experience. First, as mentioned above, there is something it's like for me to have this experience. Not only is it a matter of some state (my experience) having some feature (being reddish) but, being an experience, its being reddish is "for me," a way it's like *for me*, in a way that being red is like nothing for—in fact is not in any way "for"—my diskette case. Let's call this the *subjectivity* of conscious experience. Nagel (1974) himself emphasized this feature by noting that conscious experience involves our having a "point of view."

The second important dimension of experience that requires explanation is qualitative character itself. Subjectivity is the phenomenon of there being something it's like *for me* to see the red diskette case. Qualitative character concerns the "what" it's like for me: reddish or greenish, painful or pleasurable, and the like. From within the subjective point of view I am presented with these qualitative features of experience, or "qualia," as they're called in the literature. Reddishness, for instance, is a feature of my experience when I look at my red diskette case. It is notoriously difficult to explain this feature by reference to either the physical or formal features of my brain states. Yet, as emphasized above, that I'm having a reddish experience does seem to be both the effect of physical causes and a cause of physical effects. Thus the prospect that the qualitative character of my experience has no naturalistic explanation is extremely troubling.

While the problem of providing an explanation for qualitative character—what makes my sensation a reddish one, as opposed to a greenish one—has been the focus of most of the literature on conscious experience, a major theme of this book is that the deepest problem lies with understanding subjectivity. In fact, as will emerge in the course of my argument, the explanatory gap between physical properties and qualitative properties is a symptom of the subjectivity of consciousness. Since this is such a crucial issue and won't emerge until the latter part of the book, let me take some time now to provide the reader with a preview.

Explanation has both a metaphysical and an epistemological side to it. On the metaphysical side, to say that phenomenon A is explained by B is to say that B is responsible for A. The sense of responsibility at issue may be causal, or it may be some other relation that fits under the heading "in virtue of." The point is that it is in virtue of B, because of B, that A occurs.

On the other hand, to say that A is explained by B can also mean that by appeal to B we can understand, or make intelligible, why A occurs. Of course these two sides to explanation are related, since appealing to what is responsible for A is a way of making intelligible why it occurs, but nevertheless they are not the same thing. On my view, this becomes clear when we consider the question, What explains the qualitative character of my sensation when I look at the red diskette case? It may very well be, as I will argue in chapter 1, that what explains it, metaphysically, are the physical properties of the brain state I occupy at the time.[6] But what causes a problem is that appeal to these physical properties does not explain the qualitative character in the epistemological sense—it doesn't provide understanding of why there should be the reddish quale that there is.

It is at this point that consideration of the subjectivity of conscious experience becomes relevant. For when pushed to say just what is missing by way of an explanation of qualitative character, especially in contrast with other standard cases of explanatory reduction, we must appeal to certain distinctive features of our cognitive relation to the qualitative contents of experience, features that are definitive of the subjectivity of experience. For one thing, our conception, or the mode of presentation of a property like reddishness is substantive and determinate in a way that the modes of presentation of other sorts of properties are not. When I think of what it is to be reddish, the reddishness itself is somehow included in the thought; it's present to me. This is what I mean by saying it has a "substantive" mode of presentation. In fact, it seems the right way to look at it is that reddishness itself is serving as its own mode of presentation. By saying that the conception is "determinate," I mean that reddishness presents itself as a specific quality, identifiable in its own right, not merely by its relation to other qualities.

I argue that concepts of other sorts of properties are "presentationally thin" in the sense that their modes of presentation either contain nothing of cognitive significance beyond the bare representation of the property in question, or contain representations of other properties that are presentationally thin as well. So, for instance, consider my concept of a cat. On a purely causal/informational view, there are two candidates for the mode of presentation: my mental symbol <cat>, and the nomic relation that holds between that symbol and the property of being a cat.[7] The symbol obviously plays a cognitive role, but on this sort of view the relation does not. I need not be aware of it in order for my symbol to be about cats, and I don't explicitly include a description of the relation as part of my thought when thinking about cats. So there really is very little to the mode of presentation, and therefore it seems appropriate to call it "presentationally thin."

On other views, however, modes of presentation are not apparently so austere. On conceptual role views, various of the beliefs one holds about cats are part of the mode of presentation of cathood. But my point is that even if these views are right—and I will consider arguments pro and con in chapter 2—it is still the case that what the mode of presentation contains is really just more symbols. So, for instance, if you think it's part of my concept of cats that they are animals, then one considers the inferential link between my mental symbol <cat> and my mental symbol <animal> to be partly constitutive of the former (maybe the latter too). It's still the case, though, that what lies at the other end of the relation that secures each of these symbols to their referents is of no genuine cognitive significance; for the subject, it has the character of "whatever it is that's out there." In this sense, the mode of presentation of cathood lacks substance and determinacy.[8]

This idea, that the modes of presentation by which we come into cognitive contact with qualia are substantive and determinate, explains why there is an explanatory gap between qualia and their material bases but not between the standard examples of explanatorily reduced properties and their material bases. The epistemic puzzle arises precisely because we have the kind of cognitive grasp of qualitative character that we do. Put simply, the substantive nature of our conception provides the material for the substantive nature of our explanatory demand. There is a kind of grasp of what it is that requires explanation that is missing in other cases.

The connection between the distinctive nature of phenomenal concepts[9] and subjectivity is straightforward. The subjectivity of conscious experience is a matter of its being "for the subject." One way of elucidating what being "for the subject" comes to is that the contents of conscious experience are presented in this distinctively substantive and determinate mode. Or, perhaps one should put it the other way: what the substantive and determinate character come to is that the contents in question are genuinely "for the subject," cognitively taken up by the subject, in a way that nothing else is.

I don't think we currently have any idea how to explain subjectivity, especially not in physical, or non-mental terms. What makes the lump of meat that is my brain into a genuine subject of experience, so that its states are genuinely "for" it, something to it? It might seem as if this is really just part of the problem of intentionality. Perhaps it is, but if so, then it just means that the problem of intentionality is more difficult than we thought. It is one thing to explain how one state can acquire the property of being about another state. As already mentioned, it is very promising to treat this as a matter of carrying information, a relation that seems to be constructible from straightforward physical/causal relations. But just because state A carries information about state B, and, let's say, is thereby *about* state B, does not mean that its carrying the information that it does, meaning what it does, is in the appropriate sense "for" the subject of state A, part of what could be called the experience of that subject. All that carrying information seems to support are presentationally thin concepts that refer to the properties they carry information about. This feature, being for the subject, with all it entails, seems a substantial addition to merely meaning, being about, something in the first place.[10]

A further, and perhaps most deeply puzzling, aspect of the distinctive cognitive relation subjects of experience bear to their conscious contents is that the qualitative contents themselves, qualia, seem to have a dual character as both act and object. As we will see in the discussion of various reductionist attempts, especially "higher-order" theories, philosophers have been struggling with this problem for some time. Is reddishness essentially conscious or something that can be instantiated without my being aware of it? Is it what I'm aware of, or somehow the awareness itself? Awareness certainly seems to be a relation, which would entail that one can distinguish the act from the object of awareness. Yet when it comes to qualia, to the contents of conscious experience, the two don't come apart so easily. It does seem impossible to really separate the reddishness from the awareness of it, yet it also seems impossible to tell a coherent story about how this could be so. I wish I had the right story to tell; my aim is to press the depth and urgency of the need for such a story.

What I want to argue in this book is that the mind-body problem, at least with respect to the issue of conscious experience, presents us, in a way, with a Kantian antinomy. We have excellent reasons for thinking that mental phenomena, including conscious experience, must be a species of physical/natural phenomena. On the other hand, we also have excellent reasons for thinking conscious experience cannot be captured in physical/natural terms. The total physical/natural story seems to leave out conscious experience.

I qualified the claim above, saying "in a way" it's an antinomy, because I don't think the anti-materialist side really supports the claim that conscious experience couldn't in fact be a physical/natural phenomenon. Rather, I think the case is slightly weaker: that we can't understand how it could be a physical/natural phenomenon. That is, as mentioned above, I argue that the explanatory gap is primarily an epistemological problem, not necessarily a metaphysical one. But as will become clear once the argument unfolds, this is unlikely to provide much comfort to the materialist.

Almost everything I've asserted in this introduction is controversial in one way or another. So it's time now to defend my thesis. Adopting as I do a kind of middle position between materialist and dualist, I have two burdens of argument to bear. I must show that materialism does, in the sense I described, leave out conscious experience, while also defending materialism against dualism. Both burdens are twofold: I will attack positive proposals and defend against objections to my position. On the materialist side, this involves demonstrating that the proposals extant in the literature for explaining conscious experience fall far short of the mark, and also responding to the arguments that purport to show that to oppose these proposals on the sorts of grounds I employ entails various unacceptable consequences or downright incoherence. On the dualist side, I will argue that certain dualist proposals are unacceptable, and also defend materialism against certain dualist arguments. For the most part, however, I will emphasize my argument with materialism. It seems to me that this is still the position that commands broad consensus, and it is the one that I feel has the most going for it.

The plan for the rest of the book is as follows. In chapter 1 I will articulate and defend a version of materialism. The materialist position I favor is reductionist, but it makes a place for the causal efficacy of mental properties. In chapter 2 I defend materialism against the anti-materialist "conceivability argument," and in the process develop a position on the nature of conceptual content that will bear on what follows. In chapter 3 I argue for the existence of an explanatory gap between qualia and their material bases. It is at this point, in response to an objection that stems from my argument in chapter 2, that I introduce the idea that there is something special about the modes of presentation by which we gain cognitive access to qualia. In chapter 4 I explore various materialist reductionist strategies, especially "higher-order" theories and "representational" theories, and find them all wanting. In chapter 5 I defend realism about qualia from eliminativism; again, the substantive and determinate nature of phenomenal modes of presentation plays an important role here. Finally, in chapter 6 I revisit certain questions, especially concerning the nature of subjectivity, in the context of an exploration of various anti-zombie arguments.

1

"All in My Brain"
Materialism

1.1 Introduction

In this chapter I want to present and defend a version of materialism. In section 1.2 I will present what I take to be the essential thesis of materialism, elucidating its key concepts and providing initial motivation. In the rest of the chapter I will deal with a number of objections. Section 1.3 will address the problem of defining "material" or "physical" in a way that doesn't either trivialize the thesis or falsify it. Section 1.4 will address epiphenomenalism as an alternative to materialism. Section 1.5 will address the argument that if materialism is true, then there really isn't any causal role for mental properties to play. Finally, section 1.6 will address certain arguments for the view that the materialist project, or the "naturalization project," is wrongheaded to begin with.

1.2 The Materialist Thesis

First of all, let me deal with some metaphysical preliminaries. I am a realist about properties. I think what properties there are is an objective matter of fact, and that concrete objects enter into causal relations with each other by virtue of the properties they instantiate. So when the baseball shatters the window, it's because the baseball instantiates a certain momentum and the window instantiates a certain degree of fragility. I am not, however, making it a criterion of existence for properties that they contribute to the causal powers of the objects in which they inhere, nor am I adopting causal role as a criterion of individuation.[1]

Because I am a realist about properties, I don't accept the principle that for each predicate there is a distinct property. On the contrary, properties, like individuals, can have different names. Also, being a property realist, I don't accept the principle that for every predicate (or description) there must be a property at all, whether the same or different from the properties picked out by other expressions. Realism about a domain means thinking of it as ontologically independent of how we conceive it. It must always be open to claim that though we think of the world as containing such-and-such properties, in fact it doesn't. Thus it is only nominalism that I'm ruling out right now, not eliminativism.

There are two ways to look at the mind-body problem. We can think of it from the point of view of individuals, or objects, or from the point of view of properties. Are minds physical or non-physical objects? This is one question. Another question is whether mental properties are physical properties. Both questions require a good deal of clarification, and the answer to the first clearly doesn't entail an answer to the second. Let's look at this in a bit of detail.

When Descartes argued for dualism, he was arguing that the mind, as an object, was non-physical. Extension, the essential property of matter, did not pertain to the mind. Mind's only essential property was thought. This sort of dualism is usually called "substance dualism." However, even if one thinks that the mind and the body (or just the brain) are identical, it is possible to resist materialism by endorsing "property dualism," the doctrine that mental properties are non-physical. On the other hand, it does seem that the denial of property dualism entails the denial of substance dualism. If all properties are physical properties, then what could make an object non-physical? If thought, the essential property of mind for Descartes, weren't non-physical, Descartes certainly wouldn't have taken the object for which it is an essential property to be non-physical.

An issue that concerns both versions of dualism is what is meant by "physical." Perhaps we can define a physical object as any object that has certain physical properties,[2] but then we have to face the question of what it is for a property to be physical. For the purposes of defining "physical object" this may not be a problem, since we could always list some properties that we think any physical object must have. But when it comes to property dualism, the question is more pressing. We need not only some exemplars of physical properties, but a principle for sorting all properties into the physical and non-physical. Otherwise, it's hard to attach significance either to property dualism or its denial. I will deal with part of this problem in the rest of this section, and then more fully in the next section.

My primary concern is the stronger version of materialism, the one that denies property dualism as well as substance dualism. I think that the arguments for property dualism are more compelling than those for substance dualism, and it certainly has more adherents. Furthermore, as we will see, one needs the stronger version of materialism in order to validate the causal role of the mental, a consideration I identified in the Introduction as the prime motivation behind materialism. Let's proceed, then, to a statement of the materialist thesis.

I will just baldly state it first, and then turn to elucidation:

M: Only the fundamental properties of physics are instantiated in a basic way; all others, particularly mental properties, are instantiated by being realized by the instantiation of other properties.

Objects instantiate properties (including relations). The diskette case is red, which means that it instantiates the property [redness], and my son is taller than me, so the ordered pair consisting of him and me instantiates the relation [taller than].[3] I distinguish two ways a property (relation) can be instantiated in an object (ordered n-tuple of objects): in a basic way or by being realized by the instantiation of another property (or properties). To be instantiated in a basic way is just to be instantiated without being realized by (the instantiation of—I'll leave this out from now on) another property. So what we need to get clear about is the relation of realization.

Properties can stand in various relations. Proceeding from weakest to strongest, these relations include: accidental correlation, nomological/causal connection, realization, identity. Two properties are accidentally correlated when instantiations of one co-occur with instantiations of the other, but this is not a matter of law. A standard example of an accidental correlation is the case where all the coins in my pocket happen to be pennies. In this case the properties [being a coin in my pocket at t] and [being a penny] are accidentally correlated. If I had bothered to change a dollar into four quarters right beforehand, the connection would have been broken.

Two properties are nomologically related if there's a law that enforces the connection. Thus the masses and momenta of Earth and the Sun, together with the distance between them, nomologically determine the force of attraction acting between them. Instantiations of various properties of two billiard balls colliding determine their subsequent trajectories. Many philosophers worry about how to analyze causal and nomological relations, apparently under the assumption that if these concepts cannot be analyzed in other terms they become suspect. I do not share this assumption, and therefore take it for granted that we understand what a law and a cause is.[4] Illustrative examples should suffice for my purposes.

Now we come to realization. The instantiation of property A is realized by the instantiation of property B just in case the very fact alone of B's instantiation constitutes the instantiation of A. The best example of realization is also the one most relevant to the mind-body case: the relation between functional or computational properties and their physical implementations. Functional properties are causal role properties, properties an object instantiates just in case it instantiates a system of properties satisfying a certain description of state interactions and state relations to impingements on the object and its responses. The actual physical mechanisms that sustain the interactions and relations to inputs and outputs are the realizations of the functional properties.

So, for example, a computer program specifies a set of state transitions and outputs in response to inputs and the results of various computations. The electronic mechanisms in the computer realize the program. The same program could also be realized non-electronically, perhaps by having a person move checkers around on a super-large checkerboard. Typically, the realization relation is one-many (or even many-many, since the very same lower-level properties could realize different upper-level properties simultaneously).

I want to emphasize the contrast between nomological relations and realization. There is clearly an important metaphysical difference between saying that A causes B, or A and B are lawfully connected, and saying that A realizes B. In the former case there may be a significant ontological independence between the instantiation of the two properties. We don't think of one as constituting the other, or that the effect somehow exists by way of or through the cause. The cause's obtaining does not by itself amount to the effect's obtaining. Rather, the bringing about of the effect is itself a substantive feature of the cause, something it "does" over and above merely obtaining.

Realization, on the other hand, is a more intimate, ontological relation. In this case the instantiation of the one property does obtain by way of, or through the other. The realizing property by its very instantiation brings about the instantiation of the realized property. The electronic circuits doing what they do doesn't *cause* the program to be implemented; it *is* an implementation of the program. Though I will reserve a discussion of modal issues for chapter 2, we can capture a good part of the difference between realization and nomological connection this way: if A realizes B, then A metaphysically necessitates B, a much stronger form of necessitation than nomological necessitation.[5]

The tightest, most intimate relation is identity, of course. Realization, though it involves metaphysical necessitation, does not amount to identity. When A realizes B, we are still dealing with two properties: A and B. However, when A is identical to B, then in fact there is only one property, referred to in two different ways—"A" and "B". Realization involves metaphysical necessitation, but only in one direction: "bottom-up." If the realizers are instantiated, then the realized must be as well. However, as noted above, there can be many different realizers of the same realized property. With identity, obviously, the metaphysical necessitation goes in both directions. If A and B are identical, then you can't have one without the other.

We can now return to M. According to M, a set of fundamental physical properties serves as the realization base for all other properties. Any property that is instantiated in a basic way must be a member of this set of fundamental physical properties. Mental properties, whether it's having the thought that my diskette case is red, or having a reddish experience while looking at it, are not, presumably, on this list of fundamental physical properties. Hence, they must be realized in these properties.[6]

While mental properties are neither on the basic list in their own right nor straightforwardly identical to others on the list, one might claim that mental properties are identical to complicated constructions out of the basic ones. Perhaps to be in pain, or to have a belief, is to be in a neurophysiological state which in turn is identical, ultimately, to being in a state involving trillions and trillions of elementary particles. Whether this is the right way to view the relation between neurophysiological states and lower-level physical states is not a question I will address now. But there are strong reasons for denying an identity relation between the mental and the neurophysiological. The standard objection to identifying mental properties with neurophysiological properties is that mental properties are assumed to be multiply realizable.[7] Pains, beliefs, and desires are thought to be states that creatures quite different physically can nevertheless share. If I realize pain with brain state B, but a Martian realizes it with state C, or even a robot with state D, then to be in pain can't be identical to being in state B (or C or D, for that matter). Still, so long as in each case we have a realization relation between pain and the relevant lower-level physical state, materialism is not violated.

I want to address two questions here in a preliminary way: (1) is it reasonable to impose the condition on property instantiation spelled out in M? and (2) can we show that the condition is in fact met? With respect to (1), let me return to the argument briefly outlined in the Introduction, the argument from causal interaction. Let's take a non-mental property first, say dormativity, tending to cause sleep. Certain substances have dormative effects on people when ingested: alcohol, marijuana, and phenobarbitol, for example. So consider an episode of my imbibing several shots of Scotch and then falling asleep. Imbibing the Scotch caused me to go to sleep.

Now, let's assume being asleep can be identified with a complex neurophysiological state (or property) of my brain. The question is, how does the Scotch cause my brain to enter this state? We assume there is an answer to this question. In fact, there are two sorts of answers, both involving the provision of mechanisms: one involves intervening mechanisms, and the other involves realization mechanisms.

Intervening mechanisms come into play in explaining how it is that Scotch entering my mouth could have an effect on my brain. To explain this we tell a story about how the substance from the glass eventually ends up in my blood stream and then into brain cells. But even after we have provided the relevant intervening mechanisms, we still have a question. What is it about the stuff entering the brain cells that accounts for the cells going into the sort of states they do that is definitive of sleep?[8]

It could be there is no answer to this question. That is, dormativity might be a basic property of alcohol,[9] so there is no further mechanism to cite in an explanation of how alcohol causes sleep. It might be as pointless to seek an answer to the question how alcohol causes sleep (except, of course, for the question of intervening mechanisms) as it is (or was at some point in the development of physical theory—I'm not sure about now) to ask how negatively charged particles exert an attractive force on positively charged particles. However, given what we know about the most basic processes in brain cells, it's highly unlikely, to say the least, that there is some basic property of dormativity that affects them. Rather, what we expect to find, and indeed, I trust, do find, is that there are biochemical properties that realize dormativity, and biochemical mechanisms whereby they affect brain cells in the requisite manner.

The example of dormativity is supposed to illustrate the claim that M is plausible. What makes it plausible is this. Phenomena like sleep clearly involve the distributions of matter and energy in both brain cells and larger bodily units. For something to be a cause of sleep, it must be capable of affecting these distributions of matter and energy. But from physics we know that the only forces that can affect such distributions are those realized in the fundamental physical properties. Hence, if dormativity is going to be a cause of sleep, it must be realized in the fundamental physical properties.

Now, let's turn to a mental example. Precisely the same sort of reasoning applies. I form the intention to express the thought that the diskette case is red, and, as a result, type the sentence "The diskette case is red." My forming the intention, a mental state, causes my typing behavior. Typing involves the movement of my fingers on the keyboard, clearly a matter of changes in the distribution of matter and energy. How does my forming the relevant intention cause this to happen? Again, there are two stories about mechanisms, one involving intervening mechanisms and the other involving realization mechanisms. The former has to do with nerve impulses traveling from the relevant brain centers to the nerves in my fingers. The latter has to do with the relation between forming an intention and having certain neurons fire in my brain. If, however, the neural firings did not realize my intention, then we wouldn't know how it is that the intention caused the relevant initiating event in the causal stream that constitutes the intervening mechanism. How does an intention get a nerve impulse to travel if not by being realized by a neural firing?

I've been addressing the question whether M is reasonable. It seems to me that so long as we take mental properties to be causally relevant to the production of physical behavior, and accept the principle that the fundamental physical properties provide the only causal bases there are for changes in physical properties,[10] we have reason to believe M must be true. But it's one thing to have this sort of indirect evidence that mental properties are realized in physical properties, and another to have what Jeff Poland (1994) calls a "realization theory." A realization theory for a mental property is one that shows us explicitly how the property in question is physically realized. Presumably we have such a theory for dormativity, and also for computer programs. We can say what it is about the electronic events going on in the central processing unit of the computer by virtue of which they constitute the execution of the relevant program. But do we have a realization theory for the mind? This was the second question posed above.

I think everyone would agree that at present we do not have a realization theory for the mind.[11] But that fact alone is not very interesting. What matters is what prospects we have for eventually constructing one. For one thing, many philosophers and psychologists would argue, rightly I think, that it's premature to worry about realization theories when we are still well short of a complete psychological theory. What matters, then, is not whether we actually have a realization theory for the mind, but rather, whether the theories of mental phenomena we are now constructing are such as to plausibly yield a realization theory when enough details are in.

On this score, as I stated in the Introduction, I think the answer depends on which aspect of mentality one has in mind. To the extent rationality can be captured in formal terms—through logic, decision theory, and confirmation theory[12]—to that extent we have reason to expect a realization theory to be forthcoming. Of course we could find out that our brains can't actually support the sorts of processes specified by these formal theories, but we don't have reason to believe that now. If intentionality can be captured in terms of causal/nomic covariation, then it is clear here too that a realization theory has good prospects. All we need to do is find the physical properties that actually stand in the requisite causal/nomic relations to satisfy the specification of the intentional relation.

On the other hand, with conscious experience I think the prospects are very dim. The problem is that we can't elucidate what it is to have a conscious experience in either formal or causal/nomic terms. I will not argue for this claim here; it is the burden of most of this book. Instead, in the rest of this chapter I want to deal with various other challenges to the materialist picture presented in this section. But before closing this section, a word about the epistemological and modal status of thesis M is in order.

Materialism is usually understood to be an empirical thesis. Even if it's true, it might have been false. Now some might object that there is a general enough understanding of materialism on which it couldn't have turned out to be false, because its denial entails a kind of incoherent mysticism. I don't subscribe to this position. As I understand dualism, or anti-materialism, it is coherent and at least epistemically possible. In fact, one reasonable response to the argument of this book—one I don't share—is that it very well might be true, at least for the properties involved in conscious experience.

What about its modal status? Again, it seems to me that materialism should be seen as contingent. I don't see any reason to rule out the logical, or metaphysical possibility of dualist, or immaterial worlds (unless one collapses metaphysical and nomological possibility, which I'm not inclined to do). In terms of the formulation of materialism embodied in M, such a possibility could amount to either of the following: (1) mental properties are realized in non-physical, or as they're sometimes called, "ectoplasmic" properties, or (2) mental properties are themselves instantiated in a basic way. The latter is the more interesting case.[13] The thoughts and pains in the actual world are realized physically, but there are logically possible worlds where thoughts and pains are realized non-physically, or not at all. Whether *my* pains and thoughts could have been realized non-physically or not at all is a question I will take up later.

1.3 The Physical

I made heavy use of the expression "fundamental physical property" in the discussion above. But just what is it to be "physical"? There are those who argue that without a clear definition for the term "physical," the doctrine of materialism (or physicalism—I intend no distinction between the two) is without content. Furthermore, they claim, there is in fact no available definition of the term "physical" on which materialist doctrine both has content and is plausibly true.[14] The basic problem can be put in the form of two dilemmas. The definition of "physical" has either an *a priori* or an *a posteriori* source. If the former, it will turn out that much of what current physical theory countenances as among the fundamental physical entities and properties will be excluded, since it's hard to see how the esoteric posits of modern physics could be part of our *a priori* concept of the physical. So it appears we should derive our definition from an *a posteriori* source. The obvious source will be physical theory itself.

If we go this route, however, the second dilemma appears (it is often called "Hempel's dilemma," from the discussion in Hempel 1980). Either we define "physical" by reference to current physical theory or by reference to some future, ideally completed theory. If the former, then materialism, as embodied in thesis M above, reads as follows: All properties and relations are realized in the properties and relations described within current physical theory. But why believe that? Physics is always adding to our inventory of basic physical properties and entities, and there is no good reason to suppose this trend will not continue well into the future.

On the other hand, if we opt for future physics we fall into another trap. Thesis M would then read: All properties and relations are realized in the properties and relations described within an ideally completed future physical theory. There are two worries here. First, since we don't know what properties and entities will be included in the future physicist's inventory of basic entities and properties, the thesis that all properties are realized in members of this basic set lacks a determinate content. Materialism can't be evaluated because we don't know what it says. Second, and even more troubling, if we think of the "physical" as whatever it is that future science appeals to in its (causal) explanations, then mental properties could turn out to be physical by fiat. If physicists posited minds for elementary particles to explain their behavior, then minds would be physical. But this trivializes the thesis.

Some (e.g., Lewis 1983) try to avoid the indefiniteness of the appeal to future physics by stipulating that only "modest extensions" of current physics are envisaged by the materialist. But this doesn't seem to get at the problem. First, it still leaves materialism hostage to future revolutions in physics, even if they have nothing to do with the mind. Second, one needs a principle for what counts as "physics" if this move is going to succeed in providing materialism with determinate content. This might also be a problem for those who formulate materialist doctrine in terms of current physics, but at least they can just point to a body of extant theory and say, "*that's* what I mean by 'physics.'" But it's not clear how to determine the correct departmental classification for future theories.[15]

Chomsky is fond of putting the problem this way. In Descartes's time, the mind-body problem made sense because we had a definite conception of "body" to oppose to that of the mind. Our notion of "body" was characterizable in terms of Descartes's contact mechanics. But ever since that version of physical theory was overthrown, we have had no successor notion of "body" determinate and stable enough to serve as the contrast to "mind," and which could thus serve to provide content to the mind-body problem. To quote:

What is the concept of body that finally emerged? The answer is that there is no clear and definite concept of body. If the best theory of the material world that we can construct includes a variety of forces, particles that have no mass, and other entities that would have been offensive to the "scientific common sense" of the Cartesians, then so be it: We conclude that these are properties of the physical world, the world of body. The conclusions are tentative, as befits empirical hypotheses, but are not subject to criticism because they transcend some *a priori* conception of body. There is no longer any definite conception of body. Rather, the material world is whatever we discover it to be, with whatever properties it must be assumed to have for the purposes of explanatory theory. (Chomsky 1988, 144)

Smart (1978) and Melnyk (1997) respond to the challenge by arguing that the materialist thesis can be formulated in terms of current physical theory. To the objection that current theory is undoubtedly incomplete, or even false, each responds differently. Smart argues, citing Feinberg (1966), that when it comes to ordinary "bulk matter," we have good reason to believe that current physical theory is essentially complete. The new and esoteric entities and properties that future physics is likely to discover emerge at sizes and levels of energy that go far beyond bulk matter. The brain, and the processes that take place within it, is, for these purposes, an instance of "bulk matter." Since mental processes are reducible to brain processes, according to the materialist, the physics of ordinary bulk matter is all the physics we need care about.

Melnyk argues that the likely incompleteness of current physics does show that a materialist thesis formulated in terms of it is in fact likely to be false. Nevertheless, he endorses formulating materialism in terms of current physics. He argues that all we need claim on behalf of materialism is that it is more acceptable, more highly confirmed, than any of its (explicitly formulated) rivals, not that it's more likely true than not. He compares our epistemic attitude to materialism with our attitude to physics itself. We do, after all, endorse current physical theory over its rivals, even though we know how likely it is to be discovered to be mistaken. What is so bad, then, if our epistemic commitment to materialism is as strong as it is to physics itself?

While I find both Smart's and Melnyk's responses interesting and insightful, it seems to me that they miss something important about materialism: that it is not in fact hostage to what happens in physical theory (at least up to a point—I'll return to this below). So it doesn't matter whether the physics of bulk matter is yet complete, and in a sense we do have more reason to believe in materialism than in any particular version of physics. Now what I think is right about the spirit of their replies, as well as those who talk about modest extensions of current theory, is the idea that, as materialists, we shouldn't worry about whether current physical theory is true or complete. Something more general is at stake here, and it ought to be susceptible to fairly rigorous formulation.

I think the following two statements, one by Fodor (1987) and the other by Richard Boyd,[16] capture what is essential about materialism. Boyd said that materialism is the doctrine that what goes on in us is ultimately the same as what goes on in tables and chairs, on the assumption that they aren't themselves mental entities. If it turns out that deep down there are minds activating their behavior, then all bets are off. Similarly, Fodor says:

> I suppose that sooner or later the physicists will complete the catalogue they've been compiling of the ultimate and irreducible properties of things. When they do, the likes of *spin*, *charm*, and *charge* will perhaps appear on their list. But *aboutness* surely won't; intentionality simply doesn't go that deep. (1987, 97)

Chomsky emphasizes how we have no clear conception of "body" or the "physical." One way of taking Boyd's remarks is to say that we do have such a conception; it's ostensively defined as whatever it is that ultimately constitutes things like tables and chairs. But Chomsky would reply that the problem is that we already know that what ultimately constitutes such things is pretty far from our intuitive conception of matter, and there seem to be no constraints on how weird it could get. Chomsky is probably right about our conception of the physical, but what we should take away from Boyd's remark about when "all bets are off," as well as the quote from Fodor, is that we don't need a clear conception of the physical to formulate materialism. All we need is a clear, or even not-so-clear, conception of the mental.

What is it about tables and chairs that make them paradigmatic examples of the physical? According to Chomsky, it's their bulk, their occupying Euclidean space, their contact mechanics, all the stuff we now believe is not literally true of them (or at least their ultimate constituents). I would say, rather, it's their non-mentality.[17] As far as I know, tables and chairs, as well as rocks and avocado trees, do not support mental life. In particular, their states do not possess either representational properties or phenomenal, qualitative properties. There is nothing it is like to be a chair, nor does the chair represent; none of its states are about anything. If this is false, then tables and chairs would not be good paradigmatic examples of the purely physical. If it turns out to be false of everything, then, as Boyd says, all bets are off. Materialism and dualism would both be false.

From the quote above from Fodor the main idea that emerges is that materialism is the doctrine that mental properties—in particular intentionality and phenomenal consciousness[18]—are not basic properties. They are realized in non-mental properties. It is not important for the purposes of this thesis whether we have an adequate conception of what these basic non-mental properties are, so long as we're clear that they are not representational or phenomenal. If a future physics tells us that among the basic properties of elementary particles or fields are representing quantity x or feeling pain, then materialism is false. That's as it should be. If we can't imagine what turn physics could take that would falsify materialism, then indeed the doctrine would seem to lack content.

To reflect the results of our discussion, I now formulate materialism with thesis M′, as follows:

M′: Only non-mental properties are instantiated in a basic way; all mental properties are instantiated by being realized by the instantiation of other, non-mental properties.

M′, I believe, is sufficient for providing content to the mind-body problem, and so therefore I believe the attacks of Chomsky and others are met. It does, however, lack something present in M. M asserts that there is a proprietary set of basic properties, and we know where to look for them. They are all to be found where physics investigates. I think there is something important to this insight, and it is why so many materialists have been loath to give up on formulating materialism by reference to fundamental physics. It may be that there is a way to formulate materialism so as to give expression to this insight. Still, when it comes to the mind-body problem, I think the debate over the definition of "the physical" is in the end not to the point. Thesis M′ serves to stake out a position that is substantive and clearly the target of dualist and other anti-materialist objections. So, in what follows, though I will sometimes talk of the fundamental physical properties, it should be understood that M′ is the thesis to which I take the materialist to be committed.

1.4 Epiphenomenalism

Now that we have a better understanding of what the materialist is committed to, let's review why she should be committed to it. Suppose I put my hand on a hot burner, feel pain, and withdraw my hand quickly. This surely seems a typical example of a causal chain. Physical contact with the burner causes pain, which in turn causes the withdrawal of my hand. It also seems appropriate to ask how this causal chain came to be. As discussed above, an explanation of the causal chain involves appeal to two sorts of mechanisms: intervening mechanisms and realizing mechanisms. The intervening mechanisms would involve the excitation of nerve endings in my hand together with the afferent nerve impulses that eventuate in the relevant brain state (call it B), and, on the other end, the efferent nerve impulses from the brain that eventuate in the contracting of the relevant muscles in the hand. The question of realization concerns the pain itself, and identifying state B would presumably tell us how the pain is realized.

But why think the pain itself has to be realized by a brain state? An alternative would be the property dualist position. On this view, the events beginning with the contact with the burner and ending with state B are all physical events, each causing the next in accordance with physical law. However, rather than serving to realize the pain, state B *causes* it. Then, depending on whether one is an interactionist or an epiphenomenalist, the story continues in one of two ways. For the interactionist, the pain then causes subsequent neural events that eventuate in the withdrawal of my hand. For the epiphenomenalist, the pain plays no causal role itself. It is caused by B but causes nothing. State B then causes the subsequent neural events that ultimately eventuate in the hand's withdrawal.

Interactionism, though it was Descartes's position, does seem out of the question. So long as we find no gap in the causal stream from state B to withdrawal of the hand, we have no reason to believe that any other state is causally responsible for the behavior, and therefore no reason to believe that the pain is playing a distinctive causal role. Do we know there are no such gaps? In fact, given quantum indeterminacy, one might think we do know there are some. However, appeal to quantum indeterminacy doesn't really help the interactionist. On the standard interpretation of physical theory, on which there is genuine indeterminacy at the most basic level, the gap left by this indeterminacy is not filled by anything, including mental causes. So to posit mental causes to take up the quantum slack would violate our best physical theory.

Of course our best current physical theory could be wrong. Certainly physics has a tradition of looking for "hidden variables." But the main point is this. Events like hand movements are physical events, covered by the laws of physics. We have no reason currently to believe that the physical trajectories of the parts of the hand are causally determined in any way differently from the physical trajectories of objects for which no mental causes are ever hypothesized. If it turns out that minds are everywhere taking up the quantum slack—with tables and chairs as well as hands and feet—then, as I said before, "all bets are off." But we have not reached this point. What's more, this would be a theory we were driven to because of a more general problem in physical theory, not one that we introduced specially for human and animal bodies.

The main alternative to materialism is epiphenomenalism, the doctrine that mental properties play no causal role in the production of behavior. Notice that only in the mental-to-physical direction must the property dualist deny causal relevance. It might be thought that there is a problem in the other direction as well. After all, it does seem that a physical stimulus, such as the light reaching me from the red diskette case, causes my visual experience with its red quale. It also seems that if we deny that the red quale is physically realized, its being so caused is quite mysterious. So it might be thought that the property dualist has a problem accounting for physical-to-mental causation.

I don't deny that the physical-to-mental direction would have something mysterious about it on the property dualist view, but this mystery need not be especially problematic. Property dualism, at least as I understand it,[19] is the view that certain physical states give rise to certain mental states by virtue of their instantiating a basic law of nature. Since the psycho-physical laws involved are basic, there is no deeper explanation of their workings, no lower-level mechanisms to appeal to.[20] So long as the laws work only in the physical-to-mental direction, physical theory, in its attempt to explain the behavior of physical objects, need not concern itself with these psycho-physical laws. Yes, such laws do appear to be the sort of "nomological dan-glers" Smart wanted so much to avoid, and certainly materialism is more economical and elegant for not having them. Still, there is no guarantee the world is elegant and economical, so these grounds alone do not, to my mind, constitute especially strong reasons for dismissing property dualism.

While the property dualist can appeal to *sui generis* basic laws to make physical events, such as light stimuli on the retina, causally relevant to the production of mental states, such as my reddish qualitative experience, she cannot employ the same move to make mental events causally relevant to the production of physical events, such as behavior. It looks as if the mental events really do "dangle," caused themselves but not causing in turn. This consequence of property dualism seems sufficient reason for avoiding it if at all possible. While many philosophers would agree with this claim without argument, not all would,[21] so we need to look at the matter more closely.

One reason to avoid epiphenomenalism is that it just seems crazy—or, to put it more politely, seriously counterintuitive. Is it really a serious possi-bility that pains don't cause hands to withdraw from fires (and by virtue of being painful)? Do our thoughts not control our actions, what we say? How do we make sense of deliberation, if in fact what we're thinking about is causally irrelevant to what we do? It's clear that thoroughgoing epiphenom-enalism would have drastic consequences for our self-conception.

Of course, one needn't be that thoroughgoing an epiphenomenalist. So long as one were willing to allow that cognitive states that have no con-scious, qualitative component are physically realized, one could save activi-ties like deliberation from total causal irrelevance. Since the challenge to materialism that concerns me derives from conscious, qualitative experience, let's restrict our consideration of epiphenomenalism to qualia. Still, the charge of apparent craziness—or, again to be polite, being seriously counter-intuitive—seems apt.

In response to this charge, Chalmers (1996) has argued that the intuition that pains cause hands to withdraw, strong as it is, is just that—an intu-ition. If we have a good argument against the claim that qualia are physi-cally realized, and only an intuition to oppose to it, then the argument must command our consent. Fair enough. We will evaluate Chalmers's own argu-ment for property dualism in the next chapter. What I want to drive home in this section is just how much property dualism requires us to swallow.

Now Chalmers argues that the consequences of accepting epiphenomenal-ism are not as bad as some have made out. It is often claimed that if qualia are epiphenomenal then we couldn't have knowledge of them, or even think about them. This consequence follows from joining the claim that qualia are epiphenomenal to any version of a causal theory of knowledge and represen-tation. But these consequences can be avoided in two related ways.[22] First, if the relevant cognitive states are not themselves claimed to be physically realized—if our thoughts about qualia are non-physical in just the way qualia are alleged to be non-physical—then there's nothing to stop their being the causal consequences of qualia. The problem is with mental-to-physical causation, not mental-to-mental. Second, it's not clear that when it comes to our cognitive relation to qualia a causal theory really is in order. There may be a more immediate, intimate relation that holds between a thought about a conscious experience and the experience itself.

As I said in the Introduction, the phenomenon of subjectivity does seem to involve the existence of a rather special, first-person form of cognitive access to the contents of conscious experience. Whether appeal to this special form of cognitive access can really help vindicate epiphenomenalism is difficult to determine, given what I will argue later is our almost total lack of understanding of this phenomenon. For now, let me just say this by way of response to this defense of epiphenomenalism. Of course no one has a well-worked-out causal (or nomic covariation) theory of content, so we clearly can't assume that the correct theory of representation will be one of these. Still, given the resources present in the physical realm, I really don't see how any physically realized relation can avoid being constructed out of causal relations. What else is there?[23] So if one envisages a relation of representation holding between a cognitive state and what it's about that does not derive ultimately from some causal relation between the two, then the cognitive state in question must itself be non-physical. But if it is, then the cognitive state, as well as the conscious experience it is about, must be epiphenomenal with respect to behavior as well.

One immediate consequence of this conclusion is that deliberation looks to be in more trouble again. I think to myself, "Last time I put my hand in the fire it hurt like hell, so I won't do it this time." Either the thought that it hurt like hell is physically realized, and not actually about the pain I experience, or it's non-physical, but then incapable of causing me to keep my hand away from the fire. Either way, the process of deliberation is compromised.

More generally, even if the property dualist can make sense of the idea that one's thoughts and beliefs have contents that include qualia, I don't see how they can do the same for utterances and inscriptions. I am now writing about my reddish qualitative experience as I look at the diskette case. What do these words I'm writing—"reddish qualitative experience"—refer to? Do they in fact refer to what I intend them to refer to? It's hard to see how they could. If my intention to refer to my reddish quale succeeds because it too is a non-physical mental event, then how could it bear any causal relation to the motions of my fingers on the keyboard? But if it doesn't bear any causal relation to these motions, then, as I argued above, it's unclear how the physical symbols produced by these motions could bear any representational relation to the quale. Thus, though I think I'm writing a book about conscious experience, and maybe I am, in a sense, writing one, you, however, aren't reading a book about conscious experience.[24]

Chalmers is right to point out that intuitions alone are not arguments. But of course arguments must always begin from premises, and we must clearly start from what seems most reasonable. I contend that the consequences that flow from epiphenomenalism are very hard to accept and provide sufficient grounds to avoid it. We can't come to a conclusion on the matter, however, until we assess the strength of the arguments against materialism. For now, then, I shall leave it at this. We have very good reason for thinking materialism must be true. But, of course, it may not be, for all that.

I have assumed throughout this section that only if phenomenal properties (qualia) are physically realized can they be causally relevant to the production of physical effects. However, there is an alternative. One can argue that phenomenal properties themselves constitute the basic properties, and that what we think of as fundamental physical properties are themselves realized by phenomenal properties. This is a position that has gained adherents of late[25] and needs to be examined in some detail. I will not consider this position at length in this book, but a few words here are in order.

There are two, related problems that arise for this sort of view. First, it appears to erase the distinction between the mental and the non-mental. Everything, tables and chairs included, is constituted by mind. Perhaps this is true, but it would be incredible if it were, and, again, one would want to see evidence for the view from the behavior of the apparently non-mental objects themselves. The second problem is that it's hard to see how our phenomenal properties are supposed to be related to these very basic ones.

One argument that has been put forward to address the first problem is that the so-called fundamental physical properties are all relational, or dispositional. Charge, spin, and the like are all defined by reference to their interactions. If one takes the plausible metaphysical view that relational (or dispositional) properties cannot be basic,[26] but rather there must be intrinsic properties to occupy the relevant relational roles, then we have an independent reason to posit something more than what physics explicitly tells us there is. Why not phenomenal properties for this role?

Well, why yes? What is it about serving as the ground of the basic physical relations that requires mentality? Are we to imagine that the objects in which these properties inhere, whether they be particles or points in a field, are themselves subjects of experience? If so, then the second problem kicks in: what relation is there between me, a subject who is clearly constituted by trillions and trillions of these things, and the little subjects who serve as the ultimate bases? How is my conscious experience explained by reference to theirs? My bet is that in the end we need something like functionalism to get my mentality out of the tiny ones, and if functionalism could work then we might as well go with materialism.

To avoid the obvious threat of panpsychism, positing tiny minds everywhere in nature, some philosophers talk of "proto-phenomenal" properties as the basic properties. The challenge then is to show how genuine phenomenal experience can be constructed out of the proto-phenomenal. Again, it seems to me that whatever resources could be deployed by an adherent of this view to show how such a construction is possible could also be employed by a functionalist to show how experience can be constituted by the physical. In both cases we're constructing a subject of experience, with its experiential properties, out of things and properties that are not that subject or its properties. If there is a problematic gap here for the materialist (as I will argue there certainly is), then, I'm sure, a similar gap exists on this view. However, I do not take these remarks to be conclusive by any means. If you are attracted to this sort of view, then take my argument in this book—that neither materialism nor its denial seem fully acceptable—to constitute another reason to look at it seriously. For the reasons above I'm not optimistic.

1.5 More on Causal Relevance

I have argued so far that materialism, as embodied in thesis M, is required if we are to make sense of the causal efficacy of the mental. However, Jaegwon Kim has forcefully argued that if we accept something like thesis M, we lose the right to attribute causal efficacy to the mental. As he puts it in a recent work, "If mind-body supervenience fails, mental causation is unintelligible; if it holds, mental causation is again unintelligible. Hence mental causation is unintelligible. That then is . . . Descartes's revenge against the physicalists" (1998, 46).

We have already investigated the first horn of the dilemma. But why accept the second one? Why think that if mind-body supervenience[27] holds then mental causation is unintelligible? The basic argument is what Kim calls the "causal exclusion" argument, and it goes like this. Consider again the pain's causing my hand to withdraw from the fire. My instantiating the mental property, being in pain, is supposed to be causally relevant to the subsequent motion of my hand. We know that a certain brain state, call it B, set in motion the nerve impulses which ultimately moved the muscles in my hand. My instantiating B was clearly causally relevant. B also realizes the pain. It's supposed to be because the pain is realized in B, which causes my hand to move, that we get to say that the pain caused my hand to move. However, from the description we just gave, it seems that my (or my brain's) instantiating pain adds nothing to the causal power relevant to producing a hand motion. All the causal work is done by the neurological property B. So it looks as if being physically realized can't help to secure causal efficacy for the mental.

One way out of this predicament is to identify the mental property with its realizer. If we say pain isn't just realized in state B, but is identical to state B, then of course there is no problem about the pain's being the cause of the hand motion. However, as we saw above, identifying pain with state B is inconsistent with the claim that pain can be realized in different ways, as in Martians or robots. So a straightforward identification of pain with a brain state seems wrong.

If one wanted to secure the causal efficacy of the mental through an identity theory, and one also wanted to allow for the possibility of multiple realization, one could of course just identify the mental property with the disjunction of its realizers. Pain may not be identical to B, or to C, or to D, but it may be identical to (B or C or D). This is a move Kim (1993, 210) is sympathetic to. So long as we allow all metaphysically possible realizers into the disjunction, the mental property and its correlated disjunction will be necessarily coextensive. True, the disjunction will (most likely) be infinitely long, but it's not clear that this should matter. Being infinitely long prohibits a representation from being entertained by a finite mind, but it's not clear that being describable by an infinitely long representation does anything to undermine a property's metaphysical status. After all, if it is identical to the mental property, then we have the short, finite term "pain" (or whatever mental term is in question) by which to refer to the property.

Another possibility for securing the causal efficacy of the mental is to employ the notion of a "trope." Tropes are token instantiations of properties, like the redness in the diskette case, or this particular instance of pain.[28] We can then argue as follows. Pain, as a universal, is multiply realizable. Each instance of pain, however—each of its tropes—is identical to some trope of the relevant property universal that in that instance serves as the realizer. So this trope of pain is identical to this trope of neurological property B. To say that the property of pain is causally efficacious is just to say that its tropes are, which, since they are identical to tropes of physical properties, they will be.[29]

It's possible that either the disjunctive identity or the trope identity move will work, and thereby secure the causal efficacy of the mental. But I am not happy with them. For one thing, I just don't believe that mental properties are identical to disjunctions of their realizers. In order to refute the identity claim I would need a well-worked-out theory of property identity, which I don't have. It's not easy to say what, over and above necessary coextensivity, is required for property identity. It wouldn't be so difficult if one went all the way and endorsed the view that for each predicate there is a distinct property. However, as I mentioned at the beginning of this chapter, I am a property realist and don't think this principle is consistent with a robust property realism. So what criterion of property identity is consistent with some pairs of distinct but necessarily coextensive predicates picking out the same property and others picking out distinct properties? I think there must be one, but I can't say what it is.

Still, despite lacking a formulation of the requisite criterion, I think there are considerations that one can bring to bear on the question. It seems to me that there is a strong analogy between the relation of realized properties and their realizers, on the one hand, and properties in general and the objects that instantiate them, on the other. Corresponding to each property is the set of individuals across all possible worlds that instantiate it. Some would identify the property with that set, but this isn't really a version of property realism. To be a property realist is to endorse the view that there is something, the property, that all the members of this set have in common, and by virtue of which they are gathered together into this set. If this much is correct, it would seem perverse to say that we can identify the property in question with the disjunctive property of being this member of the set or that member of the set, or so on *ad infinitum*. The property isn't merely being this or that; rather, it's what this and that have in common.

If this is convincing when discussing properties and the individuals that instantiate them, I think the same considerations apply to properties and their realizers. There are many ways to realize a pain, but in each case what grounds the inclusion of a realizer in the set of realizers is the fact that it is realizing pain. Being a pain is what binds all the realizers together, and therefore isn't merely reducible to being one or the other of the realizers.

But even if one did identify pains and other mental properties with disjunctions of their realizers, it's not at all clear one has overcome the causal exclusion argument. The neurophysiological property B is clearly distinct from the huge disjunctive property of which it is a disjunctive component. To explain what caused my hand to move, appeal to B seems to be sufficient. So what do we need the disjunctive property for? It doesn't seem to do any work. If pain is identical to a disjunction of its realizers, then, it still appears to be out of the causal loop.

As for trope identity, I don't think it really solves the problem. A trope is a kind of particular. As such, it can partake of many universals. So this trope of pain is also a trope of neurological property B. Now it's supposed to be the case that the pain trope derives its causal efficacy from the fact that it is identical to a B trope. But it still seems as if the original question remains. By virtue of being a trope of which property does it cause the hand to move? The causal exclusion argument seems to force us to say it's by virtue of being a trope of property B. We still lack a way to bring the property of being a pain into the causal picture.

I don't take the considerations just adduced to be definitive. Perhaps the disjunctive or trope move can be made to work. I don't find them promising, however. If they don't work, then how do we secure the causal efficacy of the mental? The answer I favor includes two elements. First, we have to be satisfied with perhaps a lesser grade of causal efficacy than we might want. There is no way around it. If materialism is true, then all causal efficacy is constituted ultimately by the basic physical properties. No other property can play this role. So if by "causal efficacy" one means the kind of role that, according to materialism, only basic physical properties can play—and I won't deny that one can plausibly use the phrase that way—then of course it will turn out that mental properties, along with all other non-basic physical properties, are not causally efficacious. But so long as we also recognize another sense of "causal efficacy," a sense that applies not only by virtue of being the ultimate ground of all causal transactions, then there will be a sense in which mental properties are causally efficacious.

When we say that believing it's going to rain and wanting to stay dry cause one to take an umbrella, I don't think we intend that this is a case of basic causation, obtaining without realizing mechanisms. Rather, what makes it a genuine case of causation is the fact that there is a lawful regularity that holds between beliefs and desires with certain contents and behaviors of the relevant kinds.[30] True, there are lower-level physical mechanisms that sustain the regularity, but this doesn't itself take away from the regularity's status as a lawful regularity. It supports counterfactuals, is confirmed by instances, and, I believe, grounds singular causal claims.

I want to make two points about the (lawful)[31] regularity view. First, part of what supports the regularity view of causal efficacy is the belief that what we really care about when making causal claims is providing explanations and affording control over the relevant phenomena. If I want to know why you took an umbrella, then it is arguably a much better explanation to be told that you believed it was going to rain than to be told what brain state you occupied. There is a rational relation between the antecedent state and the behavior that is manifest on the one causal account—the belief/desire account—that is invisible on the other. Similarly, if I want you to take your umbrella, I'm pretty confident I can get you to do it by telling you it's raining.

My second point goes back to the question of whether to identify the mental property with the disjunction of its realizers. It seems to me that in order to make the regularity view plausible, we have to deny the identity of pain with the disjunction of its realizers. The reason is this.[32] Regularities, in one sense, are extremely cheap. Consider a set of arbitrarily chosen event pairs (c_n, e_n), where c_n is the cause of e_n. Now we can construct a pair of "properties," C and E, such that C is the property had by all and only events c_i, and E is the property had by all and only events e_i $(i \leq n)$. Now we have guaranteed that the generalization "C's cause E's" is true. But do we really want to say that it's being a C that's responsible for some event's bringing about an E? To say this seems to trivialize causal relevance.

However, it is plausible, especially given that our interest in attributing causal relevance is so closely related to explanation and control, that we restrict the sorts of regularities we allow to ground claims of causal relevance to those that are not indefinite and arbitrary in the way that our trumped-up C and E properties were. I don't know whether the appropriate criterion can be rigorously formulated. I will not try to do it here. But for this sort of move to make any sense we must at least distinguish the properties we do care about, like pains and beliefs, from their correlated disjunctive properties. For if we don't, then we can't distinguish the privileged class of regularities from the trumped-up ones, since all non-basic regularities will involve disjunctive properties.[33]

The regularity view may not give us all that we want, intuitively, by way of mental causation, but it is all that materialism allows. Is it enough? I think so, but I will not attempt to provide any further defense here.[34] My next concern is quite the opposite. Once we realize that all we need to secure the causal efficacy of the mental is confidence in certain macro-level, mental-physical regularities, explanatory adequacy and control, one might think that we now no longer have any reason to endorse thesis M, the doctrine of materialism. It is to this argument I now turn.

1.6 Again, Why Materialism?

If the discussion above is on the mark, then we secure the causal efficacy of the mental by noting that psychological and psycho-physical regularities possess a certain autonomy from the lower-level physical laws. Given this autonomy, the question arises why we need any account of the mental in terms of the non-mental. Indeed, why think that there *is* some regular and determinate relation that obtains, in general, between mental states and physical states?

The attempt to show how thesis M—the claim that all non-basic properties are realized in basic physical properties—can be true is a large part of the philosophical program of "naturalizing" the mind. Recently, a number of philosophers, noting the allegedly embarrassing lack of progress made on this front, have argued that the naturalization project is misconceived: there's simply no need, they say, for a *systematic* account of mental phenomena in terms of physical microstructures. I have based my argument that there is such a need on considerations of causal interaction. In this section I want to respond to the arguments offered by two such philosophers, Lynne Rudder Baker and Tyler Burge, to the effect that the causal interaction argument does not justify thesis M. Unlike the epiphenomenalist, they do not deny that mental properties play a causal role in producing behavior. Rather, they argue that their playing such a role does not require their being realized by non-mental physical properties. I'll consider each of their arguments in turn.

Baker begins her argument with a characterization of her target: a widely shared picture of the nature of mentality she calls the "Standard View." The Standard View includes the tenet that mental states—beliefs, in particular—are, in some way or other, brain states. She acknowledges that not all adherents of the Standard View adopt an identity theory, of either the type or token variety, but points out that even those who eschew identity theories will claim that token mental states are realized by token brain states. Adherents to the Standard View also hold that it is necessary to provide a "reduction" of properties like believing that p, to the extent that one can say, in non-mental, non-intentional terms, what general conditions a physical state must meet in order to realize a belief that p.

Baker next identifies several arguments that have been put forward in defense of the Standard View. I want to focus on just one of these—the argument "from causal explanation"—as this is the one I have relied on. The basic outline of the argument is simple:

(1) Unless beliefs were (realized/constituted by) brain states they could not causally explain behavior.
(2) Beliefs can causally explain behavior.

Therefore,

(3) Beliefs are (realized/constituted by) brain states. (Baker 1995, 17)

Obviously the argument is valid. Baker is firmly committed to premise (2). So the entire question revolves around premise (1).

According to Baker, one of the principal motivations for accepting (1) is the fear of dualism. If (as she puts it) "beliefs have a causal-explanatory role in behavior" (93), but are not materially realized internal states, then they must be immaterial. I (roughly) accept this line of reasoning, but Baker does not. Premise (1) is unacceptable, she argues, whatever one's reasons for holding it, because it entails that "belief explanations are replaceable by brain-state explanations" (Baker 1995, 168). Since belief explanations are not replaceable by brain-state explanations, premise (1) must be false.

I readily concede that belief explanations are not replaceable by brain-state explanations—that point was made in the last section. But I deny that any such thing is entailed by (1). Baker gets the entailment only by a subtle equivocation on "requires": she conflates the *metaphysical* requirements for a causal explanation to be *true* with the *epistemological* requirements for a causal explanation to be *acceptable*. Premise (1) as she first states it, and as I understand it, states the metaphysical preconditions of its being true that beliefs causally explain actions. This I accept: I agree that beliefs' being brain states is a condition for belief explanations' constituting genuine causal explanations. I take this to be a consequence of the requirement that whatever is cited as a cause in a causal explanation really be a cause, together with the fact—independent of the epistemological role of belief explanations— that we live in a physicalist world. But as Baker reads premise (1), it is a statement about what must be presumed to be true in order for us to be warranted in accepting the citation of a belief *as a causal explanation*. This I categorically reject: *knowledge of* the metaphysical preconditions for constituting a cause is not a prerequisite for finding acceptable a proffered causal explanation.

On my view, as on Baker's, what generally suffices to warrant the acceptance of a causal explanation is that it supports counterfactuals, and, in general, that it passes what Baker calls the "Control Test." As she says, "We know that we have an adequate causal explanation when it affords control over the phenomena of the type explained" (Baker 1995, 122). My confidence that your smiling is really caused by your good mood is intimately related to my confidence that I can get you to smile by telling you good news, which, I'm also confident, will cause your mood to brighten. Had I not told you the good news, all else equal, you wouldn't have gone into such a good mood and wouldn't have smiled.

This all seems right; it is, indeed, the ubiquity of such examples that makes eliminativism of any sort so unthinkable. Knowledge that we have hold of a controlling property—one that figures in nomic, counterfactual-supporting regularities—is all we need, epistemologically, to justify a claim to having a causal explanation. It is thus not necessary—indeed, how could it be?—that we know anything about the mechanisms by which the regularities in question are sustained, in order to causally explain behavior. Just as we can cite the application of heat to a pot of water as the explanation for its boiling without knowing any chemistry—or even knowing that there is any chemistry to know beyond that applying sufficient heat to water makes it boil—so too we can cite your good mood as the explanation of your smile without having any idea how the brain realizes a mood, or even that it does. In both cases the "explanatoriness" derives, as Baker insists, from the belief that we have a causally or nomically relevant property, and this belief can be justified in a number of ways.[35]

I insist, however, that everything I've just conceded about the epistemology of explanation is perfectly consistent with the *metaphysical* thesis that in order to be a genuine cause of behavior a belief must be (either identical to or) realized in a brain state. The citation of beliefs is explanatory (roughly) because it works; intentional explanations afford the sort of control that Baker is talking about. But a further question is certainly legitimate: *how* do they afford such control? What sustains the relevant regularities? If we are physicalists, in the sense that we endorse the principle that all basic causal powers are fundamental properties of physics, then these questions take on a more determinate form. How do physical interactions constitute mental events? What physical mechanisms sustain psychological regularities?

Baker's own example provides one last illustration of my point. In an attempt to show that the "brain explain" thesis (Baker's other name for (1)) would be false *even if* beliefs were brain states, Baker appeals to the epistemological possibility that the world could have been Aristotelian in its physics. She claims that while the difference between an Aristotelian physical world and ours would make a tremendous difference to the truth of the thesis that beliefs are brain states, it would make no difference to our ability to explain behavior by appeal to beliefs. Certainly. But the same could be said for the explanation of a pot of water's boiling by appeal to the application of sufficient heat. In an Aristotelian world, where "water" (the phenomenological analogue of water) is a simple substance, the way in which applying heat to "water" would make it boil is presumably very different from the way in which heat causes boiling in the actual world. Nonetheless, we would be just as able to explain why "water" boiled by citing the application of sufficient heat as we are in the actual world. In both this case and the actual case, we can be justified in believing that we have hold of a genuine regularity. It is up to further investigation to determine what precisely are the mechanisms, if any, that sustain the regularity, but our ability to explain events by appeal to accessible surface properties does not await the outcome of these investigations. And of course, none of this has any bearing on the claim that in *this* world, water is H_2O.

Burge appears to commit the same conflation as Baker. Averring that "mentalistic explanation and mental causation do not need validation from materialist metaphysics" (Burge 1993, 117), he apparently believes the genesis of our *understanding* of mental causation is relevant to the issue of where the "real causal work is being done."

I see no reason to think that there is anything in the idea, now common among philosophers, that in some sense the "real" causal work is being done at a lower level. I also see no reason to think that we can understand mentalistic causation through some analysis of supervenience. . . . Our understanding of mental causation derives not primarily from re-descriptions in physical terms. It derives primarily from our understanding of mentalistic explanation. This understanding is largely independent of reference to the underlying processes. (Burge 1993, 111)

I will address the question again later why there is reason to think that the "real causal work is being done at a lower level." My point here is to emphasize that *what warrants* psychological explanations, and *what makes them true* are two separate issues. What we mean by calling mental states "causally explanatory" is independent of the nature of the mechanisms by which their causal work is accomplished. While I agree that our "understanding of mental causation derives not from re-descriptions in physical terms," I insist that this fact is beside the metaphysical point.

Still, there may yet be positive reasons for thinking that the reduction of mentality to brain states is either impossible or unnecessary. Baker and Burge do argue that there is an insuperable problem for the brain state theorist. Brain states are internal states, intrinsic to the subject, but psychological states are not. My belief that water is wet is the belief it is, has the content it has, partly by virtue of my being in a world with water in it. A molecular duplicate of me on Twin Earth would share my brain states, but not my beliefs. Nor could I have the belief that the Republicans now control the Congress unless I lived in a world that shared very complicated sociopolitical conditions with the actual world. In fact, as Baker emphasizes, there are all sorts of causally relevant non-psychological properties for which local reductions seem out of the question due to the fact that their instantiations depend on the maintenance of a complex web of relations with properties and states of external objects. For instance, my having tenure certainly has causal consequences, and so is causally relevant; but clearly it doesn't supervene on any set of properties intrinsic to me.

There seem to be three worries involved here. The first is that the physical base for properties like believing water is wet or having tenure are so complex that if explanations that appealed to such properties depended on their identification they could never be employed. This worry I've already addressed: there is no need for belief explanations, or social explanations for that matter, to await identification of their physical bases in order to be legitimately employed or warrantedly accepted.

The second worry more directly addresses the possibility of a reduction. The point here is that while the properties of having tenure or believing that water is wet can causally explain one's behavior, there seems to be no property of one's brain that plays the same explanatory role. Since one's brain could be in exactly the same state even though one wasn't in a state of believing that water is wet or having tenure, the causal efficacy of these properties cannot derive from their alleged realizations in the brain. I believe that this worry can be relieved by noting a distinction of Sydney Shoemaker's (1981), between core realization and total realization. While Shoemaker was particularly interested in the relation between individual functional states and the systems within which they operated—all of which, presumably, reside within an individual subject—the distinction can be of help in addressing externalist concerns as well.

Briefly, the idea is this. According to Shoemaker, two different sorts of lower-level properties could with justice be viewed as the realizers of some second-order functional property. Let T be a theory that functionally specifies some mental property, say, the property of being in pain. Ramsifying T, we get a functional predicate of the form

$$\exists F_1 \ldots \exists F_n \; [\; T(\ldots F_j \ldots) \text{ and } \times \text{ has } F_j]$$

where F_1–F_n range over physicalistic (or at least non-mentalistic) predicates. The predicate variable F_j represents the physicalistic predicate that will replace the mentalistic predicate that is receiving a functional definition, in this case, the mentalistic predicate "is in pain." In human beings, we may suppose, F_j will be replaced by the predicate "has brain state B." Since, for human beings, being in brain state B will be necessary and sufficient for being in pain, it seems correct to say that B is the lower-level property that realizes the higher-level property pain, and thus that it is substituends of F_j that should be regarded as the first-order realizer properties of the second-order property of being in pain. Shoemaker calls these properties *core realizations*.

So, let's take the belief that water is wet, and let's assume for the moment that some version of a language-of-thought hypothesis is correct. Inside the subject is a symbolic structure, realized in a neurological structure. Let's call this structure S. We can also assume that there is something like a belief box, so that the subject stands in the belief relation to S when S is in the belief box. Given externalism, it's clear that having S in the belief box is not sufficient for believing that water is wet. To get that belief, we must also ensure that the subject is embedded in the right context—which, presumably, includes being in a world with water in it. Otherwise, though our subject has S in the belief box, it won't be a belief that water is wet that she has, but a belief with some other content.

The total realization of the belief that water is wet includes both the tokening of S in the belief box and whatever physical conditions are sufficient for realizing the context necessary to endow S with the appropriate content. The core realization of the belief will be just the tokening of S in the belief box itself. Clearly, when we say that beliefs are realized as brain states, we are talking about core realizations, but it is only *total* realizations that are, strictly speaking, fully sufficient for having the relevant beliefs. It is therefore no objection to the claim that beliefs are (core realized as) brain states to point out that two creatures could occupy exactly the same brain states while having beliefs of different contents.

This brings me to the third worry: skepticism that there is any determinate portion of the physical world that corresponds to either the total or the core realizations. The thought is that such a determinate relation between levels is quite implausible, given the complex and chaotic interactions that seem to be necessary to sustain psychological and social properties, and given the "distance" between the social/psychological and physical levels. Some connectionists have even argued that as a matter of cognitive architecture, there will be found no discrete neurological structures like S that could appropriately be regarded as core realizations of propositional attitude states. Perhaps the point generalizes: what if it takes a total world to be a total realization?

Baker and Burge insist that given the little we know about the way physical facts relate to social/psychological facts, it isn't a really good bet that the sorts of determinate, discrete relations posited by the brain state theorist are there to be discovered.[36] Yet even so, they contend, we have no reason to doubt the causal efficacy of the mental and the social: we ought to have more confidence in our judgment that good moods make people smile than we have in any metaphysical theory that demands that moods must be physically realized in order to cause anything.

There are two points at issue here. The first is whether the materialist really has any reason to demand that there be total and core physical realizations for mental and social properties. What, in other words, really justifies premise (1)? That's a fair question, but, I contend, an answer has already been given by the causal interaction argument. On the other hand, the second point has to do with burden of proof, or rather, with order of confidence. Suppose we give a good answer to the first question, that we provide good reasons for believing (1). Anti-reductionists will still say that we've offered a mere metaphysical theory, and that if it conflicts with our everyday experience of mental causation then it has to go. But this gets things backward. Suppose I have good reasons for thinking that if mental properties are causally relevant properties then they must be (core-) realized in brain states. Suppose I also have good reason—admittedly, the best possible—for thinking that thoughts are causally efficacious. Well, then, I have good reason for thinking that thoughts are realized as brain states. If the objectors retort that it is very unlikely, given the complexity and organization of the brain, and so on, that there are such states in the brain, I reply with my own order of confidence argument. I am much more confident in the causal efficacy of the mental and the reasons for thinking that physicalism must be true than I am in any connectionist or other theory that denies the possibility of brain states as core realizers of mental states, or of complex physical configurations involving brains and lots of other stuff as total realizers of mental and social states.

In fact, I just don't see why it's supposed to be so implausible in the first place that there are appropriate candidate physical states for both total and core realizations. Of course such states will be enormously complicated from the lower-level point of view, especially the total realizations. But why think complexity counts against their existence? Of course if you think, as Baker and Burge seem to, that the Standard View requires *knowledge* of the realizations before causal explanations can be legitimated, then of course the complexity is a big stumbling block. But I have already shown that this commitment is not part of the Standard View. Only if physical explanations were meant to replace belief explanations would this detailed knowledge of realizations be necessary, but as I've been at pains to make clear, no such replacement thesis is at issue.

Whenever examples are given of how supervenience fails, it always looks as if specification of more physical goings-on would make up the lack. No non-dualist, as far as I know, is prepared to deny *global* supervenience. But it's unclear that Baker and Burge ought not to. If no proper subset of the physical facts would guarantee the mental and social facts, why think the totality will? On the other hand, once one accepts a global supervenience thesis, it seems perverse to insist that nothing *less* than the truly global will do. Find a world just like ours but with a few molecules missing from a distant star: couldn't we still have tenure? Change a little more. Surely there comes a point (it doesn't have to be literally a point, so long as the area is not totally indeterminate) when a physical change *will* make a difference, and that point marks the boundary of the total realization of our having tenure. The same case can be made for core realizations, and what goes on inside one's head. Change a neural configuration in one's visual system, and you presumably haven't changed one's belief that water is wet. But continue making small neurological changes and eventually you will.

Opponents of the Standard View, such as Baker, accept two crucial elements of the Standard View. First, they accept that mental states are causes, and that mental properties figure in genuinely causal, counterfactual-supporting regularities. Second, they accept—after all, it's patently obvious—that brain states serve at least as necessary conditions for the possession of mental states. Brain-dead people don't think, lesions in certain parts of the brain cause aphasia, in other parts memory loss, and on and on. It seems a most natural question, then, to ask how the world is set up so that these causal regularities are maintained, and, in particular, to ask how the brain accomplishes these tasks.

If one thought that regularities involving mental states required *no* mechanisms to be maintained, then of course the question wouldn't arise. But we know that changes in the distribution of mass-energy in spacetime are only caused by other such changes, and since mental states cause (and are caused by) such changes it has to be that they do so by way of physical mechanisms. Discovering the mechanisms involves discovering how physical states realize mental states, for otherwise it wouldn't be clear why these physical events constitute the mechanisms we're looking for. We want to know, for example, what sustains the regularity that good moods cause smiles. Smiles involve a change in the shape of the mouth—a physical change if ever there was one. Suppose we identify the causal antecedents of the smile, or, not to beg any questions, of the change in the shape of the mouth. Somewhere in there had better be a physical configuration that realizes a good mood, or else we haven't identified the mechanism by which good moods affect changes in the shapes of mouths.

Notice that both total and core realizations play an important role in the account of the mechanisms by which mental states cause behavior (or stimuli cause mental states, or mental states cause each other). If we want to know what mechanisms sustain the nomological relation among, say, the belief that drinking water quenches thirst, the desire to quench one's thirst, and the intention to drink some water, we have to know how to realize the belief, desire, and intention in question. But the realization of a belief that drinking water quenches thirst involves more than the instantiation of a certain brain state. The total realization of this belief state will involve being in a brain state that maintains certain nomological relations with other internal states, with water in the larger environment, and with the kitchen sink, for all we know now. Clearly if we want to explain all the regularities that are exhibited in our environment by creatures that have beliefs about *water*, we'll need to have a theory of the total realization.

On the other hand, a theory of the total realization entails a theory of the core realization since the core realizer is just that state/property whose relations to everything else are at issue. The core realization, the brain state, is the one whose tokening or not constitutes—given the background conditions determined by the total realization—coming to have the belief or not. It is the core realization that actually gets the body to move, and therefore must be located within the subject. Michael Jordan could not be a *basketball* player, and thus could not shoot *baskets* were he not embedded in a certain complex social environment. Nonetheless, coaches who want their players to emulate his winning technique will focus on Jordan's individual body and individual mind.[37]

The kind of reduction I advocate can thus accommodate two important intuitions: first, that mental causes are located in the subject, and second, that what makes a mental state the state it is—what endows it with its content—involves a good part of the world outside the subject. Core realizations, which are actually implicated in token causal transactions, are inside the subject. Total realizations involve complicated parts of the world outside the subject.

Burge directly confronts this argument for a materialist reduction, but I do not find his reply satisfactory. He claims that "it would be perverse to think that mental events must interfere with, or alter, or fill some gap in, the chain of physiological events leading up to" muscular movements if they are not themselves realized by physical events. The perversity, he thinks, consists in accepting "the physical model of mental causation": thinking that a mental event must somehow transfer energy to its effect in order to count as a cause. On Burge's view, what makes mental events causal is simply their participation in a pattern of events distinctive of psychological explanation. "Neither type of explanation [mental or physical] makes essential, specific assumptions about the other. So the relation between the entities appealed to in the different explanations cannot be read off the causal implications of either or both types of explanation." (Burge 1993, 115–116).

Either these considerations reduce to the argument about the epistemology of explanation discussed earlier, or they simply avoid the point at issue. Of course there is nothing about mentalistic explanation itself that makes any assumptions about the physical, since the identity of the world's basic causal agents is not itself a psychological question; we can carry out psychological explanations of behavior in blissful ignorance of such matters. But it is not perverse to apply the "physical model of causation" to mental events if what that means is that we assume mental events have spatio-temporal location and "make a difference" to the distribution of mass-energy in spacetime. Once we discover, from the study of physics, not psychology, that only differences in the values of basic physical parameters can make this sort of difference, it then becomes reasonable, not "perverse," to wonder how mental causes are physically realized.

1.7 Conclusion

In this chapter I have presented a version of materialism, embodied in thesis M, and defended it against various challenges. Materialism is committed to the claim that all properties (at least those that play a causal role) are realized in basic physical properties. The principal reason for accepting this thesis is that only by being realized physically can a property secure a causal role at all in the physical world. Unless we want to endorse epiphenomenalism, which I have argued we do not want to endorse, it seems we are committed to materialism. Whether we can actually carry out the materialist program and provide a realization theory for mental properties, especially conscious experiences, is another matter. But before we turn to consider the problems for carrying out the materialist program, and partly as a preparation for that investigation, we need to consider in some detail what is undoubtedly the strongest basis for rejecting materialism, the conceivability argument.

2

"Lately Things Don't Seem the Same"
The Conceivability Argument

2.1 Introduction

According to thesis M, mental properties are realized by non-mental physical properties. As stated in chapter 1, realization entails "bottom-up" metaphysical necessitation. That is, if qualitative property Q is realized by physical property P, then it is metaphysically impossible for P to be instantiated without Q also being instantiated. Thus, if one can demonstrate that there is a possible world in which P is instantiated but not Q, then one would have demonstrated that P doesn't realize Q. It might be that P causes Q, or is in some other way nomologically connected to Q, but it wouldn't count as realizing it. Thesis M, the doctrine of materialism as I have presented it, would stand refuted.

There is a tradition going back at least to Descartes of arguing that the conceivability of a creature physically identical to me but without conscious experience—or a world physically identical to this one but without conscious experiences in it—provides a sufficient basis for demonstrating that such a situation is indeed metaphysically possible. Recent versions of the argument can be found in Chalmers (1996) and Jackson (1993), and slightly less recent, but contemporary versions in Smart (1959) and Kripke (1980).[1] I will argue below that the conceivability of such situations does indeed cause a serious problem for materialism, but I stop short of endorsing the metaphysical anti-materialist conclusion that some would draw. In this chapter I will present and criticize the conceivability argument, and then in chapter 3 I will show what I think does follow from consideration of what is conceivable.

2.2 Some Preliminaries

Unfortunately, the terminology for describing modal status is not standardized. People use terms like "logically possible," "metaphysically possible," "conceivable," "conceptually possible," and "epistemically possible" in different ways.[2] On my understanding of the terms "metaphysically possible" and "logically possible," they mean the same thing. To say of a situation that it is logically/metaphysically possible is just to say that it is possible; it could happen (or could have happened). This doesn't mean that it is compatible with the laws that hold in this world, so it may not be nomologically possible. But since I do not hold that our laws are themselves metaphysically necessary, incompatibility with natural laws is not a bar to metaphysical possibility. Now, I will normally refrain from using the term "logically possible," since often it is used to express what I mean by "conceptually possible," and I want to avoid any confusion.

What is a "situation"? By a situation I mean an object's instantiating one or more properties (perhaps at a time), or an ordered n-tuple of objects instantiating one or more relations. It is the sort of entity that serves as the truth condition for a statement. Situations are the subjects of possibility and necessity;[3] this could happen, that couldn't have happened, and this must happen. In all these cases we are referring to situations. What can happen, I presume, is that I quit my job tomorrow; but it can't happen that I both quit and do not quit my job tomorrow.

Situations, as I understand them, are mind-independent entities, and their modal status is a mind-independent matter; hence the appropriateness of the term "metaphysically possible." Our capacity to make modal judgments, however, is clearly not mind-independent; it is an epistemological matter. But we do not confront situations immediately. Our judgments concerning both facticity and modal status are relative to the representations used to pick out the situations in question. I am in a position to judge that my daughter, Rachel, is now twelve years old, but I cannot exercise this ability with respect to every description one might use to refer to her, since I may not know that the description in question picks her out. Similarly, I am in a position to judge both that H_2O must (of necessity) contain hydrogen and that water must contain hydrogen, but someone ignorant of the chemical composition of water might judge that it is possible for water not to contain hydrogen. In both cases the same situation is being judged fact/non-fact or necessary/not necessary depending on the representation used to pick it out.

To capture the epistemic side of modality, I employ the term "conceptually possible." I will say that a situation S is conceptually possible relative to representation R just in case S, when thought of under R, is judged possible. As a convenience, I will sometimes apply the phrase directly to R itself and just say that R is conceptually possible (or expresses a conceptual possibility), but this should always be understood as shorthand for the claim that some situation is conceptually possible relative to R. We can now connect the epistemic *a priori/a posteriori* distinction to the metaphysical necessary/contingent distinction as follows. R is conceptually possible, and thus the situation it picks out is judged metaphysically possible,[4] just in case it is not *a priori* that not-R.

I need to say more about the *a priori*, but first let me address an obvious objection. It may seem as if what I've said about conceptual possibility leaves no room for the necessary *a posteriori*. On the contrary. Consider the standard case of water. I judge that it is necessary that water contains hydrogen, yet the statement, "Water contains hydrogen" is clearly not *a priori*.

True enough. But my judgment that water must contain hydrogen is based on two premises: first, that "H_2O contains hydrogen" is *a priori*, and second, that that statement picks out the situation of water containing hydrogen. What makes "Water contains hydrogen" an example of the necessary *a posteriori* is the fact that an empirical premise, that water is H_2O, is necessary to derive the claim that the situation it picks out—water containing hydrogen—also has an *a priori* description. But without the derivation of an *a priori* description of the situation, we would not judge it to be necessary. We can put it this way: if we judge that a situation is necessary, then it follows that we have available a representation of the situation under which we judge it to be true *a priori*. This of course allows that we may also have available representations under which we know it to be true only *a posteriori*.

Obviously I cannot deliver here a full theory of the *a priori*. However, I do need to say something about what I take to be the basis of *a priori* knowledge. It seems to me that there are roughly three possible sources. The first source is logical form. I know *a priori* that I cannot both quit and not quit my job, because I know that no statement of that form can express a truth; it's a logical contradiction.[5] How do I know that logical contradictions cannot express truths? This is a deep question that I cannot take up here. Suffice it to say that, for the purposes of the mind-body debate, everyone agrees that logically contradictory statements are known *a priori* to be false, and also, that the situations they describe are metaphysically impossible.

Quineans, of course, abhor talk of the *a priori*. Quine himself, though not all his followers, also abhors talk of the necessary, so we couldn't even get off the ground if we had his scruples. At the risk of offending Quinean sentiments, I'm going to just assume that truths of formal logic are known *a priori*. I don't think any important questions will be begged. What's more controversial, and more germane to the conceivability argument, is the next alleged source of *a priori* knowledge, what I'll call "semantic form," or, more generally, information concerning the application conditions of concepts. So if I know that all bachelors are unmarried *a priori* it's because I know that nothing counts as a bachelor unless it's unmarried. Whether I do in fact have *a priori* knowledge of this sort, and how much, is a serious matter of debate.

Kant thought there was a third type of *a priori* knowledge, the synthetic *a priori*. Both logical and semantic form yield analytic *a priori* judgments, so if there is a synthetic *a priori*, it must come from another source. The most compelling example is mathematics, where it seems as if there is a direct apprehension of what must be true in some domain and it isn't based obviously on either logical or semantic form. But of course the idea that we could have epistemic access to such facts has seemed mysterious, and for that reason many attempts have been made to ground mathematical knowledge in either logical or semantic form. We needn't worry here about this problem, since it seems clear that the argument with which we'll be concerned has nothing to do with the synthetic *a priori*.

I said above that if we judge a situation metaphysically necessary, then we must have available a representation of that situation relative to which it is conceptually necessary. Another way to put the point is this: I deny the existence of "brute necessities," metaphysical necessities that transcend logic (where semantic constraints on concepts are understood to be part of logic in the relevant sense). If, for some alleged metaphysically necessary situation, there were no description of it relative to which it was conceptually necessary—no description of it (not just none that we can think of, but none at all) that manifested either formal validity or semantic/conceptual necessity—it would be hard to understand what could ground the metaphysical necessity. At the very least, I don't see how we could be in a position to judge that the situation in question was metaphysically necessary.[6]

As will become evident below, a major issue dividing advocates from opponents of the conceivability argument is the nature and extent of the second source of *a priori* knowledge, that deriving from semantic constraints. Because I am very sympathetic to the Quinean attack on the analytic/synthetic distinction I would like as much as possible to reduce the *a priori* to logical form. However, just how far I can go in this direction and still hold on to my rejection of brute necessity is unclear. Let me explain.

To begin with, consider the following objection to my account of the relation between metaphysical and conceptual necessity.[7] I claimed above that if we do have a description of a situation relative to which it is conceptually necessary, then the situation is metaphysically necessary. But take the situation of Aristotle being a student of Plato. Presumably this is not a metaphysically necessary situation, since Aristotle could have decided not to study with Plato. Yet that situation does have a description relative to which it appears to be formally valid (hence conceptually necessary), namely, "The greatest student of Plato was a student of Plato."

In reply, I think we have to recognize that the statement in question is ambiguous. On one reading it describes a general situation and on the other a singular situation. The general situation involves a relation between, roughly, the properties of being the greatest student of Plato and being a student of Plato. That relation certainly does hold in every possible world and therefore that situation is indeed metaphysically necessary. On the other reading, where we take the phrase "the greatest student of Plato" to have an implicit "dthat" operator (see Kaplan 1979), the statement represents the singular situation containing Aristotle and the property of being a student of Plato. But on that reading the statement isn't formally valid.

However, this reply immediately raises another objection, this time to the converse claim, that every metaphysically necessary situation has an *a priori* description. Consider the situation of Aristotle's being human. If one follows Kripke (1980), as I am inclined to, then this is a metaphysically necessary situation. Aristotle, though he could have failed to study with Plato, could not have failed to be human. Nothing that is not human counts as the same individual as Aristotle. Now, relative to which description is this situation conceptually necessary? One is tempted to offer something like "The human being who did such-and-such is human." That certainly seems to have a logically valid form. But given my reply to the challenge above, it looks like this statement won't do the trick. If we read "the human being who . . ." rigidly, with an implicit "dthat" operator, then it isn't formally valid, no more than is the statement "The greatest student of Plato was a student of Plato." But it's only on that rigid reading that it represents the singular situation involving Aristotle and the property of being human. So if "Aristotle is a human being," or "Dthat human being is a human being" is to count as conceptually necessary, it must be by virtue of an *a priori* principle to the effect that "human being" is a privileged sortal. That is, if the predicate applies at all to an object, then it applies to that object in every possible world in which the object exists.

It appears, then, that one can't simultaneously hold onto the following three doctrines: (1) there are *de re* necessities of the sort exemplified by Aristotle's being human; (2) there are no brute necessities; and (3) conceptual necessity reduces to formal validity. To my mind, giving up either (1) or (3) is preferable to giving up (2), and I suppose I'm most inclined to give up (3). Whether I can reconcile giving up (3) with my sympathy with the Quinean argument against analyticity depends on whether or not there is a principled basis for restricting the range of conceptual connections that can ground *a priori* knowledge to a relatively small set, one that includes the sort needed to ground our knowledge of *de re* necessities. But whatever the answer to this question, I don't believe it will have a bearing on the debate over the conceivability argument, so I will let the matter rest here.[8]

2.3 The Conceivability Argument

If we ignore certain complications not relevant to this discussion, we can say that materialism rules out the metaphysical possibility of a "zombie." A zombie is a creature that is physically identical to a conscious creature but lacks conscious experience. So my zombie twin—call him "Zjoe"—is physically identical to me but there is nothing it is like to be him. Since conscious experiences are realized in physical states, according to materialism, and since realization entails bottom-up necessity, materialism entails that Zjoe is not possible. So any argument that establishes the possibility of Zjoe refutes materialism.

The conceivability argument begins with the premise that zombies are conceivable. Not everyone would grant this premise, but it is quite plausible, and it's certainly something I want to grant. Let's be clear what this means. It's not that I think that zombies could really exist, given what I know about myself and other human beings. Since I know that I'm conscious, and also that my conscious experience depends in some way on the physical goings-on in my brain—not even anti-materialists deny that—I don't think there really could be a creature that is physically identical to me and yet lacks conscious experience. But this concession alone does not undermine the conceivability premise.

To say that a zombie is conceivable is to say that from a complete physical description of a creature like myself, and only from that description, I could not derive *a priori* that the creature was conscious (or what kinds of conscious states it had). We can put it in the terms introduced in the last section this way. Let P1 . . . Pn be the predicates that pick out the realizers of my qualia. Let Z be the statement, "There exists a creature satisfying P1 . . . Pn that has no qualia." The conceivability premise can now be stated as follows:

CP: Z is conceptually possible.[9]

Z is not formally contradictory, nor does it contain any semantic incoherence. Nothing about the conditions for applying the relevant concepts— either the physical or the mental ones—rules out the possibility envisaged. Thus CP is quite plausible.

Since arguments concerning the conceivability of zombies will receive a good deal of attention later, let me just stipulate for argument's sake now that CP is true. What I'm particularly concerned with here is whether any metaphysical conclusions concerning the nature of qualia follow from this epistemological premise.

Clearly, for the anti-materialist conceivability argument to go through, we need a connecting premise to the effect that if zombies are conceivable then they are possible. So we need PP.

PP: If Z is conceptually possible, then the situation it describes is metaphysically possible.

Obviously, from CP and PP it follows that zombies are metaphysically possible, which is the conclusion the anti-materialist needed.

2.3.1 A Digression about Realization and Identity

The argument above was couched in terms of an identity thesis—the claim that consciousness was identical to having properties P1 . . . Pn—in order to simplify the exposition. But it's crucial to point out that essentially the same objection applies if we relax the identity assumption and return to the realization thesis. Take a particular quale, say the reddish character of my visual experience of the diskette case. Let's call it R. Suppose now that R is realized by Pr. We know that means that Pr necessitates R. But does that mean that there must be a description of the situation, having Pr but not R, relative to which it is conceptually impossible? And if so, what would it be?

To the first question, I think the answer must be "yes." Given what I said above against the idea that there are brute necessities, if "if Pr then R" represents a metaphysically necessary situation, then that situation must have some other description relative to which it is conceptually necessary. To the second question, the requisite description would have to come from the realization theory for R. To understand how R is realized by Pr we need a theory that makes explicit the connection between the two properties. If we think how this is done in simple cases, such as the example of dormativity mentioned in chapter 1, we see that a crucial element of the theory will be an identity thesis. We can explain how phenobarbitol realizes dormativity in two stages. First, we identify dormativity with a certain causal role property. Second, we show that phenobarbitol satisfies that role. If this is all laid out in detail, it should be possible to logically derive that phenobarbitol satisfies the relevant causal role description from the physical description of phenobarbitol together with a description of the relevant biochemical laws.

When it comes to providing a realization theory for R, the same two stages come into play. First, we must find some redescription of R, perhaps in terms of a causal role, so that we now have an identity thesis of the form "to have R is to have X." Second, we then show how having Pr necessitates having X by logically deriving statements of the form "x has X" from "x has Pr" (together with whatever other physical descriptions are necessary). So even if materialism is not committed to a straightforward identity between mental and basic physical (or even higher-level neurophysiological) properties, an identity thesis has to come in somewhere, at some level.

Perhaps not all materialists would agree that they are so committed. But it seems to me that one can avoid this commitment only by endorsing one of two unpalatable alternatives: either give up the claim that realization entails bottom-up metaphysical necessitation, or accept the sort of brute metaphysical necessity that I rejected above. The first alternative undercuts any basis for distinguishing between realization and mere nomological connection, a connection that many anti-materialists are happy to admit. The second alternative, as I said above, just smacks of metaphysical extravagance. It's certainly not the case that we need appeal to this sort of brute necessity in order to make sense of any of our other modal claims, such as that water necessarily contains hydrogen.[10] Furthermore, I don't see how we could ever be in a position to actually embrace any particular realization thesis unless we had the requisite realization theory, and for this it seems clear you need an identity claim at least at the higher level.[11] So in what follows I will talk of identity, not bothering to distinguish between claims of neurophysiological identity and claims of higher-level identity.

2.3.2 Back to the Argument

The conceivability argument contains two premises, CP and PP. Since the argument is clearly valid, and we've stipulated that we accept CP, the only way to refute it is to attack PP, the premise that links conceptual and metaphysical possibility. On the surface, this is easy to do. As should be clear from the discussion in section 2.2, the claim that a situation is metaphysically impossible does not entail that it is conceptually impossible relative to every description of it; there need only be one representation relative to which it is conceptually impossible. There can be other representations relative to which it is conceptually possible. So the mere fact that Z is conceptually possible doesn't automatically entail that the situation it describes is metaphysically possible.

The fact that conceptual possibility doesn't entail metaphysical possibility is exemplified by the standard cases of the necessary *a posteriori*. The statement "Water does not contain hydrogen," as we saw above, is conceptually possible, but the situation it describes is not metaphysically possible. There is of course a description of that situation relative to which it is conceptually impossible—namely, "H_2O does not contain hydrogen"—but that is just the point. So long as we know of one description relative to which the situation is conceptually impossible, we are in a position to judge that it is metaphysically impossible.

We can apply this analysis to the zombie case. Relative to Z, the existence of a zombie is conceptually possible. But now suppose that in fact materialism is true, and, to simplify the case, let's assume that qualia are identical to certain complicated physical properties, say P1 . . . Pn. Now, given this identity, the existence of a zombie amounts to the existence of a creature that both has and doesn't have properties P1 . . . Pn. Clearly, relative to the description "There is a creature that both has and doesn't have properties P1 . . . Pn," the existence of a zombie is conceptually impossible, and, hence, metaphysically impossible. Thus materialism seems to be consistent with the claim that Z is conceptually possible. The crucial premise PP is not justified.

Another way to put the objection is this. One must distinguish between concepts and properties. Concepts are, roughly, modes of presentation of properties (as well as objects). In chapter 1 I claimed that it is part of a realist view of properties that one deny that a distinct property must exist for every predicate. Clearly the same thing—whether object or property—can have more than one name. Similarly, the same thing can fall under different concepts, or be presented via different modes of presentation. This explains how what is metaphysically impossible can be conceptually possible. We think of this one property under two distinct modes of presentation, and it seems possible—it *is* conceptually possible—that the property presented by the one is not identical to the property presented by the other. But since it is metaphysically impossible for one property not to be itself, this conceptually possible representation, involving these two distinct modes of presentation, nevertheless describes a metaphysically impossible situation.

Both ways of putting the objection involve emphasizing a distinction between how we think of the world—how we represent it—and how it is. Just because one way of conceiving of a situation does not reveal its incoherence, its impossibility, doesn't mean there isn't another way of conceiving of it that will. Just because we can't see *a priori* that two concepts pick out the same property—just because it isn't apparent from inspection of the concepts themselves—doesn't mean that they don't in fact pick out the same property. In the end I think this basic point is right. However, there are interesting arguments that this simple insight concerning the gulf between how we represent the world and how it is does not undermine the inference from conceptual to metaphysical possibility in certain cases, and in the zombie case in particular. So let's examine these arguments in detail.

Smart (1959) poses the challenge this way. Let's assume that sensations are indeed identical to brain states. So having a reddish experience, state Er, is identical to being in brain state Br. It's obvious that the claim that Er is identical to Br is itself *a posteriori*. What explains our inability to determine *a priori* that they are one and the same state? Isn't it, asks Smart's objector, that this one state has two distinct properties, an experiential one and a neurophysiological one, each corresponding to one of the two ways we pick it out, "Er" and "Br"? But if so, then it seems we still have a problem, since the experiential property by which "Er" picks out the sensation, its mode of presentation, will itself be a non-physical property.[12] Smart calls it an "irreducibly psychical property." Clearly, if there are irreducibly psychical properties, then materialism is refuted.

I call the account just suggested for explaining *a priori* ignorance if identities the "distinct property model" (DPM). Smart's objector goes on to point out that this model works well with all the standard cases of *a posteriori* identities, such as the identity of water and H_2O and the identity of the Morning Star and the Evening Star. In both of these cases, it's easy to see how our empirical discovery that they are the same thing (or stuff) is a matter of discovering that this one thing (or stuff) has different properties that we originally thought might be instantiated by different things. In the case of Venus, the two properties are [appearing in the morning] and [appearing in the evening]. In the case of water they are [having the molecular composition of H_2O] and [manifesting the superficial properties by which we normally identify water] (let's call this "being watery"). The point is that it's hard to find a non-controversial case of an *a posteriori* identity that doesn't fit the DPM. But when we apply the DPM to the psycho-physical case we seem stuck with "irreducibly psychical" properties.

Kripke's (1980) argument works slightly differently, though I think it comes to the same thing in the end. He asks how we normally explain the fact that a situation which is conceptually possible[13] turns out to be metaphysically impossible. In most cases we can explain the failure to detect incoherence or inconsistency in the characterization of the situation by reinterpreting what we claim to be conceiving so that it in fact describes a genuine metaphysical possibility. We can see how this reinterpretation strategy works in the standard cases like water and Venus. I think it possible that the Morning Star not be identical to the Evening Star. While this situation is not in fact possible, since Venus must be Venus, what is possible is that the star that appears in the morning not be the same star as the one that appears in the evening. Similarly, though water can't fail to contain hydrogen, there could exist a substance superficially like water—one with watery properties—that doesn't contain hydrogen. In both cases it's plausible to say that the situations we really are thinking of when we claim to envisage a possibility are the ones that really are possible.

Another way to put the argument is this. In all the standard cases, though conceptual possibility doesn't automatically entail metaphysical possibility of the situation in question, it does seem that there is a relevantly connected situation that is metaphysically possible, one that bears a semantically (or conceptually) significant relation to the representation that is conceptually possible (or, to the representation relative to which the original situation is conceptually possible). According to Kripke, the situation that is metaphysically possible is the one that would have been described by the conceptually (or epistemically) possible statement (or thought) had it been true. If the statement, "The Morning Star and the Evening Star are distinct heavenly bodies" had turned out to be true (as it was thought at one time), then it would have described a situation in which the body that appears in the morning is distinct from the body that appears in the evening. It is this situation that, despite the falsity of the statement, remains a metaphysical possibility. If this model of the relation between conceptual and metaphysical possibility holds, then there is an important entailment from what is conceptually possible to what is metaphysically possible.[14]

Chalmers (1996)[15] utilizes two-dimensional semantics to represent this model. The idea is this. Statements have two kinds of meaning, or intension, a primary one and a secondary one. Each intension is (or determines) a function from possible worlds to extensions (which, in the case of statements, will be truth values). A statement's secondary intension is the function you get by taking the situation it actually refers to around to every possible world. So the statement "Water contains hydrogen" describes the actual stuff, water, which is also H_2O, containing hydrogen. The secondary intension is necessary, since this situation obtains in every possible world. Notice, corresponding to this necessary secondary intension is another statement, "H_2O contains hydrogen," which is conceptually necessary. This fits our working hypothesis that every metaphysically necessary situation has a description relative to which it is also conceptually necessary.

A statement's primary intension is (or determines) the function you get by taking the statement (or thought) itself around to every possible world. The truth value in a world is therefore not determined by whether the situation it refers to in the *actual world* obtains there, but rather whether the situation it refers to in *that world* obtains there. As the 2D semanticists put it, when determining the primary intension we consider other possible worlds "as actual"—if the world had turned out this way, what would the concepts in question have picked out? When determining the secondary intension, on the other hand, we consider other possible worlds as counterfactual—given what the concepts pick out actually, would the statement have been true had the facts been otherwise?

According to the Kripke argument, when a statement is conceptually possible, it must be reinterpretable so that it refers to a situation that is metaphysically possible as well. This idea can be translated into the 2D framework as follows. If a statement is conceptually possible, then its primary intension cannot be necessarily false—that is, it can't determine a function that yields falsehood in every possible world. The situation(s) it would pick out in another possible world, considered as actual, serve as the metaphysically possible situation that results from the Kripkean reinterpretation strategy. Again, it's clear that this 2D framework works for the standard cases. The primary intension of "Water contains hydrogen" is contingent, since there are possible worlds, considered as actual, in which "water" picks out a liquid that does not contain hydrogen (and "hydrogen" still picks out hydrogen), so the situation referred to does not obtain, and the statement is false.

Just as we saw with the DPM, the reinterpretation strategy and the 2D model seem to provide a satisfactory account of the standard cases of *a posteriori* necessity. However, when we apply them to the psycho-physical case, we find trouble for the materialist. We've granted that statement Z— "There exists a creature with physical properties P1 . . . Pn but without qualia"—is conceptually possible. But notice that "P1 . . . Pn" are just dummy placeholders for whatever physical properties we might come up with. The idea is that no physical description substituted for "P1 . . . Pn" is going to turn Z into a conceptually impossible statement.[16] If according to the reinterpretation strategy there must correspond to Z some metaphysically possible situation, then it looks as if qualia can't be identical to (or even realized by) any physical properties, which refutes materialism. Similarly, if Z's primary intension must be contingent, there will be a possible world in which it picks out a situation that obtains, which seems to show that some property like qualitative character is not physically realized. Again, trouble for materialism.

Let's summarize the anti-materialist's argument. Zombies are at least conceptually possible. That entails that we have concepts of qualitative properties that are not *a priori* connected to any concepts of physical properties. This alone does not show that zombies are metaphysically possible. These different concepts could, after all, pick out the very same properties. This is what happens with concepts like those expressed by "water" and "H_2O," and it is this concept/property distinction that underlies the standard cases of the necessary *a posteriori*.

But the anti-materialist argues that the concept/property distinction can't help here. In every case where two distinct concepts (unconnected *a priori*) pick out the same property, they do so by way of other properties that are distinct and that serve as the modes of presentation of their common referent. All the standard cases like water and Venus satisfy this model (the DPM). Beyond the fact that the DPM seems to fit the standard cases, there is also a theoretical reason for adopting it. *A posteriori* identity, goes the argument, cannot be explained by a concept/property distinction unless it is combined with an account of how these two semantically unconnected concepts both refer to the same property. The most natural account of how these epistemically and semantically distinct paths converge on the same object/property is that they do so by ascribing contingently related properties, which, in this world, happen to be satisfied by the same object/

property. Thus whenever a statement is conceptually possible, there will be a situation (picked out by its primary intension) corresponding to it that is in fact metaphysically possible. So if zombies are conceptually possible, some zombie-like situation will be metaphysically possible, which is all the anti-materialist needs.

2.4 Various Kinds of Response to the Conceivability Argument

Chalmers (1996) categorizes materialists into two types, what he dubs "type A materialists" and "type B materialists." Type A materialists are those who just do not accept CP, the conceivability premise. They find a conceptual in-coherence in the very idea of a zombie. Type B materialists are those who ac-cept CP but resist the inference from the conceptual possibility of zombies to their metaphysical possibility. Since I have granted CP for the sake of argument in this chapter, we are only concerned with type B materialist responses.

As I see it, type B responders themselves fall into two basic categories: I'll dub them "exceptionalists" (E-type)[17] and "non-exceptionalists" (NE-type).[18] E-types generally allow that the framework developed by the anti-materialist for handling the standard cases of *a posteriori* necessities is the right one. They accept the DPM and perhaps the reinterpretation strategy. Their refusal to accept the anti-materialist conclusion is based on a rejec-tion not of that framework in general, but of its application to the case of qualia. Their claim is that when it comes to our concepts of qualia—"phenomenal concepts," as they're often called—the situation is unique, and therefore we can't assume that the DPM, for instance, applies. When it comes to phenomenal properties, qualia, it just may be that we have distinct concepts that pick them out without there being yet other properties serv-ing as the modes of presentation for these concepts. Thus, the conceptual possibility of zombies has no metaphysical consequences for the relation be-tween phenomenal and physical properties.

NE-types generally reject the DPM and its relatives. Their argument is that the conceptual possibility of zombies is on a par with the conceptual possibility of H_2O that isn't water (let's call it "zombie-H_2O"). True, they grant, we cannot derive from a purely physical description of a creature that it has conscious experience, or which conscious experiences it has. But simi-larly, we can't derive from a chemical description of what's in a glass that it's full of water either. Yet there's no problem in identifying water with H_2O. So too there shouldn't be any problem with identifying qualia with their physical correlates.

There are, of course, strengths and weaknesses to both response strategies. (It's also not out of the question to combine the two, arguing both that the DPM is not a good account of the standard cases and also that there is something special about phenomenal concepts.) E-type responses have the strength that they don't quarrel with what looks like a perfectly fine account of the standard cases. Furthermore, it does seem initially plausible that our concepts of, and our epistemic access to, our own conscious experiences might be special in all sorts of ways. On the other hand, to the extent that one accepts the DPM in the standard cases (as well as the reinterpretation condition), one is forced to show just how phenomenal concepts constitute an exception. There can easily seem to be something *ad hoc* in such a move. NE-type responses, however, don't rely on phenomenal concepts behaving differently from other ones (though they allow them to), so to that extent they are less easily accused of being *ad hoc*.

I endorse the NE-type response to the conceivability argument, and that is what I will develop in what follows.[19] First, a word about the structure, and burden, of the argument. It's clear that in the standard cases, water and Venus, there are distinct properties to serve as the distinct modes of presentation under which we think of them. Water does have various superficial properties—the watery properties—by which we normally identify it, and Venus clearly does appear at two distinct times of the day. The question at issue is whether it is this fact, the availability of these different properties, that explains the *a posteriori* character of the identities in question, water with H_2O and the Morning Star with the Evening Star. The NE theorist says that it isn't.

Since consideration of the standard cases, as they are normally presented, can go either way, the crucial test is whether or not something like "zombie-H_2O" is both conceptually possible and metaphysically impossible. If it is, then the NE-type response is vindicated. Both Chalmers and Jackson in fact pin their anti-materialist arguments on the fact that while zombie-H_2O (not their term, of course) is not conceptually possible, zombies are. So let's investigate the case of zombie-H_2O.

Consider a complete physical/chemical description of our world, with its natural laws, and combine it all into one statement; call it "P." Now take the statement, "Water fills the lakes and oceans" (or whatever is supposed to capture the most general facts about water), call it "W." By a "zombie-H_2O" world I mean one in which the statement

ZH: P & not-W

is true. This case is exactly like the normal zombie case. Corresponding to "P" in ZH, there is the physical description "P1 . . . Pn" in Z. Corresponding to "has no qualia" in Z, there is "not-W" in ZH. It's clear that the materialist is committed to the metaphysical impossibility of both situations, the one described by Z and the one described by ZH. The anti-materialist maintains that while ZH is also conceptually impossible, Z isn't, and this tells against the claim that it is even metaphysically impossible. The E-type response would admit that ZH is conceptually impossible, but argue that there are special reasons that, though Z is conceptually possible, still it represents a metaphysical impossibility. The NE-type response denies that even ZH is conceptually impossible. The two cases are on a par.

2.5 The NE-Type Response

One way to see what lies behind the NE position is to note a quite trivial sense in which the relevant statements Z and ZH can turn out to be conceptually possible. Suppose we restrict ourselves to the first of the sources of the *a priori* discussed in section 2.2, logical form. Given that the statements themselves, considered formally, are not contradictory, clearly they have interpretations on which they are true. Nobody, not even the anti-materialist, can deny that there exists a possible world in which ZH is true. Of course, in such a world the crucial terms involved, like "water" and "H_2O," might refer to anything. But if the statements themselves are formally consistent, as we must suppose they are, then of course they have models. The same is obviously true for Z. Yet this fact alone clearly doesn't show that the situations to which they in fact refer are metaphysically possible.

If we stick with this austere version of conceptual possibility, then we can endorse the DPM, the reinterpretation strategy, and the claim that the primary intension of a conceptually possible statement must yield a truth in at least one possible world. Let's take any statement that denies a true identity, say "Marilyn is not identical to Norma." If Marilyn is Norma, then of course it's not metaphysically possible that she isn't. Yet clearly our statement is conceptually possible, at least for the reason that it's formally consistent. Does the DPM apply here? Sure, at least trivially so. The two distinct properties under which we are thinking of this one person are these: being named "Marilyn" and being named "Norma." These are clearly distinct properties, and, I submit, anytime we have a formally consistent statement describing a metaphysically impossible situation, we can always find such meta-representational properties to serve as the distinct modes of presentation needed.

Notice how the reinterpretation model also applies. If "Marilyn is not Norma" is conceptually possible, according to Kripke's principle, then some metaphysically possible situation corresponds to it. Well, what about the situation of "Marilyn" and "Norma" referring to two different people? That will do the job.[20] Similarly, the primary intension of "Marilyn is not Norma" clearly includes truths in its range since there are worlds in which the two names refer to different people.

If we now turn to the zombie case, we see that there is no conflict with materialism. That zombies are conceptually possible, on this understanding, means that statement Z is formally consistent. The DPM explains its conceptual possibility despite its metaphysical impossibility by noting that there are distinct properties of any quale that correspond to its two modes of presentation, namely, being referred to by, say, "reddishness," and being referred to by a neurophysiological description. No one doubts, materialists included, that these are two distinct properties. Does Z have any truths in the range of its primary intension? Sure, if we construe the primary intension as the function that both assigns interpretations to the statement across possible worlds and then delivers truth values, then there is certainly a world in which the situation assigned as its interpretation obtains.

Obviously this way of employing the DPM and reinterpretation model is not what their advocates have in mind. The mode of presentation associated with, or expressed by, the term "water" (or mental representation <water>) is surely not as "thin" as merely being the referent of that term (the bearer of that name). When Kripke says that what's really possible is the situation that is described had it turned out that "Water contains no hydrogen" were really true, he doesn't mean merely that we find a possible world in which those very words express a truth no matter what they mean. It's supposed to be that the situation thus picked out captures what *we really had in mind* initially by uttering the statement. So the cognitive significance of the statement must be preserved in the reinterpretation. Finally, anti-materialist advocates of the 2D model don't construct the primary intension by merely taking the syntactic form around from world to world, but rather the statement, where by "statement" they mean the sentence with its meaning. It's the *concepts* that determine the primary intension, not the *words*.

In fact, it's precisely the use made of concepts and meaning by the advocates of the conceivability argument to which the NE-type responder objects. According to the NE theorist, there is very little, if anything, like conceptual content, or cognitive significance, over and above the actual symbols of the relevant representations and their referents. Perhaps, as my discussion at the end of 2.2 indicated, there has to be some minimal amount of semantic knowledge associated with a concept's mode of presentation, knowledge that would ground *a priori* judgments. The crucial point is that there need not be sufficient semantic knowledge to render ZH conceptually impossible.

What divides the NE theorist from the advocate of the conceivability argument is a general question in the theory of meaning: for most terms, do we have *a priori* access to sufficient information to determine their referent given a context (a possible world considered as actual)?[21] If one answers this question affirmatively, then, I will say, one believes that mode of presentation is in general "ascriptive"; when employing a term one has in mind, whether explicitly or implicitly, some description that would pick out its referent given a context. If one answers the question negatively, then, I will say, one believes that mode of presentation is largely non-ascriptive.

According to the non-ascriptivist, it is not part of the meaning of, say, "cat" that cats are animals. Of course it may be metaphysically necessary that cats are animals, but the crucial point is that it's not *a priori*. Mere competence with the term "cat" does not yield such knowledge. What then is the content of "cat"? In what does one's competence with the term consist, if not, at least in large part, in one's disposition to make certain *a priori* inferences and judgments? For the non-ascriptivist, the content of the term "cat" is merely the property of being a cat,[22] and one's competence consists in one's ability to use the term so as to refer to cats. If one's "cat"-term refers to cats (or the property of being a cat), then one has the concept of a cat.[23]

There are two jobs that meanings play in a theory of the mind: they determine the truth conditions for, and the rational relations among, thoughts. Ever since the Kripke-Putnam revolution, it's been taken for granted that internal meaning alone cannot determine extension, but whether it still has a substantive role to play in determining extension is a matter of debate. According to non-ascriptivism, the answer is "no." What determines extension for the non-ascriptivist are the external relations that obtain between a representation and what it represents. On most theories the relevant relation is something like causal covariation, but no theory of this form is without problems.[24]

The crucial point is this. We can think of the relation between the representation and what it represents as a kind of mode of presentation, but it's not one to which the subject has cognitive access (at least not merely by virtue of conceptual competence). I call such modes of presentation "non-ascriptive" because they don't use ascriptions of properties as determiners of extension. Such modes work, as it were, "behind the scenes."[25] So, on this view, "Cats are furry" has the truth condition that cats are furry because "cats" stands in the appropriate relation to cats, "furry" stands in the appropriate relation to being furry, and the statement has the right form for expressing the appropriate relation between the two properties.

The non-ascriptivist reduces rational relations to formal relations, since it's only the formal features of representations that play a role internally. For the non-ascriptivist the *a priori* is quite thin, exhausted (almost) by whatever is formally necessary. Of course there is no bar to explicit, or stipulative definitions. In fact, depending on how strict an atomist one is, one may allow that some terms, like "bachelor," are in fact definable.[26] If so, then one can explain the apparently *a priori* character of "No bachelor is married."[27] However, the *a priori* character is still ultimately explained by reference to an assessment of logical form; it's just that the procedure for evaluating logical form must apply after definable terms are replaced by their definienda.

According to the non-ascriptivist, then, the situation is pretty much as our trivialization of the DPM and associated models described at the beginning of this section would have it. The water facts are not *a priori* derivable from the micro-physical facts, and thus zombie-H_2O is conceptually possible (relative to ZH, of course), because "water" is not a term found among the terms of micro-physics (or basic science, whatever it is). But if zombie-H_2O is conceptually possible, and, as all agree, not metaphysically possible, then it's clear that nothing about metaphysical possibility follows from conceptual possibility. Therefore, no anti-materialist metaphysical consequences follow from the conceptual possibility of zombies. The materialist has no more to fear from mindless zombies than she has to fear from zombie-H_2O.

On the other hand, according to the ascriptivist, certain epistemic/inferential connections between concepts reflect semantically imposed constraints and are thus knowable *a priori*. It is, on this view, constitutive of one's concept of a cat that cats are animals, and therefore that cats are animals is knowable *a priori*.[28] In the case of water, it is constitutive of the concept of water that it manifest the watery properties. Thus, on this view,

W: Water is watery.

though it has a contingent secondary intension, has a necessary primary intension. For any world, considered as actual, "water" refers to whatever in
that world is watery. This reflects a semantic, or conceptual constraint on the
reference of "water." Note, if we defined the primary intension merely in
terms of the syntactic form of W it would clearly be contingent, since, if we
can vary its interpretation as we please, there are undoubtedly worlds in
which it expresses a falsehood. But if the primary intension is constrained in
the interpretation by semantic information that goes beyond the logical
form, by conceptual content, or mode of presentation, then it's possible to
have a necessary primary intension even when we don't have a formally necessary statement.

So we can frame the question that divides the ascriptivist from the non-
ascriptivist as follows: is there good reason to believe that W is *a priori*? In section 2.7 I will consider several arguments that purport to show why W must
be *a priori*, and then respond on behalf of the non-ascriptivist. But first I want
to address a preliminary matter concerning how I've framed the question.

2.6 Strong Metaphysical Necessity

Chalmers (1996) takes the type-B materialist to be committed to the existence of what he calls "strong metaphysical necessity." A strong metaphysical necessity is a statement that is *a posteriori* but nevertheless has a necessary
primary intension. From what I've said so far it isn't at all clear why the materialist (in this case, the non-ascriptivist) need be committed to strong
metaphysical necessities. As I've framed the debate between the ascriptivist
and non-ascriptivist (which, for our purposes now, corresponds to the debate
between the anti-materialist and the materialist), the question is whether
statements like W are *a priori* or *a posteriori*. True, for the ascriptivist it
means that W will have a necessary primary intension, but why should the
non-ascriptivist agree to that? If she doesn't, then she isn't stuck with any
commitment to strong metaphysical necessities, since what she claims to be
a posteriori, statement W, will have a contingent primary intension.

The question, then, is whether the non-ascriptivist can maintain that the
trivialization of the notion of primary intension outlined earlier is in fact all
there is to it. If indeed all we take with us from possible world to possible
world in constructing a primary intension is the statement itself, unencum-
bered by any semantic constraints on its interpretation, then of course every
formally consistent but invalid statement will have a contingent primary intension. However, one can certainly argue that though non-ascriptivism
is not committed to semantic constraints of the sort that the ascriptivist
envisions—epistemically accessible modes of presentation—still, there has
to be some constraint on interpretation over and above that imposed by

the mere logical form of the statement. After all, according to the non-ascriptivist there is a mode of presentation, just not one that is constitutive of the concept. This mode of presentation is constituted by whatever is the reference-determining relation, whether it be causal covariation or whatever. So the semantic constraint imposed on interpretation in the construction of the primary intension is that the terms involved must be assigned referents that stand in the relevant reference-determining relation to those terms. If we call that relation, whatever it turns out to be, "REF," then the primary intension of "water" will be constructed by determining in each possible world what stuff bears REF to "water." Interpretation is not totally unconstrained, even for the non-ascriptivist, and therefore she must allow for a more substantive notion of primary intension than the one defined purely over syntactic forms.

Given that the non-ascriptivist must allow for a somewhat thicker notion of primary intension, we can ask whether it follows that she is committed to the existence of strong metaphysical necessities (hereafter, SMNs). It's clear that for the non-ascriptivist statement W itself does not have a necessary primary intension, since she does not subscribe to the position that being watery represents a semantic constraint on what can turn out to be the referent of "water." So the fact that W is *a posteriori* does not involve the non-ascriptivist in a commitment to any SMN. But what about the following statement, W', the one that expresses precisely the semantic constraint on interpretation that she endorses?

W': Water is whatever bears relation REF to "water."[29]

Doesn't W' play the role for the non-ascriptivist that W plays for the ascriptivist? If so, doesn't she have to admit that it must have a necessary primary intension, since indeed "water" refers to whatever bears REF to it in every possible world (considered as actual)? One way to avoid commitment to an SMN here would be to claim that W', as opposed to W, is actually *a priori*. This way we still wouldn't have a case of an *a posteriori* statement with a necessary primary intension.

This is a bad move for two reasons. First, it undermines the basic motivation behind non-ascriptivism, which is to render the Fregean notion of sense largely unnecessary, so that mode of presentation can work behind the scenes, outside the cognitive content of the representation. By stipulating that W' is *a priori*, one thereby puts relation REF into the cognitive content of the term (indeed, into the content of every term). This is not a rejection of sense as much as an argument about what's actually in it.

Second, and more important for our purposes, non-ascriptivism is brought in here to help the materialist overcome the conceivability argument. But if in order to avoid commitment to SMNs she admits that statements like W' must be *a priori*, then she loses the battle over the psycho-physical case. For consider statement Q:

Q: Qualitative character is whatever bears REF to "qualitative character."

No one who took CP, the conceivability premise, at all seriously in the first place is going to buy the claim that Q is *a priori*. Notice, however, that it seems to have a necessary primary intension—at least if W' does. So clearly the materialist is better off admitting her commitment to SMNs than avoiding it by making the relevant statements *a priori*.

Making W' *a priori* doesn't seem to be a good way to avoid commitment to SMNs. I think there is another way, however. The point is quite simple. W' isn't *a priori*, but it doesn't have a necessary primary intension either. We were initially convinced that W' expressed a necessary primary intension because we agreed that, for the non-ascriptivist, it was the property of bearing relation REF to "water" that was common to referents of "water" across possible worlds (considered as actual). It is easy to slide from the claim that the primary intension of "water" is determined by the property of bearing REF to it to the claim that any statement attributing this property to water must have a necessary primary intension. But this doesn't follow! In order for W' to have a necessary primary intension, the following condition must be met:

NPIW' (Necessary Primary Intension for W'): In every possible world, the stuff bearing REF to "water" bears the relation that bears REF to "bears the relation REF" to "water."

Note that "REF" appears both inside and outside quotes. The slide from the claim that bearing REF to a term determines its primary intension to the claim that the statement expressing that fact must have a necessary primary intension is thus a kind of use/mention confusion. The point is that the only constraint on the interpretation of "bears the relation REF" is the constraint we have for every term, that whatever it refers to bear REF to it (plus whatever formal constraints we have, such as, in this case, that it be a two-place relation). There is no reason to think that only the relation REF itself would be at the other end of the REF relation to "bears the REF relation" in every possible world (considered as actual). So we have no reason to think that condition NPIW' is met. Thus the non-ascriptivist is not committed to SMN after all.

I think the argument just presented does show that it is at least not obvious that non-ascriptivists are committed to SMN. However, I want now to address what is, I think, a more significant question. Let's assume, for the sake of argument, that the non-ascriptivist *is* committed to SMN in the end. Why is this so bad? Chalmers answers as follows:

The short answer to [this question] is that there is no reason to believe that such a modality [strong metaphysical necessity] exists. Such "metaphysical necessities" will put constraints on the space of possible worlds that are brute and inexplicable. It may be reasonable to countenance brute, inexplicable facts about *our* world, but the existence of such facts about the space of possible worlds would be quite bizarre. The realm of the possible (as opposed to the realm of the natural) has no room for this sort of arbitrary constraint. (1996, 137, emphasis in original)

In a recent reply to critics, he expands on his objections to SMN as follows:

> The fundamental problem with the idea, I think, is that it rests on a false conception of modality. In particular, it ignores the deep constitutive connections between modality and rationality . . . breaking the link between conceivability and possibility breaks the link between rationality and modality. . . . [On the 2D picture that eschews strong metaphysical necessities] one modal primitive . . . gives us everything. And it must be a primitive constitutively tied to such rational notions as consistency, entailment, and ideal conceivability. . . . If our choice of primitive is a space of worlds, it is clearly the logically possible worlds that we need . . . [where this corresponds to the conceptually possible worlds]. . . . Advocates of strong necessities must reject this picture. They cannot reject a rational modality altogether, as they use such modal notions as consistency, rational entailment, and conceivability themselves. . . . So they must accept something akin to the space of logically possible worlds. . . . But they think there is a further metaphysical modality, and that not every logically possible world is a metaphysically possible world. This modality is . . . a further primitive. . . . This picture is *modal dualism.* . . . Once we get this far, it is clear that something has gone wrong. . . . The second primitive is an *invention*; nothing in our conceptual system requires it. . . . It seems to me that we do not even have a distinct *concept* of metaphysical necessity to which the second primitive can answer. (1999, 489–491)

There seem to be two points here. First, Chalmers claims that the sort of metaphysical necessity that goes beyond conceptual/logical necessity you get with SMN is "brute and inexplicable." The second point is that we need a space of conceptually/logically possible worlds in order to make sense of epistemic notions like rationality anyway, so if we had to make sense of SMN we would need to posit a separate, more restricted set of metaphysically possible worlds, and the idea that there are two sets of possible worlds seems ontologically promiscuous, *ad hoc*, and generally reprehensible. Of course the two points are related. If there were a need for the second set of worlds, then the notion that appeal to them helps to explicate would not seem brute and inexplicable.

I think this account of what the advocate of SMN is committed to is wrong, but before saying why, it's worth noting that at most Chalmers has shown there's a substantial cost to holding onto SMN. He comes close to saying the idea is incoherent in the last line of the quote above, but he doesn't really make the case. Now, if the question is whether we are willing to pay the cost of admitting this new, seemingly brute category of metaphysical necessity, we have to see what it buys us. According to Chalmers, it buys us materialism and, thereby, the wherewithal to avoid epiphenomenalism. So, which is worse—admitting this new category of metaphysical necessity or admitting that mental properties play no causal role in the physical world? Chalmers obviously thinks the benefit of avoiding epiphenomenalism isn't worth the cost of SMN, but I bet many would disagree. However, as I hope to show, it turns out we don't really have to pay so much after all.

In section 2.2 I presented my own argument against, or at least misgivings about, the idea of a brute metaphysical necessity. Much of what I had to say there is quite similar to Chalmers's objections to SMN. In that case, I was objecting to the idea that a situation could be metaphysically necessary (or impossible) and yet there be no description of that situation relative to which it is conceptually necessary (impossible). It seems to me that this would indeed be a case that merits the description "brute metaphysical necessity," because it would be completely unconnected to logical necessity. I find this notion bizarre and inexplicable, although, as with Chalmers, it's not clear I have a knockdown argument against it.[30] I agree with Chalmers that our very notion of the possible (necessary) is tied to rational and logical concepts, and therefore a modal notion that was completely independent of these concepts would be quite odd.

Where I differ from Chalmers is this: I don't think *strong* metaphysical necessity, in his sense, really amounts to *brute* metaphysical necessity.[31] So long as a situation is describable by a conceptually necessary (or impossible— let this be understood in what follows) representation, that is sufficient to ground its metaphysical necessity. It need not be the case that relative to every description it is conceptually necessary. So long as we require that to count as metaphysically necessary there must be at least one representation of the situation relative to which it is conceptually necessary, the crucial link between logic and metaphysical modality is maintained.

Chalmers, of course, wouldn't accept this way of bringing metaphysical modality into line with logic, and that brings us to the second part of his complaint against SMN. His response is this. Sure, you have explained how this particular situation can be necessary by reference to this conceptually necessary representation, but what about these other conceptually contingent representations, these other ways of thinking about the situation? Don't we need, in order to make sense of our cognitive attitudes involving them, something like a semantics of possible worlds, so that we can explain in what sense what we are thinking, the way we are thinking of it, represents a possibility? If you like, we can distinguish "notional" worlds, which correspond to how we think about the world, from metaphysically independent worlds. But this introduces an extra modal notion. We need a realm now of notional, or intentional objects, in addition to our realm of real objects. This seems metaphysically extravagant. On his 2D account, Chalmers argues, where every conceptually contingent proposition has a contingent primary intension, there is no need for more than one realm of worlds. Whatever space exists between appearance and reality in the modal realm is handled by the distinction between primary and secondary intensions.

I reply as follows. I agree that we need only one space of worlds, call it the space of "logically possible" or "metaphysically possible" worlds, as you like. Anything more is indeed metaphysically extravagant. But one space of worlds suffices for both making sense of SMN and making sense of rational notions like ideal conceivability, entailment, and consistency. The point is that all of these epistemic notions can, on my view, be reconstructed in terms of formal relations among representations. What does it mean to say that one thought is entailed by another? Simple, the representation of the one follows formally from the other, and this can be given a standard possible worlds semantics: there is no interpretation on which the other one is true and this one is false. Consistency, of course, gets its usual treatment.

What happened to SMN? On this account, the rational relations among cognitive states are explicated purely with respect to their logical forms and the semantics that goes with that. When it comes to primary intensions, though, we add the constraint on interpretation that we can only assign extensions, or properties, that bear REF (the physicalistic reference relation) to the representations. But because bearing REF works, as we said, "behind the scenes," and is not *a priori* accessible, not a part of the cognitive significance of the representation, it does not enter into the interpretation function when assessing epistemic notions like entailment, rational consistency, and the like.

On this view, then, we have one space of worlds, but three different interpretation functions, corresponding to three different jobs. The least constrained is the one that only looks at the formal features of the relevant representations, and is otherwise free to assign any extensions whatever. At this level, of course, for every formally consistent representation there will indeed be a possible world in which it's true. The next level of constraint captures the way that representations in fact hook up to the world, and this corresponds to the primary intension. At this level, there may be consistent representations that nevertheless do not get assigned possible situations. This is not any sort of mysterious new modality, just the workings of this extra-cognitive constraint on interpretation.[32] Finally, the third level reflects the outcome of interpretation in the actual world, and then we get the *a posteriori* necessities associated with secondary intensions.

2.7 Ascriptivist Arguments and Replies

At the end of section 2.5, I said the question between the opposing sides could be framed as follows: is there good reason to believe that W (the statement "Water is watery") is *a priori*? In this section I want to consider two arguments for an affirmative answer, and reply to each on behalf of the non-ascriptivist. I call these the "argument from knowledge of identity" and the "argument from explanation."

2.7.1 The Argument from Knowledge of Identity

The argument from knowledge of identity goes like this. Without appeal to the sort of analytic *a priori* connections denied by the ascriptivist we can't make sense of the standard cases of allegedly synthetic *a posteriori* judgments of theoretical identity in the first place. So, take the case of water. What justifies us in claiming that water is indeed identical to H_2O, if not a prior— that is, an *a priori*—understanding that by "water" we mean "the local watery stuff," together with the empirical discovery that H_2O fits the bill? Thus W must be *a priori*.

In reply, it doesn't seem to me that *a priori* analytic connections are necessary to justify our theoretical identity judgments. Suppose "water" has a purely non-ascriptive mode of presentation. It might seem that we lack an epistemic handle with which to connect it now to H_2O. But to get the required "epistemic handle" it isn't necessary for us to have *a priori* access to anything about either water or "water"; it's enough that we have fairly well-justified beliefs about water that are expressed with "water." That I believe very strongly that water is the local watery stuff is not in question here. Since I do, and since I discover that H_2O is also the local watery stuff, I conclude that they are the same thing. No *a priori* knowledge is necessary.

The ascriptivist might object that while it's part of the justification of the identification of water with H_2O that one's beliefs about water turn out to be about H_2O, there is still a choice left to make that the empirical discovery doesn't touch: namely, whether water is to be identified with the water role itself or with its occupant. To make this decision we have recourse to our modal intuitions, which involve judgments about what we would say under certain circumstances, such as the Twin Earth example, and this reflects *a priori* knowledge concerning our concept.[33]

Undoubtedly the objector is right that there are two issues here. First, there is the question, answerable by empirical means, about which property/substance plays the water role. As far as the metaphysics is concerned, both properties exist: the property of filling the water role, and the property of being H_2O. Second, there is a semantic question: given the existence of both the role property and the occupant property, to which one do we refer with our use of "water"? The fact that, on reflection, we would not call XYZ "water" does seem to show that we are using "water" to refer to the occupant, not the role. Does this show that "water" has an *a priori* analysis?

I don't think so. It's important, for the purposes of this controversy, that we not confuse "armchair accessibility" with *a priori* accessibility. Our intuitions about what we would say the water was if various scenarios turned out to be the case is certainly an "armchair" exercise, and therefore looks *a priori* in character. However, I think we can treat semantic intuitions—what we would say in various circumstances—the way the syntactician treats grammaticality intuitions. By considering what we would say we garner evidence for the correct semantic theory. The fact that we are inclined not to call XYZ "water" reveals to us, as evidence bearing on an empirical hypothesis, that our concept of water is of a role occupant, not a role itself. But our ability to reflect on our practice is not itself constitutive of the practice. Therefore, we still have no argument that *a priori* knowledge of a certain sort is necessary for concept possession.

One way to see this is to note the possibility of concept possessors who lack the reflective capability we have. Higher animals present one sort of example. Lacking such a capacity—to entertain hypothetical cases and render judgments about what we would say—would certainly be a hindrance for constructing a semantic theory, just as it would be for constructing a syntactic theory.[34] Nevertheless, it wouldn't show that there was nothing for such a theory to be about.[35]

Finally, it is open to the non-ascriptivist to admit that on the question of what kind of thing water is—a role-property or a substance occupying the role—we do have *a priori* access to the answer. But that isn't sufficient to render zombie-H_2O conceptually impossible, which is the point at issue here. So long as the specification of the role itself is not known *a priori*, statement ZH cannot be ruled out on *a priori* grounds.

The non-ascriptivist response to the argument from knowledge of identity relies on according an empirical status to our intuitions concerning what we would say water was, were the world to turn out various ways. The ascriptivist sees these intuitions, this ability they manifest, as an expression of our *a priori* grasp of the concept of water. To bolster the claim that this ability reflects an *a priori* grasp of the concept, the ascriptivist might argue as follows. Look what we seem to be able to do: you give me an arbitrary description of a way the world might have turned out to be (excluding explicit reference to water, of course), and I'll tell you what the water is on that scenario. How could this be a reflection of an empirical judgment, since, we can presume, all the relevant empirical information is included in the description of the scenario?

It does get tricky how to proceed here, because of course it isn't clear that, as a practical matter, I can actually do what I just claimed I can do. But the ascriptivist would claim that any inability to carry out this cognitive task would only reflect the standard, boring sorts of cognitive limitations having to do with memory and computational load. Under an appropriate idealization, she would claim, I can make the determination about what water turns out to be when given a relatively complete description of a world. It's not clear to me just how to adjudicate whether the ascriptivist is really entitled to this idealization. But let me accept it for the sake of argument.

In reply I would say that it all depends on what you count as "all the relevant empirical information." Presumably what the ascriptivist has in mind are all the empirical facts that bear on the judgment concerning the identity and composition of water. But there are two relevant domains which do not clearly fit this description, and whose content is relevant to the judgment of water's identity: confirmation theory and the theory of reference. If one believes that either, or both, of these theories is ultimately *a posteriori*, as anyone who is generally suspicious of the *a priori* on Quinean grounds, including our non-ascriptivist, is likely to, then the judgment of water's identity is still not *a priori*. There might be equally conceptually cogent, but incompatible choices about water's identity on a given scenario, depending on which confirmation function or interpretation function is correct. If the latter choice is *a posteriori*, then so is the former.[36]

The ascriptivist might try the opposite tack: rather than arguing from the possibility of empirically discovering certain identities, arguing instead from the conceptual impossibility of discovering certain other identities. For example, can one conceive of water turning out to have none of the standard properties by which we recognize it? Could scientists tell us that this stuff we drink, that falls from the sky, that fills lakes and oceans, isn't really water after all? Not, mind you, that some of it isn't.[37] Rather, what I'm talking about is a case where none of the stuff we pretheoretically picked out as water turns out to be H_2O, but the scientists tell us that water is H_2O nevertheless. Certainly in such a case we would say they were wrong. By "water" we meant this stuff in the lakes and oceans and the stuff we drink. If you're not talking about *that* when you identify it with H_2O, then you're not talking about water. But what could explain the strength of this conviction if not possession of *a priori* analytic knowledge of the meaning of "water"?

In response, one can maintain the denial of analytic connections even in the face of this argument, so long as one has an account of how certain beliefs about water can be privileged in some other way. I don't think it's hard to see how to do this. Clearly I'm prepared to find out some surprising stuff about water as a result of scientific investigation. It's enough to note in this connection an example Ned Block[38] is fond of, that glass turns out to be a liquid. But surely not all of our central beliefs, especially those that are most closely tied to the circumstances in which we apply the term/concept, could be wrong; for what would then tie our concept to the property it's alleged to be about? This isn't an appeal to analyticity, but rather an appeal to the empirical conditions necessary for maintaining whatever causal or nomic connection constitutes reference.

Furthermore, remember that what normally justifies an identification of a common property/substance, such as water, with a scientifically discovered property is the use to which that identity statement can be put in constructing explanatory arguments whose conclusions express the commonly held beliefs about it. So, an identification which contradicted every single one of these commonly held beliefs would be hard-pressed to find any justification. Again, this consideration makes no appeal to analytic connections. Rather, the inconceivability of the situation in which all of our commonly held beliefs about water are false is explained by the strength of our conviction that no theoretical identification entailing such a consequence would be justified.

2.7.2 The Argument from Explanation

This brings us to the second epistemic argument, the argument from explanation. I've argued that it is not a requirement of our possession of the concept WATER, or understanding the term "water," that we also possess some conceptually connected description of its superficial properties, a description of the water role. Yet, we do in fact possess such a description, whether you want to call it conceptually connected or not, and it clearly plays a crucial role in the epistemology of chemical discovery. In particular, it's hard to see how we could explain anything about water by appeal to its chemical composition, unless two conditions were met: first, there were descriptions of various superficial properties of water that stood in need of explanation, and second, we could derive these descriptions from the descriptions of water's chemical composition together with various chemical principles and laws.[39]

For instance, I want to know why water is liquid at room temperature. The story goes roughly like this. Room temperature is a state of matter constituted by a certain mean molecular kinetic energy, call it "r." H_2O molecules, when at r, are bonded in such a way that they display the motion syndrome constitutive of liquidity. For this to really constitute a full explanation, a description of the liquid state of water at room temperature should be formally derivable from the descriptions of the properties of H_2O molecules at r. If we couldn't, at least in principle, turn this explanation into a genuine derivation, then for all we would know it would in fact be possible to have H_2O molecules at r (and have the rest of the relevant chemical facts stay the same) without water's being liquid at room temperature. But if this is possible, then we still don't know why water is in fact liquid at room temperature. It may well be that the macrofacts supervene on the microfacts, even though we can't derive a description of the macrofacts from the microfacts. But this would be small comfort, for we would have lost the explanatory power we expected from the execution of the materialist program. Thus, to the extent we feel that we do indeed have a genuine explanation of the liquidity of water at room temperature, a derivation of the macrofacts from the microfacts must exist, and be (in principle) accessible to us.

Until now we've seen no argument that committed the materialist to an *a priori* connection between what's expressible in physical vocabulary and what's expressible in non-physical vocabulary. But the existence of successful explanations seems to provide just the argument that's needed. For now we can ask how such derivations are possible if it isn't the case that one's grasp of the concepts in the explanandum consists at least in part in knowledge of analytic connections to other concepts.

There is indeed a problem concerning explanatory derivations that could be solved by appeal to analytic connections. The problem is this. Given the difference between the vocabularies in which the microfacts and macrofacts are expressed, how do we get a derivation of the latter from the former? The ascriptivist answers that all of the terms used to describe the macrofacts— from "water" to "liquid"—have analytic connections to descriptions of causal roles which themselves involve only quantifiers and terms that are held in common with the microdescriptions (such as mathematical quantities, specifications of spatio-temporal locations, and the like). These descriptions of causal roles, given their analytic equivalence to the originals, can then be substituted for all the macroterms appearing in both the explanans and the explanandum. Once the substitution is completed, the problem of disparate vocabularies, which seemed to present an obstacle to a derivation of the explanandum from the explanans, vanishes.

The account just presented certainly provides one way of understanding how the requisite derivations are possible. However, there is an alternative account available. Suppose we just took the relevant identities as empirical premises in the derivation, your standard bridge principles. So, we have that water = H_2O, that liquidity = a certain property specifiable in micro and spatial terms, and so on. In fact, this very straightforward, simple solution to the problem fits well with our answer to a question that arose earlier: namely, what justifies the claim that water is H_2O in the first place? According to the ascriptivist, this claim is the conclusion of a derivation that contains the analytic definition of "water" in terms of the occupant of the water role together with the empirical premise that H_2O in fact occupies the water role. But the non-ascriptivist presents quite a different picture. That water is H_2O is not the conclusion of any derivation. Rather, it functions as a premise in various explanatory arguments that have descriptions of water's macro-properties as their conclusions. When asked for the justification of the premise itself, the answer is that it's justified because of the explanatory role it plays. By accepting the claim that water is H_2O it's then possible to show why water has the superficial properties it has. No analytic definition need enter the reasoning either to support the identity claim itself or to function in the various explanatory arguments from the microchemical facts to the macrofacts about water.

Notice that the microexplanation of the macrofact that water is liquid at room temperature contains three bridge principles among its premises: that water = H_2O, that liquidity = a certain spatial behavioral syndrome, and that room temperature = mean kinetic energy r. If asked for an explanation of any of these three identities the correct response is to express perplexity about what it means to explain an identity anyway. Things are what they are; there is no sense to explaining that. Let me elaborate a bit. The non-ascriptivist's response to the argument from explanation relies crucially on the premise that an identity is not the sort of fact that stands in need of explanation.[40] Of course there are identity claims that one can seek explanations for, but they always turn out really to be, if not requests for evidence, questions about how or why distinct properties are coinstantiated. So, for instance, I can express wonder that this full-grown man I am now facing is the same person as the little boy I met 20 years ago, or even that this apparently continuously divisible liquid I call "water" could be the same thing as a collection of H_2O molecules. But in both these cases it's clear that what I'm wondering about is how the very same object could instantiate these very different properties. To wonder about pure identities, how X could be itself, where no distinct properties are involved, doesn't seem intelligible.

Thus, in the explanation of water's liquidity at room temperature, the identity of water with H_2O can serve as a premise in the explanatory argument that stands in no need of further explanation itself. If one does in fact wonder how water could be H_2O in the two-property sense just described—how what appears continuously divisible, say, could have a molecular construction—we can explain that by appeal to the properties of H_2O and physicochemical laws. This would be a case of explaining how what has one property could also have another. If one wonders about how water could be H_2O in the justification sense—why we should believe water is H_2O—then the evidential question is answered by pointing to explanations of other facts, such as the fact that water is liquid at room temperature, which depend crucially on acceptance of the identity of water and H_2O.

2.8 Ascriptivist Responses

To this point I've been considering the (NE-type) materialist response to the conceivability argument that is based on a non-ascriptivist theory of meaning (or cognitive/conceptual content). I have developed this line of response at length because I am partial to it myself, and I think it brings out the issues that divide the advocate of the conceivability argument from her opponent in a particularly sharp manner. However, one needn't go all the way and buy non-ascriptivism to resist the conceivability argument.

One line of response that was mentioned earlier is the E-type response. On this view, though normally one grants that conceptual competence entails *a priori* access to primary intensions, in the case of phenomenal concepts—concepts of qualia—we lack this sort of epistemic access. So, according to this view, both zombies and zombie-H_2O are metaphysically impossible, but whereas zombie-H_2O is also conceptually impossible (even relative to ZH, the statement "P & ~W"), zombies are conceptually possible (relative to Z). Since this view accepts the DPM, the principle that when identities are conceptually contingent there must be distinct properties serving as the modes of presentation for the terms flanking the identity sign, the question is why there needn't be such distinct properties in the psycho-physical case.

What advocates of the E-type response tend to do is point out peculiarities in our concepts of, and epistemic access to, our own conscious experiences.[41] As I said earlier, I agree that there is something special going on in this case, but to my mind it actually strengthens the anti-materialist's case, though not to the point of actually demonstrating the existence of non-physically realized properties. I will develop this view at length in the chapters to follow. For now, let it suffice to note again that this is a way out for the materialist, but not one that I find promising.

What is crucial to being an NE-type response, as I intend the E/NE distinction, is that one holds that zombie-H_2O is also conceptually possible, that ZH is not *a priori* false. An ascriptivist could endorse this conclusion, so long as she thought that the conceptual contents of most macro terms like "water," "liquid," and so on were not sufficiently analyzable as to allow the derivation of their satisfaction from descriptions in a purely microphysical vocabulary. It seems to me that this is a plausible position. Let me elaborate.

Remember, one of the principal arguments for holding that primary intensions, or modes of presentation, are accessible *a priori* is our purported ability to determine, for arbitrary descriptions of possible worlds, what the water would be in that world. You tell me that it's XYZ that fills the lakes and oceans in a world (considered as actual), and I'll tell you that XYZ is water. Let's grant for now that we have this ability, and that it manifests conceptual knowledge. In particular, as the ascriptivist claims, it is *a priori* that "water" refers to whatever is watery in our world. Still, is it plausible that I could render a verdict for any description of a possible world, even if the vocabulary in which the description is couched is restricted to the terms of microphysics? Why should I believe I have that ability? It certainly doesn't seem to me that I could tell from such a description what the water would be. The problem is that I wouldn't be able to tell what the watery stuff is.

The point is that when you use terms like "lakes and oceans" and "liquid at room temperature," my conceptual competence may be such as to provide me with the requisite knowledge to determine which stuff is the water. That's because my concept of water is analyzable in those terms. But it's not clear that it's analyzable to a point that allows derivation of that analysis from descriptions in microphysics. True, my inability now to say what I would say if faced with such a global microphysical description may reflect the non-ideal character of the exercise, or mere pragmatic limitations on my computational abilities. But the burden of argument is on the person who claims that there is such a thoroughgoing analysis. At least with analyses in macro terms she can point to our manifest practice of generally answering questions like "If the world were like this, what would the water be?" But when a purely microphysical description is substituted for "this" in the question, there is no positive evidence that, but for pragmatic limitations, we could generally answer it.

It's not that the only basis for thinking that the water facts are derivable from the microphysical facts is the ability we manifest to determine what the water is in various possible worlds considered as actual. The explanation for this ability, according to this view, is that the concepts in question are causal, or functional role concepts, and this claim is supposed to apply to all the concepts epistemically connected at the macro level. So not only is our concept of water supposed to be a role concept, but also our concepts of liquidity, room temperature, and lakes.[42] If these roles are all interdefinable, so that we can Ramsify the entire network of concepts, then it might seem as if their satisfaction had to be derivable from the lower microphysical level. I grant that there is some plausibility to this view. My point is only that the phenomenon standing in need of explanation, our ability to tell what the water is when given a reasonable macrolevel description of a possible world considered as actual, doesn't demand this account, and so it's open to the NE-type theorist who is also an ascriptivist to deny that the water facts are derivable from the microphysical facts.

However, in order for that denial to be plausible, I think even the ascriptivist has to block the role analysis of the macroconcepts at some point; otherwise the Ramsification move will seem quite plausible. That is, while one might be an ascriptivist about "water" and several of its epistemic liaisons, if one doesn't want to fall into holism, there have to be some of the terms (or concepts) involved that aren't so analyzable. The problem with holism is that it makes all of a concept's inferential connections constitutive of its identity, and this makes interpersonal attributions of content nearly impossible. It's for this reason, in the end, that I prefer the non-ascriptivist version of the NE-type response to the conceivability argument. Since you've got to bring in non-analyzable concepts at some point, I don't see why they should not be brought in from the start. Still, it's worth noting that one needn't be a thoroughgoing non-ascriptivist to resist the argument.

2.9 Conclusion

In this chapter I've considered the conceivability argument against materialism. Materialists who grant that zombies are conceptually possible must face an argument to the effect that from the conceptual possibility of zombies it follows that they are metaphysically possible. Standard appeals to the necessary *a posteriori* do not automatically block this inference. There are arguments, couched in terms of the "distinct property model" and 2D semantics, that purport to demonstrate that metaphysical consequences do flow from conceptual possibilities. I distinguished two sorts of response to this argument: the E-type, which grants the general semantic account of *a posteriori* necessities, but claims that it doesn't apply to the case of qualia, and the NE-type, which rejects the general semantic account. Within the latter camp I presented two further versions, the non-ascriptivist one and the ascriptivist one. My preferred response, to which the most attention was devoted, is the non-ascriptivist version of the NE-type response.

So, if my arguments have been successful, what have I shown? From the fact that the phenomenal facts are not derivable *a priori* from the physical facts it does not follow that the phenomenal facts are not realized by the physical facts. Thus materialism, as embodied in thesis M, is not strictly incompatible with premise CP, the claim that zombies are conceivable. Still, as I've mentioned all along, I don't think this quite gets materialism off the hook. While materialism may be true, and, as I argued in chapter 1, I think we have excellent reasons for thinking it must be true, there is still an important sense in which we can't really understand *how it could be true*. It is to the task of making this case that I now turn.

3

"Actin' Funny, but I Don't Know Why"
The Explanatory Gap

3.1 Introduction

In defending materialism against the objections of Baker and Burge at the end of chapter 1, I relied heavily on the distinction between the metaphysical thesis M and any epistemological theses regarding explanation. I argued that we could be in an excellent epistemic position to assert both that mental properties are causally efficacious, and that their causal efficacy stems ultimately from underlying physical mechanisms, without knowing anything about the way in which they are realized physically. However, now I want to turn to the question of explanation. In particular, I want to argue that there is a problem for materialism lurking here.

Though I stand by my argument against Baker and Burge, I do believe that if materialism is true, there ought to be an explanation of how the mental arises from the physical: a realization theory. While we may not require possession of such a theory to certify claims regarding mental causation, such a theory should be in principle accessible. Science is in the business of explanation. We want to know not only that such-and-such is the case, but also *why* it is the case. If nature is one large, lawful, orderly system, as the materialist (or naturalist) insists it is, then it should be possible to explain the occurrence of any part of that system in terms of the basic principles that govern nature as a whole.

The problem, however, is that there are good reasons for thinking that, unlike other macro domains, when it comes to qualia, we are not lacking merely enough detail to provide the requisite explanation, but any idea of how such a theory might go. That is, there is an explanatory gap between the physical and the mental (at least when it comes to qualia). In this chapter I will present the case for the claim that such a gap exists.

In section 3.2, I will briefly survey some of the principal ideas in the literature on scientific explanation, so that we can establish criteria for what an explanation of qualia in physical terms should include. In section 3.3, I'll present the argument for the explanatory gap. In sections 3.4 and 3.5 I'll discuss various attempts to bridge the gap, and try to show why they fail. My discussion of these attempts in this chapter is not meant to constitute a full-fledged response. Rather, my remarks here should be taken more as softening-up arguments, intended mainly to locate just where the serious problems lie. In chapter 4 I will delve into my criticisms of certain current views in more depth.

3.2 Explanation

There are several relatively orthogonal issues that cause controversy when it comes to scientific explanation. First, there is the question whether explanations should be thought of as deductive arguments, or arguments of any sort. Second, there is the question of the relation between basic physical science and the special sciences when it comes to explanation. Third, there is the question whether explanation applies primarily to the occurrence of individual events, or to regularities, or to properties, and so on. I will take up each of these questions in turn.

Wesley Salmon (1989) divides the major theories of scientific explanation into two major competing conceptions: the "epistemic" conception and the "ontic" conception. (Actually he includes a third, the "modal" conception, but for our purposes the first two will suffice.) The principal idea behind the epistemic conception is that explanations are forms of argument that serve to exhibit the explanandum (the event, or whatever, to be explained) as "to be expected" in the light of the explanans (the statements that do the explaining). Two of the most influential theories that come under this heading are Hempel's (1965) "deductive-nomological" model of explanation (hereafter the "DN model"), and the "unification theory" advocated by Michael Friedman (1974) and Philip Kitcher (1989).

Briefly, Hempel's view goes like this. Suppose we want to explain the occurrence of some event *e*. We do this by constructing an argument that has the following form: (1) it includes (essentially) among its premises a statement of a law; (2) it includes among its premises a statement describing specific conditions obtaining in some spatio-temporal region; and (3) the premises jointly entail a statement to the effect that *e* occurred. The premises constitute the explanans, and the conclusion the explanandum.

Hempel extended his model in two significant ways. First, he allowed that we often seek explanations of regularities as well as of particular events. In that case, a statement describing the regularity would constitute the conclusion of the argument, and, as before, at least one law statement must occur in the premises essentially. However, depending on the regularity, there may be no need for any statements regarding specific conditions in some particular spatio-temporal region.

Second, Hempel also wanted to allow for explanations that involved only statistical laws. We might want to explain the occurrence of some event by reference to a law and a statement of initial conditions from which it doesn't strictly follow that the event will occur, though it is highly likely. So someone's becoming infected with HIV may be explained by their sexual behavior, even though not everybody who engages in such behavior is so infected.

Hempel calls such explanations "inductive statistical" (IS) explanations, and considers them similar in spirit to DN explanations; that is, where DN explanations show that e, given the explanans, had to occur, IS explanations show that e, given the explanans, was quite likely to occur. The "to be expected" character of explanation, and therefore the defining condition of the epistemic conception, is present in both models. What's more, both models involve characterizing an explanation as a form of argument.

A number of objections to Hempel's model have been presented over the years, a sampling of which follows. First, there is the problem of accounting for explanatory asymmetry. If explanation is just a deduction from laws and descriptions of specific conditions, then it should be possible to explain an event that happened in the past by inferring its occurrence from laws and conditions that obtain in the present. Or, take Sylvain Bromberger's case of the flagpole.[1] We can just as easily deduce the height of a flagpole from the length of its shadow (together with the relevant laws about light propagation and the angle of the sun, etc.), as we can the length of the shadow from its height. Yet only the latter counts as an explanation.

Second, there is the problem of statistical explanation. On the one hand, the epistemic relativity that attends IS but not DN explanations is troubling. This arises from the fact that IS explanations are not strict deductions, so additional premises can undermine the degree to which the explanandum is to be expected in light of the explanans. If being a good explanation is a fully objective notion for the one case, it seems odd that it should not be for the other as well. This is especially troubling if, as seems to be the case, the fundamental laws of nature turn out to be irreducibly statistical. On the other hand, the high-probability constraint, which is responsible for the epistemic relativity in the first place, is itself open to doubt. If we know that under conditions C, there is a 90 percent chance that event E will occur, do we have any less of an explanation of E's non-occurrence (when it doesn't occur) than we do of its occurrence (when it does occur)? We knew there was a 10 percent chance it wouldn't happen. Isn't that an explanation too?

According to Salmon, these objections strike at the core of the epistemic conception of explanation. If to explain is to render an event "expectable," then of course we need a high-probability requirement, for, by definition, a low-probability event was not to be expected. Also, since the notion of expectability is cashed out in terms of an argument, the problem of asymmetry is going to arise quite naturally, since one can argue in any direction at all (both temporally and conceptually). Salmon argues that these problems show the need for an ontic conception of explanation, on which to explain is to exhibit the mechanisms that are causally responsible for the event (or regularity).

On the ontic conception, by revealing the causal mechanisms responsible for an event or regularity, whether or not citing those mechanisms renders the event expectable, we thereby explain it. So the reason you can't explain an event in the past by reference to events in the present, or explain the height of a flagpole by reference to the length of its shadow, is that the purported explanans events or conditions are clearly not the causally responsible agents. (Of course if backward causation is possible, or if you tell the right sort of story about the flagpole [e.g., that someone built it a particular height so it would cast a shadow of a certain length], these could count as explanations on the ontic conception. But then, of course, they just might be good explanations, so that won't be a problem.) Also, once one has isolated the relevant causal mechanisms, and supposing them to be statistical in nature, one can explain improbable events by reference to them just as well as highly probable events. All that matters is that we be acquainted with the causally responsible mechanisms.

Another problem with the DN model, presented forcefully by Friedman (1974), is that it seems to leave out what ought to be most central to the notion of explanation, namely *understanding*. Explaining a phenomenon should yield understanding of the phenomenon. While understanding ought to be especially emphasized on the epistemic conception, it seems to be missing, argues Friedman, from Hempel's account. After all, on the DN model, we explain an event E merely by subsuming it under a lawful regularity. But this doesn't obviously supply understanding. Just to be told that events like E always occur in conditions C doesn't tell us *why* they occur.

The ontic conception would seem to address Friedman's concern. Revealing the causal mechanisms responsible for an event does render the event more intelligible, better understood. However, Friedman takes a different line, one that is developed by Kitcher and is clearly a version of the epistemic conception. This is the "unification theory" (UT) of explanation. According to Friedman and Kitcher, we explain an event, or a regularity, by showing how the argument pattern that predicts the event can be unified with argument patterns that predict other events, in a way that reduces the number of independent laws, principles, and patterns that we must accept in order to account for the totality of our store of data. Understanding is achieved when we show how this event or regularity is just a special case of some more general phenomenon.

I will take the UT as the prime example of the epistemic conception of explanation. It shares with the DN model the notion that explanations are kinds of arguments, or argument patterns. However it doesn't easily fall prey to the sorts of objections against the DN model that we surveyed above. As just discussed, it was explicitly introduced by Friedman to fill a gap in the DN model's account of scientific understanding. When it comes to the asymmetry objection, Kitcher argues that the bad explanations one wants to rule out can be ruled out by the requirements of unification. The idea is that the argument patterns involved in the bad explanations do not unify with those that are involved in good explanations. Finally, when it comes to statistical explanations, there is no need from the point of view of the UT to adopt the high-probability constraint, so therefore the epistemic relativity that attends the maximal-specificity constraint is also unnecessary. As the argument pattern establishing the high probability of E's occurring is the same one establishing the low probability of not-E's occurring, we have an explanation of either outcome.

Both the ontic conception and the epistemic conception face an objection from the pragmatic approach to explanation, on which explanations are whatever people accept as answers to certain questions. The objection is that we never in fact produce explanations of events (or regularities) that exhibit the causal mechanisms in their entirety, or that exemplify the full argument pattern from which a description of the event could be deduced. Hempel's response to this sort of objection was that most actual explanations were really "explanation sketches," enthymemes that left out hard-to-state but generally acknowledged premises regarding background conditions and the like. Railton (1981) has revived this idea with the notion of an "ideal explanatory text." An ideal explanatory text is one that describes the causal mechanisms responsible for producing an event in their entirety. The goal of actual explanations is not to approximate the ideal text, but rather to fill in various gaps in the text. We have a full explanation of an event not when we actually produce the entire ideal explanatory text—that would be practically impossible—but when we are in a position to fill in any arbitrary portion of it. Thus, to the objector who cites the fact that no one actually produces an explanans from which the explanandum could be literally *deduced*, one could reply that this doesn't show that explanation doesn't involve deduction. So long as it is possible to fill in any missing premise that might be questioned, the merely ideal existence of the full explanans doesn't impugn the status of the actually proffered explanation (sketch).

There is one more general issue concerning explanation that needs to be mentioned before we can turn to the bearing of this material on the mind-body problem. Some philosophers, notably Cummins (1983), have criticized the DN model of explanation for its nearly exclusive focus on the explanation of events. As we've seen already, it is not much of a stretch to apply the model to the explanation of regularities. (Friedman made the point that science (especially natural science) is almost never in the business of explaining individual events anyway.) But even with adding regularities, the model is too narrow. The problem is that aside from individual events and regularities holding between event types, another type of phenomenon requires explanation: namely, the instantiation of properties.

Cummins is most concerned with the question of psychological explanation, so he emphasizes examples from that domain. In psychology we are often interested in explaining psychological capacities, such as the capacity to learn one's native language, the capacity to extract information about the three-dimensional layout of external objects from the two-dimensional display on the retina, or the capacity to remember one's name and address. If we think of such capacities as properties of the subject displaying the capacity, then the question is not "Why did such-and-such occur?" or even "Why do events of this type generally occur in these conditions?" but rather "How is this object able to do this?" or "How is this property instantiated in this object?" Cummins claims that a quite distinctive sort of theory—a "property theory"—is necessary to answer this sort of question, and it's not the sort that lends itself to the DN model of explanation, a model that implicates "state transition" theories.

I'm very sympathetic to Cummins's argument; in fact, I began this chapter equating the sort of explanation we're looking for with the provision of a realization theory, and, arguably, what Poland has in mind by "realization theory" is very much like what Cummins means by a "property theory." But I don't see that it's all that hard to incorporate the Cummins/Poland insight into either the epistemic conception, as embodied in the UT, or the ontic conception. With regard to the latter, Salmon himself distinguishes between what he calls "etiological" and "constitutive" explanations, which correspond well to the distinction between explaining events and explaining the instantiation of properties. In both cases, he argues, what is at issue is to uncover underlying causal mechanisms. In the one case the mechanisms at issue are those that produce an event, in the other they are the ones that realize, or constitute the capacity or property in question.

With regard to the UT, what might seem most damaging is its taking explanations to be a kind of argument, with descriptions of events, or event regularities as conclusions. Yet there is no reason that the sort of explanation by functional analysis that Cummins favors couldn't be couched in the form of an argument as well, and one subject to the constraints on unification characterized by Kitcher. Suppose we want to know how O has capacity C. We analyze C into its functional units, showing how the job definitive of C is accomplished. Then comes an argument to the effect that if a creature instantiates the relevant functional units, related in the appropriate manner, then it will manifest capacity C. No special problem for the epistemic conception, or the UT more specifically, arises from the explanation of capacities, or property theories more generally.

From the brief survey of current theories of scientific explanation just presented, I think the following claim can be justified: in a good scientific explanation, the explanans either entails the explanandum, or it entails a probability distribution over a range of alternatives, among which the explanandum resides. In other words, I take explanation to essentially involve deduction. Let me elaborate.

At least on the epistemic conception, it is clear that to explain something is to in some way render it expectable. In other words, we achieve understanding when we can see why, given the information cited in the explanans, the phenomenon cited in the explanandum had to be; or, to put it another way, why the relevant alternatives are ruled out, inconsistent with the explanans. To accommodate the idea that we can explain an irreducibly statistical phenomenon as well, we can modify this slightly to include cases where we achieve understanding when we see why, given the information cited in the explanans, a certain range of phenomena should have the probability distribution they have. Either way, a deductive relation rests at the base of the explanatory relation.

However, it may seem as if my claim would come into conflict with the ontic conception of explanation. For one thing, Salmon emphasizes that on the ontic conception explanation is not a form of argument, so the relation of entailment is not appropriate. For another, Salmon also insists that it is not necessary for the explanans to render the explanandum in any way likely or expectable. Once we have exposed the causal mechanisms underlying the production (or constitution) of the explanandum, we have done all there is to do.

However, I don't think either of these considerations actually reflects an incompatibility between my claim and the ontic conception. Let's take the second consideration first. I am willing to grant Salmon's point that when we are dealing with a fundamentally statistical phenomenon, exhibiting the causal mechanisms responsible for the statistical regularity is sufficient to explain both high- and low-probability events. But if that is all Salmon is concerned with, then he should have no quarrel with the claim I made above, since knowledge of the requisite causal mechanisms should, even on his view, supply knowledge of the probability distribution covering the phenomenon to be explained. What I am ruling out is the idea that one could explain a phenomenon by reference to the causal mechanisms that produce (or constitute) it, and yet where nothing follows at all about the occurrence of the explanandum from a description of these mechanisms, whether it be the probability of its occurrence or its occurrence *simpliciter*. I see nothing in Salmon's argument to contradict this.

As for the first consideration, that on the ontic conception explanations aren't arguments, in fact not a relation among propositions at all, but a relation among phenomena, this requires only a slight modification in the way the claim above is couched, nothing more. If we think of the explanans and the explanandum as actual phenomena, not statements, then the claim must be stated as follows: in a good scientific explanation, a description of the explanandum, or of a probability assignment to the explanandum, should follow from a description of the explanans.

It's not just that there is nothing in the ontic conception as Salmon presents it that contradicts my claim. It seems to me that this claim is squarely in the spirit of the ontic conception. For instance, suppose we want to explain the boiling point of water at sea level. On the ontic conception, this means we cite those underlying causal mechanisms that are responsible for the boiling point of water at sea level being what it is. So, we would cite the chemical composition of water, the kinetic energy of water molecules, the effects of atmospheric pressure on the surface of the water, and the like, in the explanation. Now, if we really have cited all the relevant mechanisms, it should follow from a description of these mechanisms that water boils at 212°F at sea level. If a description of these mechanisms does not entail the boiling point of water, then the fault must lie with one of the following: either (1) we haven't specified a sufficient amount of the ideal explanatory text, particularly the background chemical theory, or (2) boiling points are a stochastic phenomenon, so it only follows from even a full description of the relevant causal mechanisms that the boiling point will be within a certain range, or a certain value with a certain probability, or (3) there are as yet unknown factors that are partially responsible for the determination of boiling points. Alternatives (1) and (2) have already been shown to be consistent with the general deductivist claim I wish to defend. Alternative (3) is precisely an admission that we don't have an adequate explanation.

Let's return now to the problem of qualia. I claimed at the beginning of this chapter that if materialism is true we have reason to expect that any phenomenon can be explained by reference to the physical laws and principles that govern nature as a whole. Adding the basic deductivist claim about explanation, it follows that we should be able to show how a description of the phenomenon to be explained can be deduced from an ideal explanatory text that includes all the laws of physics, together with whatever constitutive principles are necessary to bridge the vocabulary of physics with the vocabulary within which the description of the phenomenon to be explained is couched. Thus, what we should expect is bottom-up necessity, both metaphysically and epistemologically.

Is this a reasonable demand, and does it really arise naturally from a consideration of the project of naturalizing the mind, in particular? I think so. Again, let's take some particular psychological phenomenon, say my ability to tell someone my name when asked for it. Let's suppose that our favored version of materialism, expressed by M, is true. So then it follows that the process I go through from first being stimulated by the airwaves that realize the question to my producing the airwaves that realize the answer is a physical process. What makes the relevant physical events realizations of the corresponding psychological events in the psychological process of understanding the question, retrieving the information, intending to respond, and finally producing the speech event, is the fact that they form part of a system that realizes the functional analysis of the task in question (as well as many others, of course). If this is so, and if we haven't left out any crucial mechanisms involved in the realization of the psychological process, and if the psychological account is itself adequate to explaining my ability to carry out the task, then a specification of the basic mechanisms will entail my ability to carry out the task. The expectation of epistemological bottom-up necessity, derivability, and not just metaphysical bottom-up necessity, falls naturally out of the explanatory demands on materialism.

3.3 The Explanatory Gap Introduced

In the Introduction I briefly presented what I see as the main obstacle to acceptance of materialism. While we seem to have some idea how physical objects, or systems, obeying physical laws, could instantiate rational and intentional properties, we have no idea, I contend, how a physical object could constitute a subject of experience, enjoying, not merely instantiating, states with all sorts of qualitative character. As I now look at my red diskette case, I'm having a visual experience that is reddish in character. Light of a particular composition is bouncing off the diskette case and stimulating my retina in a particular way. That retinal stimulation now causes further impulses down the optic nerve, eventually causing various neural events in the visual cortex. Where in all of this can we see the events that explain my having a reddish experience? There seems to be no discernible connection between the physical description and the mental one, and thus no explanation of the latter in terms of the former.

There are several ways to make the point about the explanatory gap.[2] One particularly compelling way is exemplified by Frank Jackson's story of Mary, which he employs in presenting his "knowledge argument" against materialism. The story goes like this:

> Mary is a brilliant scientist who is . . . forced to investigate the world from a black and white room *via* a black and white television monitor. She specializes in the neurophysiology of vision and acquires . . . all the physical information there is to obtain about what goes on when we see ripe tomatoes, or the sky, and use terms like "red," "blue," and so on. . . .
>
> What will happen when Mary is released from her black and white room or is given a color television monitor? Will she *learn* anything or not? It seems just obvious that she will learn something about the world and our visual experience of it. But then it is inescapable that her previous knowledge was incomplete. But she had *all* the physical information. *Ergo* there is more to have than that, and physicalism is false. (Jackson 1982, 130)

As is clear from the passage, Jackson takes his story to demonstrate a metaphysical thesis, that materialism is false.[3] For the same reasons I do not accept the conceivability argument, I do not accept the knowledge argument. Knowledge is clearly sensitive to how we conceptualize the object of knowledge, and from the fact that we can't find the right sort of connection between one conceptualization and another doesn't entail that they aren't, nevertheless, conceptualizations of the very same phenomenon, or situation. This, in a nutshell, was the argument of chapter 2.

Even though I do not accept Jackson's metaphysical conclusion, I do think Jackson's story of Mary does show something important about Mary's epistemic situation; in particular, her ability to *explain* qualia in physical terms. For if Mary could really explain the character of sensory experience by reference to the underlying physical processes, then it seems that she shouldn't learn anything new when she finally experiences red for herself. She should have expected it to be like that. The fact that it seems so clear that she would learn what it's like to experience red is testimony to the explanatory gap that separates physical theory and conscious experience.

Another way to see a manifestation of the explanatory gap is in our deep puzzlement over the question of attributing conscious experience to creatures somewhat different from ourselves. In other words, we aren't really sure how to solve the "problem of other minds." With other human beings, or with animals sufficiently like us, we presume that they have conscious experiences, and ones that are pretty much like our own, based on their physical (as well as behavioral and functional) similarity to us. It's not necessary for us to understand how certain neural processes produce, or constitute certain conscious experiences in order to use them as evidence of their presence. It's enough that we have grounds for believing that qualia are physically realized—perhaps for reasons like those outlined in chapter 1—and that we ourselves have qualia. Using these two bits of evidence, we then have a basis for projecting our qualia onto others who share our physical constitution.

However, once we depart from extensive physical similarity, we are at a loss to determine whether a candidate creature has conscious experience. Just how similar to me—physically or functionally—does something have to be in order to have an experience like my reddish experience right now, or any experience at all? We seem pretty sure that "minds" made up of people passing notes to each other[4] do not constitute genuine subjects of experience and that minds constituted by normally functioning human brains do, but where we draw the line in between seems quite up for grabs.

It's not merely a slippery slope problem, a problem of drawing a sharp line. What we lack is a principled basis for determining how to project the attribution of conscious experience. I submit that we lack a principled basis precisely because we do not have an explanation for the presence of conscious experience even in ourselves. We know, perhaps, or at least have good reason to believe, that its presence is due to something about our physical constitution. But without an explanation of how our physical constitution gives rise to consciousness, we can't use that knowledge as a basis for determining what else has it. Were we to understand how neural firings realized reddish experiences, then we would know what to look for in other creatures to tell whether they had these, or any, experiences as well. We would look for just those properties of neural firings that were responsible for the reddish qualitative character. It might turn out that only brains like ours have those features, or it might be that they are widely shared by systems of varied physical constitutions. The point is, we would have a way to tell. The fact that we don't really know what to look for is, as I said, a manifestation of our explanatory ignorance.

3.4 Conceivability and the Explanatory Gap

Both of the manifestations (or symptoms) of the explanatory gap just described are intimately related to the conceivability of zombies and of qualia inversions. In chapter 2 we saw an argument—the conceivability argument—which tried to establish that there is a metaphysical gap between physical phenomena and conscious experience. I argued there that the anti-materialist metaphysical conclusion did not follow from the conceivability premise. Here I want to use the conceivability premise to help articulate the epistemological problem for materialism. But it isn't a straightforward matter. I will proceed first by laying out the case in a fairly intuitive way, and then deal with the necessary complications that derive from the discussion in chapter 2.

It seems to make sense that a creature could instantiate the same physiological states as me and yet have different qualia, or none at all.[5] The fact that we cannot derive that a creature has qualia, or some particular quale, from the claim that it satisfies the realizing physical states is a manifestation of our not having an explanation of how these states realize qualia, or that quale. If we had a realization theory for qualia, we would be able to derive a creature's qualitative state from his/her/its physiological state. The conceivability of zombies is thus the principal manifestation of the explanatory gap.

I say it's the principal one because the other two described in section 3.3 are derivative from it. If we possessed the ability to derive qualitative states from physiological states, we would know whether or not other creatures shared our qualia. The realization theory would guide our projection of qualitative attributions onto creatures physically dissimilar from us. If Mary, sitting in her black and white room, had a realization theory for reddishness and greenishness, when she emerged into the world of color she would be able to predict from her knowledge of the relevant physics and neurophysiology what the qualitative characters of her experiences would be. The claim that zombies and qualia inversions are conceivable amounts to the claim that we don't have the requisite realization theory.

Intuitively, one can see a contrast here between the case of qualia and the case of water. What is explained by the theory that water is H_2O? Well, as an instance of something that's explained by the reduction of water to H_2O, let's take its boiling point at sea level. The story goes something like this. Molecules of H_2O move about at various speeds. Some fast-moving molecules that happen to be near the surface of the liquid have sufficient kinetic energy to escape the intermolecular attractive forces that keep the liquid intact. These molecules enter the atmosphere. That's evaporation. The precise value of the intermolecular attractive forces of H_2O molecules determines the vapor pressure of liquid masses of H_2O, the pressure exerted by molecules attempting to escape into saturated air. As the average kinetic energy of the molecules increases, so does the vapor pressure. When the vapor pressure reaches the point where it is equal to atmospheric pressure, large bubbles form within the liquid and burst forth at the liquid's surface. The water boils.

I claim that given a sufficiently rich elaboration of the story above, it is inconceivable that H_2O should not boil at 212°F at sea level (assuming, again, that we keep the rest of the chemical world constant). But now contrast this situation with a physical reduction of some conscious sensory state. No matter how rich the neurophysiological story gets, it still seems quite coherent to imagine that all that should be going on without there being anything it's like to undergo the states in question. Yet, if the physical story really explained the qualitative character, it would not be so clearly imaginable that the qualia should be missing. For, we would say to ourselves something like the following:

Suppose creature X satisfies physical description P. I understand—from my physical theory of consciousness—what it is about instantiating P that is responsible for its being a conscious experience. So how could X occupy a state with those very features and yet *not* be having a conscious experience?

3.5 Explanation and Identity—An Objection

While I think that the conceivability of zombies is indeed the principal manifestation of the explanatory gap, and that there is a real contrast between the psycho-physical case and the standard cases of reduction, like water to H_2O, it should be clear that the account just presented must be significantly modified to accommodate the materialist counterargument of chapter 2. Remember that I argued there that zombie-H_2O was conceptually possible. If all the conceivability of zombies amounts to is the conceptual possibility of statements like Z ("There exists a creature satisfying P1 . . . Pn that has no qualia"), then there doesn't seem to be a genuine contrast between the qualia case and the water case. After all, we can't derive the water facts from the physical facts either, and yet there isn't any explanatory gap here. So the conceivability of zombies must amount to something more than mere conceptual possibility.

Furthermore, in chapter 2 we explicitly addressed the issue of explanation, and what we had to say there makes the claim that there is an explanatory gap in the psycho-physical case even more dubious. Remember, the crucial move in replying to the "argument from explanation," which was supposed to support the DPM (distinct property model), was the claim that identities *per se* do not stand in need of explanations. But if identities on their own do not require explanations, then perhaps materialism isn't even in epistemological trouble after all. Perhaps the problem with qualia is that there's just nothing to explain.[6] Let me elaborate.

Take my current visual sensation as I focus my attention on my red diskette box. Call that token sensation "r." I'm also in a certain brain state that corresponds in some way to r, call it "b." Now, many philosophers, even anti-materialists, would agree with identifying r and b. These are the same token state. So we have (1) $r \equiv b$.

Okay, let's consider the state types of which r/b is a token. We can think of these as properties, being a state of type R and a state of type B, where "R" stands for the reddish qualitative character of the visual sensation, and "B" stands for its neurophysiological character.[7] Many philosophers, again even anti-materialists, would agree with the claim that every token of R is a token of B, and vice versa, at least as a matter of law. So we have (2) It is at least nomologically necessary that $(\forall x)(Rx \equiv Bx)$.

The real question, then, is whether to go ahead and identify properties R and B. Should we adopt (3) $R = B$ (taking "R" and "B" here as singular terms referring to properties)? Let's see how this question comes up in the context of seeking an explanation. One explanatory question I could ask is this: why am I in state r when I look at the diskette case? Answer: there's a physical story that starts from the light reflecting off the diskette case and ending with my occupying state b. If we adopt the hypothesis that r = b, then I can explain why I'm in r, so I have good reason to accept (1), and I have my explanation.

Of course the anti-materialist will insist that this isn't the relevant question. The question she wants an answer to is this: why does the state I'm in have property R? Here's one answer: since the physical story explains why it has B, and since we already accept (2), it follows that it will have R. The anti-materialist will of course not accept this dodge, but will press further: okay, what explains (2)?

If (2) doesn't have an explanation, then that can be for only one of two reasons: either we've reached a basic law, or it isn't a matter of law at all, but just follows from (3). With respect to the first alternative, the point is this. If all (causally relevant) properties are indeed realized in basic physical properties, as thesis M affirms, then there really can't be any basic or brute laws above the level of fundamental physics. If one thinks it is consistent with thesis M that there be macro-level brute laws, then I submit that their exclusion should be added as another fundamental tenet of materialism. It seems clear to me that the basic idea of materialism is that the fundamental physical properties and laws determine all that happens (to the extent there is determination, that is). The anti-materialist is happy to admit the basic nature of (2) as a reason for its lacking an explanation, but then insists, rightly I think, that admitting (2) to the class of basic laws is really to abandon materialism.

So now we see the importance of (3). Can we use (3) as we used the identities of water with H_2O and liquidity with its peculiar spatial behavior syndrome? Suppose we argued that by adopting (3), we can explain (2). The reason every instance of B is an instance of R is because R and B are the same thing. That's what explains the correlation. You can't go on to ask why (3) is true, because, as we claimed above, identity facts, unlike law facts, aren't the sorts of facts that stand in need of explanation. Things are what they are. You can ask why one should think that the identity statement is true, of course, and this is just to ask for one's evidence. In this case, the ability of (3) to explain (2) would be the answer. But you can't ask what, metaphysically speaking, makes it true. That question has no sensible answer. There can't be an explanatory gap if there's nothing (relevant) to explain.

3.6 Gappy Identities

As I argued in chapter 2, I generally endorse the claim that pure identities are not suitable candidates for explanation. Yet, when we look more closely, it seems that things are not quite so straightforward. In particular, there is a sharp epistemic contrast between various standard cases of identity claims and the case of an identity claim like (3) R = B. With the standard cases, once all the relevant empirical information is supplied, any request for explanation of the identities is quite unintelligible, as the considerations just adduced would predict. In the case of (3), however, it still seems quite intelligible to wonder how it could be true, or what explains it, even after the relevant physical and functional facts are filled in. This difference calls out for explanation.

To illustrate the distinction I have in mind, consider three cases: one involving natural kinds, one involving indexicals, and one involving demonstratives. Take indexicals first. It's notorious that no purely descriptive, qualitative statement can entail one containing an indexical (see Perry 1979). No matter how full a description there is of what's happening to a certain body in a certain spatio-temporal location, it won't follow logically that it's happening to me here now. Yet, of course I can explain why I have a cut on my hand now by citing events describable in terms like "This body at time t encountered a knife while cutting a bagel." I don't get a derivation, of course, without bridge principles, like "That body is mine" and "Now is soon after time t," and so on. But neither the materialist nor the anti-materialist will claim that the inability to derive "My hand is cut now" from non-indexical premises shows the metaphysical irreducibility of the properties, being mine and being now.

More significant than the issue of metaphysical irreducibility, however, is the question of the epistemic status of the bridge principles. After being informed that the body referred to is mine, and the time t is shortly before now, would there be any sense to the question "How could that be my body?" or "How could t be now?"? Of course I can think of circumstances that might give sense to these questions, but they involve ascribing properties to the body referred to in the premise different from those I believe my body to have. What there really doesn't seem to be is any cognitively significant content to the notion of being mine, pure and simple. "Mineness" (or "me-ness"), as a notion in its own right, seems quite "thin." Thus to wonder how the body referred to in the explanans could have it (i.e., being me, or mine) doesn't seem to have any cognitive substance.

Similarly, take the following example, involving a demonstrative. I point blindly in front of me and say, "I wonder what that is." I have no more substantive idea of what I'm pointing at than that it's an object occupying space. I open my eyes and see that the object in the line of sight from my pointing finger is my red diskette case. Is there any sense to be made of my now wondering: but how could my red diskette case be *that*? I don't see any. Once I've determined that it's the red diskette case that occupies the relevant contextual niche, there's just nothing more to wonder about.

Notice that there is still no way of deriving the statement "That = Joe's red diskette case" from premises containing only non-demonstrative terms. Somewhere along the derivational route one needs to encounter a premise to the effect that *that* is what Joe is pointing at. So the lack of a demonstrative-free derivation is not sufficient to show that there is still some sense to wondering how *that* could be my red diskette case.

Finally, turning to natural kinds, consider again the case of water and

H_2O. Earlier we determined that there was no way to derive statements containing the term "water" solely from premises that did not contain the term. Yet, once we discover that H_2O is indeed the substance that lies at the other end of the contextual reference-determining relation from "water," it does seem that there is little sense to be made of my wondering how H_2O could *be* water. "But what do you have in mind?" one is tempted to ask of me. Of course I may answer that I don't see how H_2O could play the water role, how it could be liquid, transparent, quench thirst, and so on. These questions do have sense, but then they also have an answer in terms of underlying chemistry. It's after all is said and done, the chemical explanations are all in place, and I still persist in my wonderment, that one is absolutely puzzled as to what substantive content there could be to my wondering. At that point it just seems as if I'm holding on to the word with nothing in mind that it signifies.

In stark contrast to these three examples stands the case of qualia. I am told that my concept of reddishness is really about a neurophysiological or functional property. I then wonder, as I ostend the reddishness of my visual experience, how could a functional or physiological state be *that*? In this case, even if one is convinced by the identity claim, one wouldn't be mystified as to what it is I'm wondering about. There does seem to be a substantive content to my puzzlement. Finding out that a particular neurophysiological or functional property stands at the other end of the contextual reference-determining relation from my representation "reddishness" doesn't settle all there is to be settled, as it seems to with "water."

So, we are faced with the following contrast. Once all the standard superficial properties of water are explained by reference to the structure of H_2O molecules and general chemical laws, there seems to be no substantive cognitive significance to the question how water could be H_2O. On the other hand, even after all the causal role properties of experience are explained by reference to its neurophysiological or functional structure, still there seems to be genuine, substantive cognitive significance to the question how reddishness could be a neurophysiological or functional property.

It might be thought that the contrast between water and reddishness could be explained this way. In the case of water, we start out with a host of property ascriptions along with the contextual feature. Again, it doesn't matter whether one incorporates the property ascriptions into the meaning of "water," as in an ascriptivist theory of meaning, or just allows that whatever the cognitive content expressed by "water" itself, even if it's non-ascriptive, it's still the case that we possess a rich web of associated beliefs concerning it before scientific investigation gets off the ground. Thus, when scientific investigation yields a candidate to which these beliefs apply, we find the identification irresistible, and this explains the apparent lack of sense we find in questioning the identification. However, with "reddish" there isn't the same web of associated beliefs. Our primary cognitive contact with this property, when presented introspectively, is purely contextual. We just ostend it as we instantiate it. Thus there is bound to be a residual sense of inappropriateness about the suggestion that it is identical to some richly described theoretically posited property.

In reply I would note the contrast with our other examples, especially the "blind" use of "that" mentioned above. It seems to me that what the materialist is suggesting in order to explain the contrast between water and reddishness is that qualitative concepts are essentially "blind" demonstratives. They are pointers we aim at our internal states with very little substantive conception of what sort of thing we're pointing at—demonstrative arrows shot blindly that refer to whatever they hit. But just as it seemed unintelligible to wonder how water could be H_2O after learning the relevant chemistry, it is similarly unintelligible to wonder how my red diskette case could be *that* when I point blindly and am told that I've pointed at my red diskette case. If the materialist were right about my concept of reddishness, it should behave just like this case of blind pointing. But, as we've seen, it doesn't.

In fact, I would suggest that the contrast between the modes of presentation associated with phenomenal concepts and other concepts is precisely the reverse of what it is often taken to be in the literature. Where E-type materialists are willing to grant a cognitively substantive, or "thick" mode of presentation for concepts/terms like "water"—an ascriptive mode that describes water's causal role—I see a very "thin" one that merely labels a phenomenon/substance in the world. It is this non-ascriptive, "presentationally thin" view of the concept expressed by "water" that simultaneously explains why the water facts are not strictly derivable from the physical facts and also why, nevertheless, requests to explain the identity of water with H_2O, once the relevant physical facts are known, are unintelligible. There isn't enough cognitive substance associated with "water" to make sense of this request for explanation.

On the other hand, with phenomenal concepts, such as our concept of a reddish quale, there is a "thick," substantive mode of presentation. We are not just labeling some "we know not what" with the term "reddish," but rather we have a fairly determinate conception of what it is for an experience to be reddish. This is, as I described it in the Introduction, a reflection of the subjectivity of conscious experience, the fact that my qualia are "for me" in a cognitively substantive and determinate way. When we compare this substantive and determinate conception with what is represented in a physical description of the neural processes underlying color vision, there is genuine cognitive significance to our wondering how these two conceptions could be conceptions of the same thing. Qualia present a problem for reductive explanation precisely because there is a real content to our idea of a quale, and not, as the E-type response would have it, because it is merely ostensive. The intuitive contrast between identities involving mere demonstratives and indexicals and those involving phenomenal concepts testifies to this difference.

Let's call an identity claim that admits of an intelligible request for explanation a "gappy identity." Some philosophers who advocate what I consider E-type responses to the conceivability argument have tried to explain the peculiar cognitive content of phenomenal concepts in a way that might seem to explain the gappiness of phenomenal-physical identities, though this is not their way of putting it. I have in mind in particular the views of David Papineau (1995) and Brian Loar (1997). As Papineau presents the argument, what makes psycho-physical identities like (3) seem so difficult to accept is that one side of the identity, "R" in our case, is a representation that one can token only by also tokening an instance of the state it represents. When I imagine a reddish experience, I can do so, in the relevant first-person sort of way, only by actually putting myself in a state that is qualitatively similar to a reddish experience. Rather than actually seeing something red, of course, I may only be calling up a visual image. But even with this fainter image, it's still the case that something reddish is going on inside me. What's more, there is physiological evidence that when I form a reddish image some of the very same neural states are involved as when I see something red.

So the reason that (3) causes epistemological puzzlement in a way that water = H_2O doesn't is this. When I entertain "R," I am using the state I'm representing, R/B, to represent it, whereas this is not the case with "B." Since "B" doesn't involve R/B itself whereas "R" does, it appears to me that they couldn't be referring to the same thing. But this is an illusion brought on by the peculiarly intimate relation between "R" and R/B. It doesn't show that "R" and "B" don't refer to the same thing, nor that the identity (3) R = B stands in need of explanation any more than any other identity claim.

Brian Loar argues that phenomenal concepts are "recognitional concepts," concepts that are exercised directly through the recognition of their instances. I'm not sure I completely understand Loar's view. Taken one way, he seems to be assimilating phenomenal concepts to demonstrative ones, a move that won't work, as I have already argued. But he claims not to be doing this, and a crucial part of his view is the idea that phenomenal properties serve as the modes of presentation of phenomenal concepts. Whereas with most other concepts we use other properties as a mode of presentation of the target object/property, in the case of a property like reddishness, it itself is the mode of presentation of our concept of reddishness. It is this peculiar fact about the concept of reddishness that explains our peculiar cognitive relation to any psycho-physical identity claim involving reddishness, and therefore the gappiness of the identity.

Of course I myself, in the Introduction, claimed that part of what's involved in the subjectivity of qualia is the fact that they seem to serve as their own modes of presentation. However, I don't pretend to understand clearly how this can be so, and it's certainly unclear to me how appeal to this idea can help explain the gappiness of psycho-physical identities in a materialistically respectable way. Again, a view like Papineau's, where the instantiation of the property is a necessary condition for application of the concept, might be a way of spelling that out.

With regard to Papineau's position, I don't see that appeal to the coinstantiation of R with "R" really makes any difference. After all, consider yet again my example of the blind demonstrative. The demonstrative can't refer to anything that isn't there, so it's clear that the diskette case must be there in order for the demonstrative to refer to it, a requirement that doesn't attend the description "my red diskette case." The principal problem is this. The mere fact that a representation of a sensory experience involves re-creating a facsimile of the experience in order to represent it doesn't explain how the facsimile itself somehow makes a cognitive difference—how it enters into the cognitive significance, or content of the representation. We still seem to have two elements involved here: a pointer and the thing pointed at. But what is it about internal pointings—in contrast to external pointings—that gets us into the sort of cognitive contact that can cause puzzlement about an identity claim? In the end this is not different from the demonstrative move we saw above.[8]

I believe a similar problem attends Loar's position. Before one can adequately assess his argument, it's crucial that one get clear on what it is for reddishness to serve as the mode of presentation for "reddishness." If it comes down to anything like Papineau's model, then what I just said applies to Loar as well. Perhaps my point could be put this way. Yes, it does seem as if the very property of reddishness is somehow present in the concept, making a cognitive contribution that endows the content with genuine substance and explains the gappiness of the identity. But how do we explain that on a physicalistic model? How does a property referred to by a mental representation get cognitively incorporated into the representation in the way it seems to with phenomenal concepts and properties? The model of demonstratives, perhaps embellished in the way Papineau does it, seems to be the only model we have, and that doesn't seem to do the job.

What emerges from our discussion is that the explanatory gap is intimately connected to the special nature of phenomenal concepts. E-type materialists try to save materialism from the conceivability argument by arguing that phenomenal concepts are special in some way. Well, I grant that, but then we have the problem of providing an explanation in physicalistic terms of that very specialness, and we don't seem to have one. If we could explain the explanatory gap, then either it would go away or we would just learn to live with it. But it seems we can't do that without a good account of phenomenal concepts, and that's something we don't have. We lack both an account of phenomenal properties and phenomenal concepts.

3.7 Metaphysics Again

Back in chapter 2 I mentioned that once we looked carefully at the different cognitive features of phenomenal and other concepts, rather than weakening the argument, as E-type responders would have it, the argument would be strengthened. I want now to consider that question. Does the notion of a gappy identity give the anti-materialist more ammunition for her metaphysical conclusion? I think so, but not quite enough to deal materialism a death blow.

What explains the gappiness of an identity claim? There seem to be two possibilities: either the identity claim is true, and what we need explained is how this one thing could instantiate some particular pair of distinct properties we believe it to have; or the identity claim is false. The point is that an intelligible request for explanation seems to entail a distinction in properties somewhere. If it isn't to be located in the properties of the one thing we're representing on both sides of the identity sign, then it must be that the terms flanking the identity sign themselves represent distinct things.

Notice, again, that it isn't sufficient merely to cite the concept property distinction and insist that what explains the gappiness is the fact that the two terms flanking the identity sign express different concepts, and that this entails nothing about a difference in properties. What we need here is an account of the conceptual distinction, and this is what we've been investigating at length. One account takes the difference in concepts to consist principally in the syntactic difference between the two different representations—a difference in labels—together with distinct causal paths between representation and referent. But this leads in the end to non-gappy identities. The mere difference in labels can't support an intelligible request for explanation, and the difference in non-ascriptive modes of presentation—the distinct causal paths—isn't cognitively significant in itself, since this is not part of the conception entertained by the subject. These causal connections work, again, "behind the scenes."

But what other account of conceptual difference is there, except appeal to distinct ascriptive modes of presentation, which brings with it appeal to distinct properties? We can put it this way. To say two cognitively distinct concepts A and B are both about C involves a burden to explain how they both secure reference to C. Either they do so by "behind the scenes" connections, non-ascriptive modes of presentation, or by describing satisfaction conditions for C, their referential target. The former is not cognitively significant. The latter involves distinct properties.[9]

Now, let's apply this result to the question of conceivability. In general, the connection between explanation and conceivability is straightforward. An explanation is called for whenever it is conceivable that it could have gone the other way. I want to know why most objects fall when unsupported. My question is intelligible precisely because we can conceive of their not falling. But now let's explicitly draw a distinction between two grades of conceivability in terms of the distinction between gappy and non-gappy identities. I'll call a situation "thinly conceivable" relative to R just in case it's conceptually possible relative to R. This is the sense of conceivability that was employed in CP of the initial argument presented in chapter 2. I'll call a situation "thickly conceivable" relative to R just in case it's conceptually possible relative to R, and any derivation we can construct from R to a conceptually impossible representation R′ will include gappy identities in its premises.

In chapter 2, I put the materialist reply to the conceivability argument this way: "Just as zombies are conceptually possible relative to the standard descriptions, so is zombie-H_2O (i.e., H_2O that isn't water, even given all the relevant microphysical facts). If the conceivability hypothesis amounts only to the conceptual possibility of zombies, then it poses no threat to materialism." However, now the anti-materialist can argue that there is a crucial difference. Granted, zombie-H_2O is conceptually possible, or thinly conceivable, and this poses no threat to the identification of water with H_2O. But zombies are not only conceptually possible, they're thickly conceivable, since the only way to derive a contradictory representation of a zombie is to use gappy psycho-physical identities as bridge principles.

In a way, the anti-materialist is using the materialist's own argument against her. The materialist argues that just as zombies (under the appropriate description) are conceptually possible, so too is H_2O without water, or the corresponding non-indexically described situation without its indexically described counterpart. Since we're not tempted to posit any irreducible properties there, or find any explanatory gaps, there's no reason to in the case of qualia. But the anti-materialist insists that it's of the utmost significance that we aren't tempted to find irreducible properties or explanatory gaps in the water or indexical cases, but we are in the qualia case. The difference requires an explanation. The best explanation available is that in the case of qualia we're dealing with genuinely independent properties.

We can now reconstruct the anti-materialist conceivability argument as follows:

CP': Zombies are thickly conceivable.
PP': Thickly conceivable situations are metaphysically possible.

Therefore,

Zombies are metaphysically possible.

The new argument is stronger than the initial one in two ways. First, the justification of PP' doesn't rely on the DPM, so the availability of non-ascriptive modes of presentation to explain the inability to derive certain identities *a priori* doesn't help. We need an explanation of gappiness, which is something more than mere inability to produce an *a priori* derivation. Second, the compelling analogy with the other empirically grounded identities breaks down over gappiness and thick conceivability. While we have nice examples of thinly conceivable situations that are nevertheless metaphysically impossible, we don't have any examples of thickly conceivable situations that are metaphysically impossible. At least, so the anti-materialist argues, and it's hard to think of an example to prove her wrong.

Before turning to evaluate this new argument in section 3.8, I want to present one final argument in favor of there being an important distinction between the standard cases of empirically grounded identities and the case of qualia. This argument, which has the form of an "open question" argument, bears directly on the question of the alleged metaphysical independence of qualitative properties. Consider again the problem of attributing qualia to other creatures, those that do not share our physical organization. I take it that there is a very real puzzle whether such creatures have qualia like ours, or even any at all. How much of our physicofunctional architecture must be shared before we have similarity or identity of experience?[10] This problem, I argued above, is a direct manifestation of the explanatory gap. But now I want to see if it has metaphysical implications as well.

The contrast here with the case of water is instructive. We are faced with XYZ and with an alien creature, and we have to decide whether XYZ is water and whether the alien creature experiences reddishness. In both cases, let us suppose, we have all the relevant information concerning physical structure and causal role. We know that XYZ is a different molecular structure from H_2O, and that on Twin Earth it plays the water role. With respect to the alien, we can suppose that we have a relatively complete map of its functional organization and the way that organization is realized physically.

Now, the questions are: Is XYZ water? Does the alien experience reddishness? Earlier I conceded to the defender of the DPM that the former question is essentially a semantic one. We know what there is to know about XYZ; we just have to determine whether the term "water," as used by us, applies to it. To decide this, I said, we consult our linguistic intuitions. If those intuitions don't determine an answer, then it seems quite open to say that it's now a matter for decision whether we should extend our application of the term "water" to XYZ. As it happens, I think the argument that our linguistic intuitions settle the matter are persuasive, but nothing of substance here hangs on that.

But the second question clearly isn't merely a semantic question at all. I'm not asking whether or not to extend my use of the term "reddishness" (or its mental equivalent) to the alien, and the answer to the question doesn't seem to lie in consulting my linguistic intuitions. I want to know whether or not it has this sort of experience, whether or not it instantiates a certain property. Furthermore, the idea that, failing to find sufficient grounds for answering the question either way, we might resort to just deciding whether to say it has reddish experiences seems preposterous. You don't just decide matters of fact. If one feels there really is a contrast here, as I do, then it seems to commit one to the claim that reddishness is a genuinely independent property. The point is that only if reddishness is distinct from either a physical or a functional property does it seem that there could be more than a semantic question left to decide.

3.8 Materialism with an Explanatory Gap?

As with the initial conceivability argument, various options are open to the materialist by way of reply. First, she can reject the conceivability premise itself, CP′. Now that we're talking about thick, as opposed to thin, conceivability, this move is much more plausible. Many philosophers who buy the thin conceivability premise, CP, do so because they aren't comfortable with any claims involving *a priori* analyses of concepts. To the extent that thick conceivability goes beyond the mere denial of such analyses, they may very well fail to accept it. If one isn't moved by the contrast between the cases of water, demonstratives, and indexicals on the one hand and qualia on the other, this is the place to block the argument. But I take the argument of section 3.6 to reveal the existence of a genuine explanatory gap, a genuine distinction between gappy and non-gappy identities. Therefore, I'm interested in what metaphysical conclusions can be drawn if we accept CP'.

So suppose we accept CP'. Must we accept PP'? As a first step, notice that one can accept the inference from CP' to the non-identity of qualia with any physical or functional property, and still reject PP', so long as one insists that the relation between physical properties and qualia is metaphysically necessary. The point is that distinctness isn't sufficient; qualia must be only contingently related to their physical or functional correlates to get the metaphysical possibility of zombies out of their thick conceivability. But now the challenge is to make sense of the claim that though qualia are distinct from their physical correlates, they are metaphysically necessitated by them nonetheless.

In chapter 2 I argued that this challenge would be very hard to meet, that it required embracing a notion of brute metaphysical necessity that goes beyond even the "strong metaphysical necessity" to which Chalmers objects. To review quickly, the problem comes in two stages. First, to avoid commitment to brute metaphysical necessity, I argued that for a situation to be metaphysically impossible, it must be that there is a representation of it relative to which the situation is also conceptually impossible. Second, in order to meet this requirement we would need a realization theory that in the end is based on some identification of the target property so that a re-description of it enables the relevant conceptual necessity to be expressed.[11]

So it looks as if materialism is committed to some sort of identity theory. Maybe reddishness is not identical to a strictly physical, or even biological, property, but it must be identical to—that is, it must *be*—a property that admits of a description susceptible to derivation from physical descriptions. Our problem is that the only values for "X" that we can imagine substituting into "R = X," if we accept the argument of section 3.6, yield gappy identities. So long as we maintain that gappy identities entail a distinction in the relevant properties, we seem to be in trouble.

I see three possible strategies for the materialist to adopt in response to these considerations: hold out for a value of "X" in "R = X" that would deliver a non-gappy identity; explain away gappiness by adopting a form of eliminativism; or just deny that gappiness must be explained by a distinction in properties. The first strategy really is a version of what I described earlier, rejecting CP', the thick conceivability premise. The second is one I haven't touched on as yet. Both of these strategies will be examined at length in the next two chapters. I will end this chapter by briefly examining the third strategy.

Suppose we challenge the assumption that to explain a gappy identity we must appeal to a distinction in the properties of the target object/property. It's not that the assumption lacks plausibility; quite the contrary. In cases of non-gappy identities, such as "water = H_2O," while there is no *a priori* route from the "H_2O"-described facts to the "water"-described facts, still there is the definite sense that when all the chemical facts are in, the whole story has been told. As we argued above, no sensible question about how H_2O could be water remains. Thus the claim that the mere formal consistency of denying "water = H_2O" doesn't entail that there is a genuine distinction between the properties involved seems fairly easy to accept. However, with the proposed identification of reddishness with a physical or functional property, where a substantive question does remain, the temptation to believe that there has to be some genuine distinction in properties corresponding to the representations of reddishness and its physical correlate is cognitively irresistible. Furthermore, we have the argument about extending our concept to new cases. The only way it seems plausible to distinguish cases where it seems to be a matter of semantics from those where it seems to be a matter of fact is to claim that extra, metaphysically independent properties are involved in the factual cases.

I find these considerations intuitively compelling, and I must admit I find it hard to see how qualia could actually be identical to physical properties. Yet, despite these intuitively compelling considerations, the assumption they support—that gappy identities indicate distinct properties—does come into conflict with other considerations that are equally compelling. In particular, it seems to be based on a kind of Cartesian model of access to the facts, one that blurs the line between epistemology and metaphysics.

The point is, how can I tell, merely from facts about my own cognitive situation, including facts about various conceptual relations among my representations, that what one representation refers to is distinct from what another one refers to? The argument is supposed to be that only a distinction in the relevant properties could explain the gappiness of an identity. But gappiness is a matter of what I find intelligible, which in the end is a matter of how I represent the world. The bottom line is that my representations seem to present me with two distinct properties. But the possibility that distinct representations really refer to the same thing must always be an open one.

Suppose, then, we reject this crucial assumption underlying the inference from thick conceivability to possibility: that gappy identities reveal distinct properties. Now we are left with a different puzzle, namely, how to account for the distinction between gappy and non-gappy identities. The problem can be put this way. In both the gappy and non-gappy identities, we have two representations of the very same property, both of which involve non-ascriptive modes of presentation.[12] Non-gappiness is readily explained by the "behind-the-scenes" nature of non-ascriptive modes of presentation. If what we have in mind when we think of water is really just our mental representation of water, then we would expect there to be nothing cognitively left over after all the chemical and contextual facts were in. But gappiness is really puzzling. Causal or nomic relations seem ill-suited to explain the sort of cognitive relation we have to qualitative character. On the other hand, causal or nomic relations seem to be all the materialist has available to account for the representation relation.

I think the explanation of gappiness is a very deep problem, and, as I said at the end of section 3.6, the problem of explaining how the physical gives rise to the phenomenal and the problem of explaining the peculiar cognitive features of phenomenal concepts are intimately connected, if not the very same problem. As we investigate the first two strategies described above, we'll have occasion to examine this connection in more depth. For now, then, I leave the matter as a further puzzle, and turn to a more in-depth examination of various attempts to bridge the explanatory gap.

4

"Don't Know If I'm Comin' Up or Down"
Reductive Strategies

4.1 Introduction

I've argued that there is an explanatory gap between the physical and the mental, at least with respect to conscious experience. That argument has been based largely on considerations of what's conceivable. It is the fact that we can easily conceive of creatures satisfying certain physical conditions but lacking qualia, or having radically different qualia, that testifies to the explanatory inadequacy of physicalistic theories. In this chapter I want to survey various attempts at explanatory reduction and show why they don't succeed in closing the gap. I'll begin, in section 4.2, with some general remarks concerning the status of qualia as either intrinsic or relational properties. In section 4.3 I'll explore the intuitive resistance to relational theories, specifically traditional functionalism. In sections 4.4, 4.5, and 4.6 I'll turn to two more recent reductive strategies, "higher-order" theory and "representationalism."

4.2 Intrinsic or Relational

It seems to me that a lot of the literature about qualia over the past two decades can be seen as a pendulum, with various proposals bouncing back and forth between treating qualia as intrinsic and treating them as relational, but none overcoming the basic structure of this dilemma: qualia as intrinsic properties can't be integrated into a naturalistic framework, but no proposal to treat them as relational seems at all compelling. We've seen the first horn of the dilemma already. If we consider a property like the reddishness of a visual experience, it certainly seems to be the paradigm of an intrinsic property. Yet, if it is, what property is it? Materialists must say that it's a neurophysiological property, and it's precisely this hypothesis that is vulnerable to the explanatory gap objection. The only hope for a successful explanatory reduction seems to be in identifying qualia with suitable relational properties.[1]

Before we explore the problems with relational theories, it's important to address an objection to the argument presented so far. It has been objected to this sort of argument that the apparent explanatory gap between the neurophysiological and the qualitative is merely that—apparent. It is an artifact of our current ignorance of the neurophysiological mechanisms underlying conscious experience. As we learn more about the brain and the various sensory mechanisms responsible for our qualitative experience we'll come to understand why being in various neurophysiological states is experienced the way it is.[2]

Of course it is always open to someone to appeal to what may yet be discovered—who knows what that may be? But if we assume that we're dealing with the sorts of neurophysiological properties with which we are already familiar—the sorts of electro-chemical properties exhibited by the firings of neurons, along with the excitatory and inhibitory connections among them—then I don't see how appeal to such properties could explain qualitative character, so long as it's considered an intrinsic property of experience. To put the point starkly: what is it about the firing of a neuron, or the nature of a synaptic connection from one neuron to another, or any complicated assembly of such connections and firings, that could explain the reddishness of my experience of the diskette case? It seems to me that we have only four options, none of which works.

Option one is to admit that no progress can be made if we consider qualitative character to be an intrinsic property of experience, and to argue that it ought to be analyzed as a relational/functional property instead. This of course just means confronting the other horn of the dilemma, and we'll do that presently.

Option two is to appeal to correlations as the basis for identification. For instance, suppose we find that whenever someone is experiencing a visual sensation of type R (the reddish qualitative character I have when looking at my red diskette case) there is a particular pattern of neural firing occurring in their visual cortex. Or suppose that whenever someone is having a conscious sensation, a 40 Hz oscillation pattern is occurring in the relevant cortical areas (see Crick and Koch 1990). We might then appeal to this discovery as a basis for the claim that to have an experience of type R is just to have the relevant pattern of firing in the visual cortex (similarly for having a conscious sensation and the presence of the 40 Hz oscillation pattern).

While a robust correlation of the sort envisaged might provide grounds for identifying the properties in question, it certainly doesn't explain anything on its own. Is it really just a brute fact that certain neurophysiological states constitute qualitative experiences? That seems very hard to swallow. There are two ways of thinking about correlations as brute facts. One might have in mind that the correlation is not a matter of identity, but of a basic lawful connection. If so, then, as I've argued already, this amounts to a kind of dualism. On the other hand, one might have in mind that qualia just are the neurophysiological properties with which they are (apparently) correlated, and the bruteness we find in the identification is just the bruteness of identity itself. This too, I've argued above, is inadequate. Phenomenal-physical identities are gappy; requests for explanation clearly make sense here and demand some sort of answer.

So, instead of resting on brute correlation, option three is often preferred.

According to this view, what legitimates the identification of R with PR, its neurophysiological correlate, is the fact that PR provides the mechanisms by which the functions we associate with R are performed. Color perception involves selective sensitivity to fairly complicated properties of the light reflected from physical surfaces, and we now know a lot about how that sensitivity is implemented in neural hardware.

The problem is that the theory of neural implementation, as important and interesting as it is, basically comes down to the theory of how certain states bear information about other states. What we find out from studies of the neural pathways leading from retina to the visual cortex is how information about various properties of the light are processed. But informational content is a relational property *par excellence*. If we are still committed to treating qualitative character as an intrinsic property of experience, then it isn't reducible to the property of bearing such-and-such information about the distal (or even the proximal) stimulus. It may in fact bear such information (presumably it does, or what's it good for?), and indeed the description of the neurophysiological mechanisms underlying vision may explain its ability to carry such information, but that doesn't amount to there being a neurophysiological explanation of qualitative character itself.

Option four for closing the explanatory gap is to build the explanatory connection out of isomorphic structure. For instance, Hardin (1988) and Van Gulick (1993) have argued that one reason qualia are thought to be inexplicable is that they are thought to have no structure. The idea is that the only way to explain the instantiation of one property in terms of the instantiation of other properties is to exhibit the structure of the explanandum property and show how the explanans properties realize that structure. If the property to be explained is simple, then the most you get from the alleged explanation is a brute correlation between that property and the ones in terms of which it is supposed to be explained. They then argue that though qualia appear at first blush to be simple properties, they are in fact quite complex, structured states, and therefore susceptible of an explanatory reduction to neurophysiological states.

A very simple example of the sort of thing they have in mind is this. A visual experience of orange might at first blush appear simple in character. Yet, upon reflection it seems to have a reddish and a yellowish component. Now, suppose we find that light reflected from orange objects tends to excite both the neural correlates of red and of yellow (something like this appears to be the case); then we could see why such light would cause the experiences it does. If we could analyze every experience of color into a complex, multidimensional property, then perhaps we could see how it is that its neurophysiological correlate constituted the type of experience it did.[3] We would have transcended brute correlation for genuine explanation.

My problem with option four—I call it the "complexity gambit"—is that it either doesn't address the real challenge, or else it reduces to option one. The idea is supposed to be that by finding structure inside qualia we will better be able to connect qualia to their underlying neurophysiological realizations. But why is this *internal* structure necessary anyway? Why isn't it sufficient that each quale maintains a complicated set of external relations to other qualia (as well as to stimuli, behavior, and other mental states)? We can then link each quale to its neurophysiological correlate by exhibiting how the properties of the latter explain the external relations maintained by the former.

Obviously, the problem is that if we intend to get our explanatory punch from the external relations maintained by a type of qualitative character, then we are back to options one and three. Either we've given up on analyzing qualitative character as an intrinsic property, or we have to admit that though we can explain the way a state with property R relates to other states by appeal to PR, we still cannot explain the nature of R itself in this manner. Hence the move to find structure *internal* to qualia, so that there will be more for those explanatory hooks to grab onto.

The problem is that this just displaces the explanatory gap, instead of removing it. Structure is a matter of relations among elements, which are themselves either structured or simple. To avoid an infinite regress, it is clear that whatever set of relations individual qualia are analyzed into, the relata must themselves be simple elements of experience. Whether red is a simple, or warmth is, something experiential has to be. So long as the experiential primitives are themselves intrinsic properties of experience, the explanatory gap will remain.

4.3 Qualia as Relational

It seems that the only way to explain qualitative character is to first analyze it as a relational property and then show how our neurophysiological mechanisms realize the appropriate relations. But, as I mentioned above, the problem is that relational accounts of qualia are so plainly implausible. In this section I want to explore the reasons for this (allegedly) patent implausibility, extracting certain general themes from the arguments and counterarguments that have been presented over the last two or three decades.

Functionalism is the view that mental states, including qualia, are definable in terms of their causal roles—their causal relations with stimuli, behavior, and other mental states.[4] So a state would have the property R, of being reddish, just in case it was normally caused by viewing red things, it tended to cause judgments to the effect that something was red, and it generally related to other mental states—in particular through similarity judgments—in the way that is typical of experiences of red. Let's call the functional role in question "FR."

The basic objection to functionalism is that it just seems intuitively plausible that FR and R could come apart. The mismatch goes in both directions. That is, according to the famous "absent qualia" and "inverted qualia" hypotheses, it seems quite possible that a creature could satisfy the conditions for being in FR even though not experiencing R, or, for that matter, having any qualitative experience at all. On the other hand, and this is less emphasized in the literature, it also seems quite possible that a creature could experience R even though most of the causal relations normally maintained by R were absent.[5]

An example of the first sort of problem is the well-known "inverted spectrum" thought experiment. If we assume that color space is appropriately symmetrical, then if one person's experience underwent a transformation so that she experienced the complement of what everyone else experienced, she would satisfy the same functional description yet her experience would possess a different qualitative character.

An example of the second sort could occur if someone's normal functioning were disturbed, so that various relations between her color experience and memory, belief, and the like no longer held. It seems possible that this could happen while the qualitative character of her experience remained the same. One concrete case of this is color blindness. The fact that someone can't distinguish red from green obviously affects the structure of their color space, yet it isn't obvious that this makes their experiences of blue any different from mine. In fact, I think we could take this to an extreme and imagine someone whose entire visual experience involved just one hue, and that one was qualitatively similar to the one involved in my experiences of type R. Why shouldn't this be (at least conceptually) possible?[6]

There have been two basic responses to these anti-functionalist arguments. The first is to grant their cogency and claim that for qualia, as opposed to cognitive states like belief, functionalism is wrong and the traditional type-identity theory is right.[7] But then one is back with the explanatory problems confronting the intrinsic theory.

The second sort of response is to attempt to undermine the intuitive resistance to a relational account represented by the absent and inverted qualia hypotheses. Numerous such attempts have been made, but I want to focus on two related strategies in particular. I think they both fail, but their failure is especially instructive.

The basic idea behind the first strategy is to argue that an appropriately chosen and sufficiently rich relational description can uniquely identify a type of qualitative character, and thereby get around the sorts of counterexamples just discussed. So Austen Clark (1993) argues that each type of color quale can be identified with a point in a multidimensional color space, so that it is defined by its relations to other color experiences, and nothing else. It may well be that only that particular type of color quale could occupy that point in the space. If so, then there can't be inverted color qualia.

The second strategy is exemplified by Van Gulick (1993, 147–149), in his discussion of the absent qualia argument. He notes that the absent qualia hypothesis seems to assume that a state's being conscious is not necessary for playing its functional role. In fact, there is some evidence, for example, from blindsight cases, that consciousness is necessary. For instance, blindsight patients tend not to initiate action with respect to the objects that they can passively detect in their blind field. If, as such cases suggest, consciousness is essential to the performance of certain functional roles, then it isn't possible for a non-conscious state to play the same functional role.[8] Hence, absent qualia aren't possible.

Both strategies, finding a function that a quale is uniquely suited to perform and finding a definite description sufficiently rich to uniquely specify it, suffer from the same defect: namely, an unwarranted assimilation of role player to role. However complex the description of the functional role played by, or network of relations maintained by, my reddish visual experience of the diskette case, it seems like the right way to characterize the situation is that the reddish experience is *playing* a certain role, not that it *is* a certain role. The point is that you don't show that a property is itself relational merely by finding a relational description that uniquely identifies it. It might still be that the property is itself intrinsic; it just turns out that only it satisfies the relevant description.

Thus, in response to Van Gulick, I grant, for the sake of argument, the possibility that there may be jobs, or roles, that only conscious states can fill. That still doesn't mean that filling that role is what it is to be conscious. In fact, that very way of putting it—that being conscious is essential, or necessary to playing the role—seems to imply just the reverse: that being conscious is one thing, playing the role quite another. Suppose it turned out that being red was essential to some plant's playing the ecological role it played; nothing that was not red could do it. We wouldn't say that being red *is* to play that role, but rather that being red is what makes the plant in question especially suited to play that role. It seems to me the same goes for being conscious in the scenario envisioned.

There is an interesting similarity here between the way that being conscious fills a role and the way that neurophysiological properties fill a role. In both cases, it seems, we have a role, relationally defined, and then we find something that plays it and determine that certain of its intrinsic properties are the ones that enable it to play the role. Whether it's being conscious or resonating at 40 Hz, the explanatory structure seems to be the same. In fact, this very similarity in the way that qualitative and neurophysiological states enter the explanatory picture is just what makes the identity theory so tempting in the first place.

So, for instance, suppose the role in question is the "binding" of different features of a percept into a unified visual experience. On the one hand, as some speculate, the resonating at 40 Hz might be the relevant neurophysiological cross-referencing property. On the other, conscious awareness certainly also seems to bring the various perceptual features together into a unified experience. Thus identification of the consciousness with the resonating seems almost irresistible. Of course, as I argued above, so long as consciousness is understood as the role *player*, and not the role itself, we can't explain *its* character by reference to the neurophysiological property. All that we could explain by identifying it with the neurophysiological property would be its ability to play the role.

This sort of confusion between role and role player, and the way this clouds discussion of the explanatory adequacy of neurophysiological reductionist accounts of qualitative character, is exhibited in Owen Flanagan's (1992, chapter 3, section 6) discussion of the neural coding of sensory qualia, and in the way he employs his distinction between "informational" sensitivity and "experiential" sensitivity. Informational sensitivity is an organism's ability to respond selectively to stimuli. So, in the case of blindsight, though the subject claims to be unable to see anything in a certain region of her visual field, she displays informational sensitivity by "guessing" correctly at the identity of objects displayed there. Experiential sensitivity is the ability of an organism to respond to stimuli with phenomenal experience, a state that has not only an informational content but also a qualitative character. It is the presence of this sort of sensitivity that distinguishes normal sight from blindsight.

Now, with respect to qualia, Flanagan proposes the following: each qualitative difference to which we are capable of consciously responding (like the difference in taste between Coke and Pepsi)—each instance of experiential sensitivity—must correspond to a difference in the activation vector of the relevant sensory pathway. Now this seems right, since the only way the difference can be detected is by way of its effect on sensory mechanisms. No difference in the latter, no difference in experience.

But then Flanagan goes on to propose that we take the next step and identify the relevant quale with its corresponding sensory vector. The reasoning seems to be that since the ability to distinguish between the tastes of Coke and Pepsi is explained by the difference in activation vectors, these vectors explain the nature of the experienced tastes themselves.

But this is wrong. What the vectors explain is precisely informational sensitivity, because they provide avenues for preserving information about the difference in chemical composition between Coke and Pepsi. Of course *any* system of units capable of taking on the activation vectors that neurons take on, and capable of responding with just those vectors to just those chemical properties, would do the job just as well. What's essential here is precisely the job of information transfer, not the means by which it is done. Furthermore, we can think in the same terms about our experiential sensitivity. That is, what our consciousness of the difference between the taste of Coke and the taste of Pepsi enables us to do is to detect a difference in the stimuli—between Coke and Pepsi. That is, the qualitative difference serves to preserve, or transfer information concerning the chemical difference. Again, the qualitative character is here playing the role of information carrier; it isn't reducible to the very fact of information carrying itself. The qualitative difference and the vector difference are on a par here, as implementations of a task. They both explain how we detect the difference between Coke and Pepsi. That they are correlated in doing this job is undeniable. But what I do deny is (1) that the activation vector itself explains the qualitative character, and (2) that the qualitative character is identifiable with the job it is carrying out.

What I hope to have established so far is not that qualia are definitely intrinsic properties, but that at least one sort of strategy for convincing us otherwise is inadequate. That is, devising definite descriptions in relational terms for identifying qualia is not sufficient for establishing that the properties themselves are relational. An inherently intrinsic property may be uniquely describable in relational terms, though not constituted by them. In particular, I have argued that many functionalist moves only work if we blur the distinction between *role* and *role player*. If we keep these two notions distinct, then the functionalist moves lose much of their claim to plausibility.

In addition to the role/role player argument just presented, I think there's another way of looking at what seems wrong about the case for treating qualitative character as a relational property. Earlier I argued that it certainly seemed possible that someone could experience a sensation with a reddish quality even if they were incapable of experiencing sensations of other chromatic types. In response the relationalist might argue that reddishness is essentially a matter of occupying a certain point in color quality space. Not to be related to other color qualities in this particular way is just not to be reddish.

But even if we grant that the structure of color quality space is somehow essential to its occupants, it still doesn't follow that there couldn't be creatures who experience only a subset—perhaps even only a singleton subset— of the entire set of color qualities. Perhaps the property R is necessarily related to the property G (greenishness) in a certain way. That doesn't entail that someone who experiences R must also be capable of experiencing G. It might mean that if she does experience both, these experiences must be related in a certain way, but nothing requires that the antecedent of this conditional be satisfied.

To be more concrete, I can see that in some sense it may be essential to red that it be similar to orange, a complement of green, and so on. I'm not sure this is true, but let's grant it for the sake of argument. In a sense, then, we can be holists about the space of color qualia. Still, individual experiences may be of the requisite type—say R—without the subject of that experience herself being capable of experiencing more than a limited range of all the possible color qualia. But if this is indeed possible, then how does the relational analysis of R as a point in color quality space help us with our predicament? It turns out that Jones, who, to take an extreme case, can experience only R and G, is not herself in a state that satisfies the rich relational description that characterizes R's position in color quality space as a whole. So it can't be by virtue of occupying a state within such a structure that she counts as having such an experience. Hence, R itself, as a property of her experience, has not been shown to be a relational property, and we're back where we started.

My purpose in this section has been to explore the reasons why relational analyses of qualia are so intuitively unconvincing. In the spirit of this exploration of the intuitive domain, it might be informative to investigate other cases where what seemed intuitively to be intrinsic properties were reanalyzed in relational terms. Consider two in particular: weight and color.

At first it seems as if an object's weight is intrinsic to it. The only way to change it would be to alter the object itself. But then we learn that weight is a matter of the attractive force between the earth and an object near its surface, so it turns out to be a relational property. In other words, I can change the weight of my red diskette case both by changing it and also by changing the mass of the earth (or its distance from the center of the earth). Of course what is intrinsic to the diskette case, and in some sense captures what was originally thought to be the intrinsic property weight, is its mass.

Let's turn to color, which is closer to our primary interest here. The diskette case is red. It's also three inches from the computer. Again, normally I would say its redness is an intrinsic property and its distance from the computer is a relational property, because to change its color something would have to be done to it, whereas I could change the distance from the computer by moving the computer and leaving the case where it is. But now along comes a color theorist who tells me that color is itself a relational property. How so? Well, to be red is to be such as to excite certain visual experiences in normal observers under appropriate circumstances. We can change the color of the case, then, by changing the human visual system.

Here too, as in the case of weight, the reanalysis of color from an intrinsic property to a relational one involves substituting another intrinsic property that captures what was originally thought to be intrinsic about color. In this case, it's the color quality of the visual experience. We can put it this way. We've pushed the color, what we originally took to be intrinsic, back into the head. As far as the relational analysis of objective color is concerned, this subjective color, which was pushed back into the head, is still intrinsic.

It seems that when we start with an intuitively intrinsic property and reanalyze it as a relational property, that the process involves an intrinsic residue. In the case of color it's our visual response to the light coming from the object. In the case of weight, it's mass. These are plausible intrinsic substitutes for the original intrinsic properties. Perhaps what seems so problematic about the case of making qualia relational is that there isn't a plausible intrinsic substitute. The intrinsic buck seems to stop here.

To see the force of this problem, consider the sorts of intrinsic substitutes that have generally been offered for qualia. According to traditional functionalist theories, a quale is defined by its relations to inputs, outputs, and other mental states by a Ramsey-style method of definition. Here the intrinsic residues are the inputs and outputs—stimuli and behavior.

Despite the appeal to other mental states, this sort of functional analysis suffers from its behavioristic flavor. It displaces the core of the identity of an experience from what is going on inside to how it contributes to behavior. It just seems to be a contingent, not a criterial fact that experiences with a reddish quale cause me to say "red." And qualifying the conditions under which it causes me to say this with reference to attention, understanding, desire, and so on doesn't really help. I see the inverted qualia hypothesis as just a concrete way of expressing the contingency of this relation.

Of course some other versions of functionalism don't take stimuli and behavior to be the ultimate points by which functional identity is pinned down. For instance, one might view qualia as primarily representational, a view we will look at in some detail later in the chapter. On this view, to occupy a state of type R is to represent an object as having a certain property—presumably, being red. The intrinsic residue, then, is redness itself. While I put off until later a general discussion of representationalism, I want to pursue here just a couple of points concerning this theory and the problem of finding a plausible intrinsic residue.

There are two *prima facie* problems with identifying redness itself as the intrinsic residue. First, redness itself was analyzed as a power to cause R experiences, so now circularity threatens. Also, we need to distinguish representational experiences from plain representational states, such as beliefs that something is red.

With regard to the threatened circularity, there are two possible responses. First, maybe redness isn't itself a power after all. Maybe it can be identified with something like a surface spectral reflectance.[9] Second, even if it is understood to be a power, so long as we can analyze what is distinctive about an experience of type R in terms of conditions internal to the subject, it's still possible to count the relational property of the external surface as the intentional object of the experience.[10] Of course this gets us out of the circularity, but at the price of removing the property of the external surface as the intrinsic residue for which we're searching.

So it all comes down, then, to the nature of the internal response. Well, what makes a visual response experiential, as opposed to merely judgmental or cognitive? There are two possibilities. One, pin the experiential nature on the particular neurophysiological mechanisms that subserve the response. Second, pin it on the pattern of relations to judgment, memory, emotion, and the like that is characteristic of visual experience.

On the first option we are essentially giving up on the relational analysis and back to identifying qualitative character with a neurophysiological property. On the second option, the intrinsic residue is to be found in judgment, memory, and the like. But surely analyses of these states will lead us right back out to either stimuli and behavior or properties of external objects, none of which provide plausible candidates for the intrinsic residue we're looking for.

Another source, then, for the implausibility of relational analyses of qualitative character is revealed by our comparison with the cases of color and weight. Unlike these cases, with qualitative character there is no plausible intrinsic substitute for the original. Mass does seem sufficiently like what we took weight to be for the relational analysis of weight to make a lot of sense. Properties of visual experience—subjective colors—also serve as an intelligible, plausible replacement for the intrinsic objective colors. But judgment, memory, behavior, or any of the other functionalist candidates seem totally foreign to experience itself. Rather than an analysis of qualitative character, functionalism amounts more to an elimination of it.

In this section I've presented various reasons why relational treatments of qualia are not intuitively compelling. As I said above, these considerations do not constitute knockdown arguments, nor were they intended to. Rather, what I've attempted here is a fleshing out of the strong intuitive resistance to functionalist treatments, and to show that they have a basis. So let me now turn to the question of the state of play, or burden of argument.

First of all, a word about the role of intuition is in order. When one speaks of "intuitive resistance," it's tempting for one's opponent to accuse one of "mere intuition mongering" or even mysticism. On my view, intuition has no special epistemic status; it's not a faculty in its own right, nor are its dictates to be treated as incorrigible. As far as I can see, intuition is just reasonableness. That is, to say that something is intuitively wrong or odd is to say that it strikes one as unreasonable, implausible. One could be wrong about this, and the basis for this response should always be sought out to the degree possible, but sometimes one just has to rest on the fact that some hypothesis seems blatantly implausible. In the philosophy of mind there is often a tendency to take the anti-Cartesian denial of epistemic privilege for intuition to an unwarranted extreme.[11]

But now what about the case of our intuitions about qualia? I agree in principle that it could turn out—intuition notwithstanding—that qualia are actually relational properties. This follows for me from the general (and anti-Cartesian) principle that I accept—namely, that *anything* (perhaps excluding outright contradictions) could turn out to be the case. But on what basis ought we to accept a relational analysis of qualitative character in the face of its apparent implausibility? I can see only two, neither of which, at this stage in the process (and philosophers have been attempting to make the materialist world safe for qualia for a long time now), seems very promising. The first is conceptual analysis, and the second is theoretical analysis.

I don't mean to claim that a very sharp line exists between these two forms of analysis; sometimes drawing a line is quite hard. Furthermore, I'm not sure that there really is such a thing as conceptual analysis.[12] But it does seem to me that there are basically two avenues along which to discover that the way we originally characterized a property has to be changed. Either through reflection on what we had in mind, we become clear that it is really different from what we originally thought; or we make a theoretical discovery to that effect. What else could there be?

If we consider the various relational analyses of qualia that have been discussed above, it doesn't look like they could be convincingly established in either way. As conceptual analyses they just don't capture what we have in mind by our notion of qualitative character. This is the burden of the sorts of considerations that I've advanced above, as well as the point of the inverted and absent qualia hypotheses that go hand in hand with those considerations. To say that my conception of R is really a conception of a functional role is just not credible. As I have tried to show in this section, the standard arguments that have been advanced on its behalf are unconvincing, once we make the necessary distinctions.

Perhaps, then, it's a matter of theoretical discovery. But what sort of discovery is this? Suppose we have discovered precisely what information about the light hitting the eye is registered by an experience of type R, and also by what neurophysiological mechanisms this information-processing feat is accomplished. In what sense does this constitute a theoretical discovery to the effect that to be in state R is just to register this information? What the theory tells us is that information of such-and-such a sort is registered, and how it's done. But how can it tell us that doing so captures the essence of property R?

The theory could do this if it explained why R was experienced as it was. It could do this, in turn, if we already had an analysis of R in relational terms. If we knew pretheoretically that R was a state that interacted with light, the eyes, memory, belief, and so on, and we just needed to know precisely what information about the light it detected, and just how it interacted with these other systems, then the theory would explain how we experienced R as we do. Of course this whole scenario depends upon a prior analysis of experiencing R in functional-relational terms. If we don't have such an analysis ready to hand, then I don't see how the theory is going to provide it. It can tell us a lot about the functional role that R plays, and by what mechanisms that role is realized. It can't tell us that that's what R *is*.

Again, these are not conclusive considerations. But I do think they show that the challenge facing the relationalist is quite severe indeed. In the remainder of this chapter I'll look more closely at recent versions of relationalism to see whether there has been significant progress in meeting these challenges.

4.4 Subjectivity and Higher-Order Theory

There are two questions a materialist theory has to answer: (1) what distinguishes conscious experiences from mental states (or any states, for that matter) that aren't experiences? and (2) what distinguishes conscious experiences from each other; or what makes reddish different from greenish, what determines qualitative content? The first question specifically targets subjectivity, there being anything at all it's like to occupy a certain state. In this section we'll look closely at a prominent theory of subjectivity, the "higher-order" theory, and at the end briefly consider some alternatives.

The basic idea behind higher-order theory (HO) is that consciousness is a matter of awareness, so to be in a conscious state is essentially to be aware of the state one is in.[13] What distinguishes my visual experience of the red diskette case from my non-conscious states that might also be caused by my exposure to the red diskette case is the fact that I'm aware of the experience, whereas I am not (directly, at least) aware of these other states. In other words, what makes my visual state an experience is its being the representational object of some other state, not something about its intrinsic character.

There are two versions of HO: the "inner-perception" model (IP) and the "higher-order thought" model (HOT).[14] According to IP, there is an internal scanner that works in a way like one's externally directed perceptual systems, and monitors various mental states. For a state to be conscious is for that state to be monitored or scanned by this internal device. According to HOT, for a state to be conscious is for there to be another state, a thought, whose content is that one is in the original state. I will mostly ignore the differences between IP and HOT in what follows.

While HO provides an account of what it is to be a conscious experience, of subjectivity, it isn't an account of qualitative character, in that it doesn't explain how particular qualia differ from each other. When I look at my red diskette case, I have a reddish conscious visual experience, of type R, and when I look at the can of Sprite sitting next to the diskette case, I have a greenish conscious visual experience, of type G. According to HO, what makes them both conscious states is the fact (roughly) that some other mental state represents my occupying these states. But what distinguishes the qualitative character of R from G? On this, HO is silent. However, this is seen by HO's adherents as a virtue of the theory.

Their point is this. First, one of the factors that they claim contributes to the unclarity clouding the discussion of conscious experience is that there are many different phenomena being assimilated; and the most egregious example is the question of qualia and the question of awareness. Qualia (or, better, states with qualitative character) are what we are aware of, so a theory of what it is to be aware of a quale ought to be distinguished from a theory of what a quale is. On their view it makes perfect sense to talk of unconscious states that have qualitative character.

In fact, they say this sort of thing happens all the time. For example, suppose I drive my car as it were on "automatic pilot," unaware of what I'm doing because I'm lost in thought.[15] Despite my apparent obliviousness to the task of driving, I obviously perceive the road, the color of traffic signals, and the like. The difference between my visual experience of the red light that causes me to stop and my visual experience of the red diskette case is not anything intrinsic to either state. Rather, it's the fact that I'm aware of the latter, but not the former. Thus what distinguishes my visual experiences of red and green traffic lights while driving on "automatic pilot" isn't relevant to what it is that makes these states conscious when I'm paying attention to my driving.

Of course one still wants to know what determines qualitative content. HO theorists have recourse to various options here, none of which is essential to being an adherent of HO. They can identify qualia with neurophysiological properties, functional properties, or, the option to be discussed below, with representational contents. Of course whatever problems attend these answers to the second question will affect their theory accordingly.

Let's consider now the overall plausibility of HO. Its distinctive feature is the way it splits off subjectivity from qualitative character, and the problem is that it is precisely this feature that seems so implausible. Consider again my visual sensation of the red diskette case. The reddishness of the experience is not merely a matter of an object occupying a state that instantiates a certain property, but, as we characterized at the start, the reddishness is "for me," or "presented to me." It seems very odd to think of the reddishness being present without its also being "for me," or subjective, in this way.

To elaborate on the oddity for a moment, consider three mental states: my state as I deliberately stare at the diskette case, my perception of a red light while driving on "automatic pilot," and the clearly unconscious state of my early visual processing system that detects a light intensity gradient. According to HO, the first two states both instantiate the same qualitative character, and for the second and third states there is nothing it is like to occupy them; they are both unconscious, non-experiences. One oddity, then, is the fact that, on HO, the very same qualitative feature possessed by my perception of the diskette case can be possessed by a state that is as unconscious as the intensity gradient detector.

Furthermore, does the intensity gradient detector itself possess qualitative character? HO faces a dilemma. To say such states have qualitative character seems to rob the notion of any significance. To deny them qualitative character requires justification. What one would normally say is that to have qualitative character there must be something it is like to occupy a state, and the qualitative character is what it's like. But the advocate of HO can't say this, since states there is nothing it is like to occupy have qualitative character on this view.

Another objection to HO also has to do with states like those that detect intensity gradients. The problem is that we want our theory of subjectivity to deny it to them, but it's not obvious that there aren't higher-order states of the requisite sort within the computational system that carries out visual processing.[16] But then what are clearly unconscious states would count as conscious.

With regard to this last point, the HO theorist might just bite the bullet here and grant that if there are such monitoring states in early visual processing, then their objects would count as experiences.[17] We aren't aware of them as experiences simply because our higher faculties have no access to them. They are experiences for the visual system, not for us. This seems to make being an experience a little too cheap and common, easily programmable into any computer with a camera attached.[18] However, this doesn't seem to me a decisive objection.

What is more significant is the issue raised by the first objection, since this goes to the heart of HO's basic strategy, which is to divorce subjectivity from qualitative character. Can qualia be instantiated in non-conscious states, or is being conscious essential to being a quale? On the face of it the idea that a state could have a reddish quality without being reddish for any subject seems absurd. Rosenthal explicitly addresses this concern. He writes:

> Reflection on what it is like to feel sensations does, however, suggest an important source for doubt about whether nonconscious sensations can occur. We classify sensory states and discriminate among their various tokens on the basis of what it is like for us to be in those states. . . . And

there is no such thing as what it is like to have these sensations unless the sensation is conscious. One might conclude from this that there is no such thing as a sensation's having some distinctive sensory quality unless that sensation is conscious. . . . [In reply:] The distinctive qualities by means of which we type sensations form families of properties that pertain to color, visual shape, sound, and so forth. The members of these families resemble and differ from one another in ways that parallel the similarities and differences among the corresponding perceptible properties of physical objects. . . . So we have no basis to deny that sensory qualities can occur nonconsciously. The distinctive sensory properties of nonconscious sensations resemble and differ in just the ways that those of conscious sensations resemble and differ. (1997, 733)

What Rosenthal seems to be saying is this. Qualitative character is whatever it is that we use to classify sensations. Since we classify sensations by what they're like for us, it might appear that qualia are essentially objects of awareness. However, according to Rosenthal, this is a confusion. Of course we classify by how sensory qualities appear to us when conscious, but that doesn't mean that the properties we are aware of are themselves essentially objects of awareness. Both when we are aware of them and when we're not, the properties at issue are individuated by their place in the relevant similarity space, of the sort proposed by Clark (1993), discussed above. Thus the notion of a non-conscious state's being reddish makes perfect sense.[19]

If indeed a quale could be identified with a location in a similarity space, then I think Rosenthal's reply to the objection might work.[20] If what I'm aware of when I'm having a reddish conscious experience is that I'm in a state that occupies a certain position in the relevant similarity space, then it makes sense to suppose that the property I'm aware of is a property that the state very well could have in the absence of any awareness. But, as argued in the previous section, I deny that that's what I'm aware of. Rather, it seems clear that I have a more determinate and substantive conception of what it is to be reddish, a conception that is not exhausted, or adequately captured by the rather formal description of a location in a similarity space. Again, this is why the idea of inverted (or absent) qualia makes clear sense.

Of course it doesn't follow immediately from the fact, assuming it to be a fact, that *reddishness* is an intrinsic property, that consciousness is also an intrinsic property. What Rosenthal is concerned to deny is the latter claim. What's at stake is whether being conscious is a property of the conscious state, essential to its having the qualitative character it has, or whether its having the qualitative character it has is one thing and its being an object of conscious awareness another. Merely claiming that reddishness is itself intrinsic doesn't settle this question.

However, my claim is not just that the particular relational analysis of qualitative character suggested by Rosenthal doesn't work. It's also clear that no intrinsic property of an internal state will do, either, again for the reasons discussed above. Rather, when we contemplate what this determinate idea of reddishness is that we have, we see quite clearly that it is an idea of an experiential property; reddishness, as I think of it, is a "way things appear to be," where that it's an appearance, and thus for a subject, is intrinsic to what it is. This is even clearer with feelings like pain. It isn't, as Rosenthal suggests (1997, 732), merely a semantic fact about our use of the word "feeling" (though no doubt the word does imply awareness). There really is something about our conception of the property itself, the pain itself, that makes it essentially a mode or kind of experience.[21]

Another way to see what's wrong with the HO strategy of dividing consciousness, or subjectivity, from qualitative character is to consider an objection of Karen Neander's (1998).[22] Neander argues that there is a basic problem with what she terms the strategy of "dividing phenomenal labor." The problem can be brought out with the following example. Suppose I am looking at my red diskette case, and therefore my visual system is in state R. According to HO, this is not sufficient for my having a conscious experience of red. It's also necessary that I occupy a higher-order state, say HR, which represents my being in state R, and thus constitutes my being aware of having the reddish visual experience. So far so good.

The problem is this. Whenever we are dealing with a representational relation between two states, the possibility of misrepresentation looms. Suppose, because of some neural misfiring (or whatever), I go into higher-order state HG, rather than HR. HG is the state whose representational content is that I'm having a greenish experience, what I normally have when in state G. The question is, what is the nature of my conscious experience in this case? My visual system is in state R, the normal response to red, but my higher-order state is HG, the normal response to being in state G, itself the normal response to green. Is my consciousness of the reddish or greenish variety?

Whatever one answers, there is a problem. Suppose we say that my experience is of a greenish sort, because that is what I'm aware of, in the sense that my higher-order state is so representing my experience. Well, then it looks as if the first-order state plays no genuine role in determining the qualitative character of experience, and in a sense HO now collapses qualitative character and subjectivity back together again. On the other hand, if we say that the qualitative character of the conscious experience is still reddish, despite the misrepresentation at the level of the higher-order state, then it looks as if we've collapsed the two together again as well, this time back onto the first-order state. After all, we now have a reddish conscious experience, the consciousness of which could not be constituted by the mistaken higher-order state.

There are other options, of course. One is to say that when this sort of case occurs, there is no consciousness at all. This seems *ad hoc*, and not really well motivated even within the context of HO theory itself. A better option is to ensure correct representation by pinning the content of the higher-order state directly to the first-order state, say by endowing it with a demonstrative content. If the higher-order state says, in effect, "I'm now in *that* state," pointing to R (in our case), then the sort of mistake we're imagining couldn't occur.[23]

But there are two problems with this move. First, what if the higher-order state is triggered randomly, so that there's no first-order sensory state it's pointing at? Would that entail a sort of free-floating conscious state without a determinate character? Second, and more crucial, it's not clear how this really overcomes the basic problem. What Neander's objection shows, I think, is that it just doesn't work to divide phenomenal labor. We have a reddish experience, a certain state of consciousness that has a determinate character. The character is a feature of the state of consciousness. What HO tries to do is split off the character from what it is the character of. We've seen that when you do this by putting a representation of the character into the higher-order state, you just get the character itself back into the same state.

On the other hand, if you opt for this demonstrative move, what's not clear is how the character that is outside the state of consciousness itself is supposed to now get into it. The very problem we saw earlier in chapter 3, the problem that attends various E-type attempts to account for the special character of phenomenal concepts, attends the demonstrative move on the part of the HO theorist. Whatever there is on the other side of the demonstrative, the higher-order state only has an indeterminate, "pointing" content. What we need an account of, and what it's unclear HO can deliver an account of, is how the fact that there is an R-state being demonstrated, as opposed to a G-state (or none at all), is supposed to make a cognitive, and conscious, difference.[24]

If we accept the thrust of these objections to HO, it turns out that subjectivity and qualitative character are internally, necessarily linked. Rosenthal (1997) argues that if we take this line, we are going to be forced to admit that consciousness cannot be explained, since only if consciousness can be reduced to a relation between non-conscious states is there a hope of providing an explanation of the phenomenon. What's more, he argues, the idea that consciousness is inherently part of qualitative character smacks of the view that qualia are "self-intimating," a view of Brentano's (1973) Rosenthal claims is rightly disparaged by Ryle (1949).

I accept both of these consequences of linking subjectivity and qualitative character. I think we don't in fact know how to explain subjectivity, and the fact that we don't is due partly to its paradoxical, self-intimating nature. This is a theme I will return to in chapter 6. What's more, our inability to explain qualitative character is due largely to its connection to subjectivity, a point I've been making frequently throughout our discussion. There is something special about the nature of our cognitive relation to qualitative character that underlies the explanatory gap. I differ with Rosenthal only in not seeing these consequences as a reason to deny the phenomena. There is of course no transcendental argument that qualia and consciousness must be explicable. And in the end, what matters is whether the account that rids consciousness and qualia of their obstructive link is plausible; if it's not, as

I've argued it isn't, then the fact that it's the only explanatory game in town—if indeed it is—doesn't really help.

Suppose we grant that HO is fundamentally flawed in its attempt to split off subjectivity from qualitative character in the way that it does. It's still worthwhile to see how it compares to alternative theories of subjectivity. Relevant materialist alternatives seem to come down to two: the "identity theory" and some other version of functionalism. Is it plausible that the crucial difference between my visual sensation of the diskette case, which has subjectivity, and the state detecting an intensity gradient, which does not, is a matter of the former's possessing, and the latter's lacking, a particular type of neurophysiological property? A functionalist answer certainly seems more plausible here.

HO, of course, is a version of functionalism. So an alternative to HO must involve some other aspect of functional role. The alternatives divide into two types: those that focus on subjectivity, trying to capture what it is for a state to be "for the subject," and those that focus more on trying to capture what it is to be sensory rather than conceptual. Of course combinations of these two are possible.

Examples of the first sort are: being available for verbal report,[25] being located within certain specific memory systems,[26] or being richly embedded in a web of relations involving the control of behavior and cognitive function.[27] Examples of the second sort usually involve representational views. Qualia are distinguished from other mental representations by their format. It might be a matter of being more imagistic, as opposed to conceptual, or being located within a sensory module.[28]

All the functionalist alternatives to HO share the problem that it seems possible to instantiate that particular feature without there being anything it is like to occupy the state in question. But this is the general absent qualia problem. More specifically, they do not have the consequence that states like my visual perception of the diskette case count as non-experiences when not the object of a higher-order state. Being available for report and being located within a particular memory or sensory module do not entail being the object of another state's intentional content. To the extent one finds such a consequence troubling, the alternatives to HO are at an advantage.

On the other hand, an advantage of HO over these alternatives is that its account of there being something it's like to have an experience seems at least connected to the phenomenon we have in mind, even if many find it ultimately inadequate. It analyzes subjectivity as a kind of awareness, after all. But why should being located in a certain memory or sensory module make there be something it's like to occupy that state? The connection between representational format and subjectivity is equally obscure. Thus it's not clear that any functionalist account of what makes a state a conscious experience has a decisive advantage over its rivals.

In fact, I think there is a way of seeing the issue that essentially removes the major difference between HO and other functionalist theories of subjectivity. HO tries to give a direct theory of subjectivity in terms of first-person awareness of one's own mental state. Other functionalists want to allow that states that are not the object of another state's content might still count as subjective or conscious. However, when one objects as above that the functional feature they choose doesn't seem to have anything to do with the "what-it's-like" property we're interested in, the response is to explain our inability to see that the favored functional feature really is the property we're interested in by reference to there being different ways of accessing that property. The theoretical description, of the sort surveyed above, is one way, and our first-person introspective way is the other one. So instead of directly explaining subjectivity in terms of internal access, they explain our puzzlement about subjectivity—the fact that it seems to be a special property inaccessible to functional or physical reduction—in terms of internal access. Either way, the special character of first-person, higher-order representation is carrying a large part of the explanatory burden. I have already, in my discussion of gappy identities, expressed skepticism that such "architectural" moves can work, but there is more to be said on this score, and I will return to this topic below, after we look at eliminativist strategies.

4.5 Representationalism: Externalist Version

Representationalism is the view that qualitative content is intentional content.[29] The idea is this. My visual experience of the red diskette case represents the world outside as being a certain way, namely, as there being a red diskette case in front of me. The reddishness of the experience is just my internal representation of the red color of the diskette case. What distinguishes reddish from greenish experiences, then, is like what distinguishes the meanings of the words "red" and "green."

Representationalists divide over one big question: what sort of intentional content is qualitative character to be identified with—narrow or wide, internal or external? According to the externalist view, which seems the more popular, the reddishness of my visual experience is the property of representing the distal object as having objective redness, which, we'll assume, is something like a particular surface spectral reflectance. On the internalist view, the intentional content at issue is something like conceptual role. There is also a third option, which merges with eliminativism, and which I'll reserve for discussion in chapter 5.[30] In this section I'll discuss externalist versions of representationalism, which I'll just call "externalism" for short, and in section 4.6 I'll deal with internalism.

On externalism, my reddish experience is a state that represents the diskette case as being a certain way, and the reddishness of the experience is just the property of representing the diskette case as being that way. There is a certain initial plausibility to this view, and certain clear philosophical advantages if it can be made to work. First, perceptual states do seem to represent distal objects as being a certain way, and the reddishness of my experience certainly seems to be telling me something about the diskette case.

Second, whenever I try to describe the qualitative character of my experience, I seem to be able to do it only by reference to the properties of external objects—as in, "By 'reddish' I mean the way that diskette case looks to me now." Furthermore, representationalism in general has the advantage of uniting all mental phenomena under the rubric of intentionality, and externalism has the added advantage of obviating the need for an account of so-called "narrow content," a troublesome question it would be good to avoid if possible.

With respect to the first point, it's important to keep the following in mind: one doesn't have to be an externalist, or even a representationalist, to credit the claim that qualia are representations. Any view, even one that treats qualitative character as an intrinsic property of an internal state, can allow that that property serves to represent some distal property. But on views other than externalism, that reddishness, say, represents objective red is a contingent fact. Had the world been different, it might have represented objective green instead. For the externalist, however, all there is to being reddish is to be a representation of objective red. The externalist takes what on other views is a contingent relation and turns it into a conceptually necessary one. I submit that this takes us beyond the initial plausibility that attaches to the idea that qualia are representational states.

Notice that for externalists the inversion problem is especially serious. Whereas traditional functionalists, as we saw above, can appeal to the complex web of relations constitutive of color quality space to pin down a particular quale, this move, as limited as it is, isn't available to the externalist. On the latter view, it shouldn't matter to the question of intersubjective similarity of qualitative character whether two creatures share a complete, or even relatively large range of their quality spaces. So long as they are both in states that represent the same distal property, their qualia should be identical.

Ned Block (1990) has constructed an example, the "Inverted Earth" scenario, that presents the problem vividly. Imagine there is a world where all objective colors are inverted with respect to those here on Earth. Also imagine that spectrum-inverting lenses can be implanted on one's eyes. Now suppose I were simultaneously to be fitted with such lenses and transported to Inverted Earth. It seems pretty clear that everything would look to me as it does on Earth, given the compensating inversions of the external environment and the lenses. My qualitative states would be the same when looking at fire engines and grass as they were on Earth.

On the other hand, what would be the representational contents of my visual states? Would my experience be representing fire engines as red or green? Block admits that at first, despite the regular causal connection between green fire engines and my reddish experiences, it would make sense to say that my experiences were misrepresenting the fire engines as red. So long as we say this there is no problem for the externalist with this scenario. However, assuming that I stay for many years on Inverted Earth, and the inverting lenses remain permanently adhered to my eyes, Block maintains that the representational contents of my perceptual states would change to reflect the new causal regularities between them and the distal properties of my environment. But it seems bizarre to think that as the representational contents changed so would the subjective qualitative character of my experiences. Why would they change? Nothing has changed inside me, and therefore, presumably, I would notice no change.[31.] But if we accept this judgment, then qualitative character isn't constituted by external representational content.

Of course externalists have offered replies. The most common reply is to deny that the representational contents of my visual experiences would change despite the years of residing on Inverted Earth. One might appeal to teleological considerations to back this up. So, for instance, the historical fact of my sensory organs having been the product of evolution on Earth might make them always the representers of what they detected on Earth. Also, the alien nature of the lenses might come into play. My sensory organs are the product of an evolutionary process that did not include inverting lenses. All in all, the idea is that, to use Dretske's way of putting it, what my visual states represent is what they are supposed to detect, what they have the function of detecting.[32]

This doesn't completely take care of the objection, since, in a certain way, the fact that it is me throughout the story, from residing originally on Earth, traveling to Inverted Earth, and then residing there for many years, is inessential. We could tell an alternative story this way. Suppose Inverted Earth were Putnam's Twin Earth, where my twin resides, with everything just like Putnam's story except for two items: we have the environmental inversion of Inverted Earth, and we also have inverting lenses on my twin. To make the case a genuine counterexample to the teleological story, let's imagine that twin-humans evolved with lenses that inverted colors. So when I'm looking at a fire engine, I'm in the same internal neurological state as my twin, but his state represents the engine as green and mine as red. Intuitively, our qualia should be the same. If one judged mine were the same before and after the long sojourn on Inverted Earth in the original story, then why not in this case, given the (relevant) physical identity between me and my twin?

The externalist would have to say that in the second version of the story the qualia were really different. In fact Dretske (1995), for one, is quite explicit in endorsing this consequence. But this seems quite odd. How could physically identical states constitute different qualia? How could qualitative character be a matter of what's going on outside, or what went on with one's ancestors? Since I think Dretske (1995) has the most developed reply to this objection, I'll focus on his discussion of this point. I believe whatever points emerge in connection with his discussion will apply more generally to the externalist position.

Dretske takes his task to be to respond to one who is willing to allow externalism for thought and belief, but not for experience. So, take the second Inverted Earth story. Both Joe and twin-Joe are watching firefighters battle a fire by spraying it with water from a hose attached to the truck. The colors of the two trucks are inverted with respect to each other, and also twin-water is made out of XYZ, not H_2O. According to Dretske's opponent, though Joe's and twin-Joe's beliefs that water is being sprayed on the fire have different contents in virtue of their different environmental circumstances, still their visual qualia when looking at the fire trucks are the same. Dretske argues, on the contrary, that if one is willing to accept an externalist account of conceptual representations, so that Joe's belief is about H_2O and twin-Joe's about XYZ, then one ought to accept such an account for qualia as well, attributing a reddish experience to Joe but a greenish one to twin-Joe. The argument goes like this.

Dretske uses his distinction between two senses of phrases like "the fire engine looks red to Joe": a purely perceptual sense he calls "looks$_p$" and a more cognitive, or doxastic sense he calls "looks$_d$." For instance, a fire engine can look$_p$ like a fire engine to my dog even though my dog has no concept of a fire engine. However, it doesn't look$_d$ like a fire engine to her, since she doesn't have the concept of a fire engine; she isn't disposed to judge that it's a fire engine as a consequence of her perceptual experience of it. On the other hand, to me the fire engine both looks$_p$ and looks$_d$ like a fire engine.

Now, consider again Joe and twin-Joe. Joe's visual state represents red, whereas twin-Joe's state represents green. According to Dretske their states have different qualia, whereas on the internalist position they have the same qualia. Dretske presses against the internalist as follows. What is it for Joe to know about his qualitative character? If one thought that introspective knowledge were a matter of perceiving an internal object, then of course it would be hard to see how Joe and twin-Joe could think differently about their perceptual states, since the natures of any internal objects certainly supervene on whatever is going on inside.

However, clearly there are no internal red or green objects to be perceived. Rather, any knowledge of the character of one's perceptual states is dependent on the way the external object is being perceived. So, the question to ask about Joe (or twin-Joe) is, how does the object look$_d$ to him? What else could there be to each's knowledge of what his experience is like than his knowing how what he's looking at looks to him? But to know what something looks like, in the sense that yields knowledge, is to know how it looks$_d$.

Once we've transformed the question of how Joe's (twin-Joe's) experience seems to him into the question of how the perceived object looks$_d$, then, assuming an externalist theory of conceptual representation, we're home free. For the objector already grants that how something looks$_d$ is externally determined, in the sense that the belief caused by the perceptual state is content-individuated by external features. So to Joe the object looks$_d$ red, and to twin-Joe it looks$_d$ green. If there is any feature their experiences are supposed to have in common, it's not one they have a concept of, and therefore not one they can come to have knowledge of. But now it appears that the internalist is stuck with saying that qualitative character is something

neither Joe nor twin-Joe can know about, and this now becomes the counterintuitive position.[33]

This argument rests on the following dubious assumption. For S to know
what looking$_p$ F is like is for S to occupy a state that involves something's
looking$_d$ F to S. That is, Dretske assumes all I can know with respect to my
reddish qualia is how red things look$_d$ to me. This is made plausible by
using the "looks like" locution to capture qualitative character in the first
place, since what the thing I'm looking at looks like is clearly a matter of
the properties of an external object. But knowing about qualia is plausibly
a matter of knowing how things look$_p$, and this is different for Joe and
twin-Joe.

To put the point another way, suppose we take looking$_p$ F to be not a matter essentially tied to F, but rather only contingently tied to F, as is clearly
the internalist's intent. So what we mean by the "look" of an F is not necessarily anything F-ish, but rather an intrinsic (or at least internal) feature that
experiences of F things normally have. This feature could just as easily have
been a feature of experiences of G things. We use "F" here non-rigidly to pin
down the feature.

Once we characterize "knowing what it looks$_p$ like" in this way, then the
argument that one must have the concept of F in order to know even that
one's experience is of the looks$_p$-F variety doesn't go through. Whatever this
feature of looking$_p$ F is, it is only contingently characterized by reference to
F. There are perhaps other ways of characterizing it, and therefore other concepts that can afford one knowledge that one's experience has this feature. So
both Joe and twin-Joe can know that they have this qualitative character to
their experiences, and it's the same one for both of them, even though Joe
would call it a "reddish quality" and twin-Joe a "greenish quality." Their use
of these terms is merely a matter of their not having a better way to communicate it to others, so they use this contingent feature, being the normal effect of red/green objects, to pin it down. But that doesn't mean they can't
have their own internal concepts that characterize precisely this quality.

If I'm right in my objection to Dretske's argument, then we are still faced
with a standoff. The question remains whether the "internalist intuition,"
Dretske's term for the intuition that qualia are supervenient on what's inside
the head, is, as he claims it is, just a brute intuition. Of course without
Dretske's argument against it, brute or not, it's pretty compelling. But let's
see if we can do more than merely appeal to intuition, compelling as it is.
Let's see if we can articulate at least some of what underlies the intuition.

To start with, note that what Dretske calls the "internalist intuition" isn't
really about what's inside or outside, at least if those terms are understood
spatially. I am prepared to find out that what my experience is like is determined by goings-on quite far outside my body, quite far from where I take
my conscious experience to be occurring. This is the lesson we learn from
Dennett's (1978) ingenious example, when he finds himself staring at his
brain in a vat. That the causal ground for consciousness might be spatially
distinct from where the conscious mind takes itself to be is not a problem for

the internalist. This could be either because the brain is really "over there," not "here," as in Dennett's case, or because, for some strange reason having to do with weird laws of nature, certain brain states are causally dependent on remote events in the requisite ways. Maybe only when I look at red objects am I capable of seeing redly. This doesn't seem to be the case, but it certainly could have been.

So the point of internalism is not to deny that the causal basis for conscious experience could be spatially extended beyond the body. Rather, the "inside" at issue is whatever it is that is the causal basis for the mind. Assuming that a single mind has boundaries, however spatially disconnected they may be, the claim is that what the experience of that mind is like is not constituted by what happens outside those boundaries. In other words, only that which directly causes a change in the structure that core realizes the mind can bring about a change in qualia. The problem, then, with cases like Inverted Earth, on the externalist interpretation, is that a qualitative change is supposedly brought about without any causal interaction with the structure that is serving as the causal basis of experience.

While I think this is on the right track, it doesn't go far enough. True, we seem to feel strongly that you can't effect a change in my experience without doing something to *me*; it's not enough to change the outside world. But what drives this feeling? I think in the end it's a matter of epistemology. If externalism were correct, then I could be mistaken in my belief about the qualitative character of my experience by virtue of facts that lie quite beyond me. That seems bizarre, to say the least. Let me elaborate.[34]

Imagine the following scenario. Suppose that when looking at red objects, say within a certain very narrow range of shades (those in the neighborhood of my diskette case), there was a certain variation in one's experience from time to time. Sometimes the objects looked one shade, and other times they looked another. We can suppose that one of the shades, call it "special red," was more fine-grained, was located in between two shades that, when special red was not perceived, constituted a just noticeable difference. This in-between relation was determined by subjective judgments. Some people saw special red most of the time, others just some of the time, and others never did.

Now, imagine that two hypotheses arose in the community to account for this phenomenon. Some people assumed that seeing special red was determined by one's spiritual state. Gurus claimed to be able to teach people to attain the height of spiritual awareness necessary to see special red. Others, more hard-nosed scientistic types, insisted that there was some physical difference in lighting conditions, background, or whatever, that accounted for seeing special red. After years of research, scientists discovered that there is no systematic difference in the stimulus conditions that give rise to experiences of special red. Rather, a random switch in the brain changes certain values on some occasions of stimulation by red objects within the relevant range and not others.

Notice that in this case, since there is no stability to the circumstances that produce experiences of special red, there is no basis to include some distal property into the representational content.[35] Both reddish experiences and special-reddish experiences indicate, and represent the same external properties. Thus, on the externalist view, we must say that there really is no qualitative difference between the two. But imagine the situation of those awaiting the results of the research. They surely seem to experience a qualitative difference. Now they're told that if the research comes out one way, they really do experience such a difference, but if it comes out the other way, then they don't. Does this make sense? Would people be prepared to give up their claim to a difference in the qualitative character of their experiences based on the results of this research?

It's important not to confuse this argument "from inside" with any claim to infallible or incorrigible knowledge. I can tell from inside that my special-reddish experiences are different from my reddish experiences. The opponent might try to rebut this argument by characterizing it as an appeal to privileged access and incorrigible knowledge. After all, maybe you're mistaken about the difference between your experiences. Isn't a mistake of that sort possible? Couldn't empirical research convince you that you'd made such a mistake?

The answer is, "yes," or, more cautiously, "yes, as far as this argument goes." I'm not appealing to privileged access. My point is this. While there can be mistakes about what's going on inside, and so there isn't incorrigible knowledge, what doesn't seem possible is that everything should be as it appears as far as what's going on inside—so no internal mistake is being made—and yet, for reasons totally external to the subject, it turns out she's wrong about whether or not her experiences are of the same quality. That's what seems absurd.

While the foregoing certainly seems convincing to me, there is still a line of reply available to the externalist that we need to address. Dretske, remember, is arguing against the idea that externalism is appropriate for cognitive content but inappropriate for qualitative content. The point is that the very same epistemic argument we used against externalism about qualitative content has been used against externalism about cognitive content (e.g., Boghossian 1989). Are we really in doubt about the contents of our water thoughts until we find out the chemical composition of water? If this sort of objection doesn't bother us with water thoughts, why is it more problematic with reddish experiences?

In fact, it might easily appear that the standard reply for the water case would work as well for reddishness.[36] The idea is this. What is it to know what the contents of my thoughts are, anyway? It's to have another thought that represents them. Well, when I think to myself that I'm having a water thought, I use the very representation of water that also occurs in the first-order thought about water. Thus whatever my representation of water turns out to refer to, it will be the same for both the first-order thought and the second-order one representing the content of the first-order one. Thus I'm guaranteed knowledge of the contents of my water thoughts.

Similarly, in the case of qualia, it might seem as if the same reply could work.[37] I'm guaranteed knowledge of the qualitative contents of my experiences since my second-order thoughts about those contents are expressed using the very same representations as the first-order experiences themselves. When I think things look red to me, "look red" refers to whatever my reddish experiences refer to, so there's no possibility of error, at least from purely external sources.

However, this line of reply won't work. There is an important disanalogy between the water case and the case of qualia; or, rather, the analogy is really quite different from the way it is presented by the objection. The anti-externalist about cognitive content objected that when I think that water is wet certainly I know what I'm thinking. To that objection, the reply that my knowing what I'm thinking employs the same representation as the lower-order thought itself is quite appropriate. But notice a crucial element of this example of self-knowledge. If pressed concerning what I can really determine about my thought that water is wet merely from introspection, I have to admit that nothing about the real nature of the object of my thought is transparent to me. I can detect which representations, both images and words, I am tokening, and that's about it. So it isn't all that bizarre in the end to be told that which class of objects my thought is really about cannot be read directly off the thought itself.

On the other hand, when contemplating the possibility that water is H_2O, while I can't determine introspectively that water and H_2O are distinct substances, I certainly can determine that "water" and "H_2O" are distinct representations. Nothing about the external situation is going to show me wrong about that. My claim is that qualia function for these purposes more like the representations "water" and "H_2O" than like water itself. Let's return to my example of special red. I can determine introspectively that reddish and special-reddish experiences are different, and it seems bizarre to think that information about the external environment can show me wrong. It may turn out they indicate the same external property, the same surface spectral reflectance, but they aren't the same experience. In the same way, the fact that water is identical to H_2O doesn't undermine my claim to know that my thought that water is wet is a different thought from my thought that H_2O is wet.

The externalist defense presented above, that the second-order thoughts employ the same representations as the first-order ones, only works against the objection that externalism entails we don't know what we're thinking about. The externalist then rightly points out that "knowing what one's thinking" is itself a matter of representing one's thought in a certain way. But my objection to externalism about qualia is that, if it were true, we couldn't tell from within when two qualia differ, and to that objection the standard externalist defense is not an adequate reply. The problem is that we manifestly can tell the difference, and no purely external information is going to convince us we're wrong.

Here's one final way to put the point. Whenever we are dealing with a relation between representations and the world, the possibility of a "Frege case" arises: that we have two distinct representations of what, unbeknownst to us, is the same thing. We can never tell, merely from reflection on the representations themselves, that they don't in fact refer to the same thing. However, no discovery about what they refer to is going to show that the representations themselves are not distinct. If qualia are the referents, then it must be possible to discover that what we thought were distinct qualia are in fact the same, just as the Morning Star turns out to be the Evening Star. But this seems absurd. What makes it absurd is that the qualia aren't the referents, but the representations themselves, and just as the discovery that the Evening Star is the Morning Star doesn't show that the term "the Evening Star" is identical to the term "the Morning Star," so too a discovery that, say, green is red wouldn't show that greenish is identical to reddish.

4.6 Representationalism: Internalist Version

Let's turn now to the internalist version of representationalism. According to the internalist, qualitative character is that aspect of a perceptual state's intentional content that is internally determined. As Stephen White (1994) calls it, it's the state's "notional content." We can explicate internal content through conceptual role, or through a more abstract notion of that which determines a function from contexts to external contents. This sort of view isn't going to violate internal supervenience, so the sorts of objections we've been dealing with above won't apply. However, it still shares with externalism the essential idea that qualitative content is intentional content, and that what unifies all mental phenomena is intentionality.

Given internalism's immunity from the Inverted Earth scenario, why would anyone prefer externalism to it? I can think of at least three reasons. First, as mentioned above, many philosophers who work on the problem of intentionality don't believe that there is a viable notion of internal, or narrow content. For one thing, because of threats of holism, they don't think it can provide a stable enough property to capture what all thoughts with a given content have in common. For another, some don't feel it gives us a genuine kind of content at all, since they think of content as what's represented, and narrow content specifically excludes the object of representation.

The second reason is related to the holism problem. While there are inversion scenarios that challenge externalism in a way that they don't challenge internalism, the reverse is true as well. The internalist has to delimit a range of internal relations that are constitutive of a type of quale. The problem is, as we saw above in section 4.3, that unless one restricted the range to a very great extent—in which case one might as well treat qualia as non-relational—it seems as if there are always going to be cases where we want to say that it's possible for there to be qualitative identity (or similarity) despite important differences in the web of internal relations sustained by the states in question. This is similar to the objection to holistic doctrines, or even restricted conceptual role doctrines, that it seems possible for two people to share belief contents even though their inferential roles are significantly different. Externalists, who pin qualitative identity on the identity of the distal properties detected, don't have this problem.

The third reason to prefer externalism, however, is probably the most fundamental one. Representationalism can be seen as a bold attempt to overcome the materialist tug-of-war between intrinsicalism and relationalism, but only on the externalist reading. On the one hand, qualia seem to be capable of multiple realization, which diminishes the plausibility of any theory that identifies qualia with intrinsic physiological states. On the other hand, they also seem to be intrinsic properties, which leads to all the problems with finding a plausible relational alternative.

As we've seen earlier, philosophers have gone back and forth along this path with no stable resting place. Externalist representationalism, however, seems to combine multiple realizability with intrinsicality, by displacing the intrinsic property onto the external object. So we can allow many different types of physical states to count as realizations of reddishness, since all they need share is their serving as representations of objective redness.[38] The property of reddishness, of course, is still a relational property. But our intuition that something involved here is intrinsic is accommodated by the claim that objective redness, the content of reddishness, is an intrinsic property—not of one's mental state, but of the object of one's mental state. To put it in the terms of our discussion in section 4.3, objective redness serves as the intrinsic residue we're looking for.[39]

For all the reasons discussed above, it's hard to make this move work.[40] But it's not hard to see why it's very tempting, and why internalist representationalism might look too much like old-style functionalism to promise any real progress. However, since externalism does face such overwhelming problems from individualist supervenience considerations, and since representationalism does seem to hold promise as a unified theory of mind, let's explore deeper into internalism and see if the problems just presented can be overcome.

As I mentioned above, most representationalists are externalists. Internalism has been defended in print, as far as I know, only by White (1994) and Rey (1997 and 1998). I'm going to base my discussion mainly on Rey (1998), since he seems to address the problems mentioned above most directly.

First of all, consider the objection that narrow content is not really content, since it abstracts from what is represented. Rey asks us to consider the case of indexicals, such as "I" and "now." There are interesting psychological generalizations that seem to involve these indexicals essentially, and in a contentful way, but which cannot be understood in terms of their reference. For instance, take the egoist hypothesis that people always act out of self-interest, or the economic principle that people discount future utility. Certainly it isn't by virtue of the objective time or person that these generalizations hold, since under relevantly different descriptions they wouldn't hold. It's because I conceive of myself as my*self* that my action counts as self-interested, not because I conceive of myself as Joe Levine. Similarly, I discount some future pleasure because it's after *now*, not because it's after March 19, 2000. Only on a narrow construal can we capture the essence of the generalization, and also only on that construal does it apply intersubjectively.

Furthermore, it's overwhelmingly plausible that whatever role uniquely marks out a symbol as a "self" or "I" symbol—similarly for "here," "now," "that," and so on—is a matter of the symbol's content. It's only qua content, after all, that it enters such generalizations as the ones mentioned above. Thus here we have at least one example of a narrow content that seems to count as a genuine content.

It's important to note here that the role played by the example of indexicals in the argument is that of providing an analogy, or an existence proof. Some theorists, as we have seen, have gone further and tried to utilize the special properties of indexicals and demonstratives directly in an analysis of qualitative experience, specifically with regard to the phenomenon of "knowing what it's like." This is not what Rey is doing here (if I understand him correctly). The crucial difference is this: Rey wants to assign to qualia themselves a kind of content that is analogous, with respect to being narrow, to the kind of content we assign indexicals. The other theorists, however, want to use indexical or demonstrative representations in an account of how we know about our qualia. I have already presented my objections to that view, though I will have more to say later on. For now it's just important that we see that it's not the move under consideration.

Aside from indexicals and demonstratives, another plausible example of internally determined content is that of the logical constants. If we ask of some symbol, say "&," what makes it a representation of conjunction, the answer isn't likely to be that it stands in a certain nomic relation to the appropriate truth function. After all, how could it do that?[41] Rather, what we say is that it plays the appropriate role. For instance, when the system in which it is used tokens a symbol of the form "P&Q" it is also likely to token P and also Q. Again, it seems as if functional role is the relevant content-determining relation here.

Given that indexicals and logical operators are serving here as examples, we need to know what the analogue of these functional roles in the case of qualia is supposed to be. According to Rey, it's what he calls their "characteristic processing." To instantiate a qualitative state of type R is to token the relevant symbol, say <r>. But merely being an instance of <r>, described physically, isn't sufficient to instantiate R. (Or, better, being in a certain physical state isn't sufficient for counting as a tokening of <r>.) Rather, only when the relevant physical structure is actually involved in the characteristic processing definitive of the narrow content of <r> is one having an experience of type R. In fact, it is the entire processing event that is really the realization of R.

The appeal to characteristic processing is supposed to provide a principle for avoiding the holism that threatens functional role views. Not just any aspect of functional role is content-determining. Of course defenders of non-atomistic views of content have struggled mightily to provide plausible principles for distinguishing those features of functional role that are meaning-constitutive from those that aren't. This has often led them to attempt to resurrect some version of the analytic/synthetic distinction, and then run afoul of Quinean arguments.

While not everyone is convinced by the Quinean arguments,[42] Rey's job is easier here than taking on Quine in general. For there are anyway plausible arguments that sensory systems should be treated as "informationally encapsulated modules."[43] The idea is that the computational architecture of the mind is such as to prevent the free flow of information between one's storehouse of beliefs and the processing of sensory stimuli. This explains such phenomena as the persistence of visual illusions, such as the Mueller-Lyer illusion, even after one has been shown that it is an illusion. Given this informational barrier between sensory modules and "central systems," and, presumably, each other, restriction of the content-constitutive functional relations to those inside the module is principled in a way that restrictions of content-constitutive relations to a proper subset of a central system's inferential connections might not be.

Appeal to characteristic processing and modularity helps with the holism problem, but of course it doesn't solve it. As we noted in section 4.3, it seems plausible that one could have a reddish experience even if most of the connections to other color experiences were severed, or non-existent. Still, let's say, for the sake of argument, that Rey's proposal does indeed cut the holism down to manageable proportions. Another problem for internalism, mentioned above, was that narrow content didn't seem to really be a matter of content. Rey's examples of the narrow contents (essentially like Kaplan's "characters") of indexicals and demonstratives, as well as the functional roles of the logical connectives, are plausible examples of internal contents. But how does this transfer to the characteristic processing of visual representations? What is it about their functional roles that is especially content-like?

Rey isn't very explicit about this, but I assume that the sort of processing he has in mind is that which bears on judgment. So, for instance, he does mention certain associations between colors and other aspects of experience, such as whether a color is warm or cool, as the sort of relation he has in mind. Presumably similarity judgments would also be in there. Those aspects of processing that weren't connected with judgment—say the precise algorithm for computing surface reflectance, or something of the sort—wouldn't be constitutive of the representation's narrow content. Thus what would go into the content is, as with traditional conceptual role views, the representation's inferential connections, except that they would be restricted to those that obtain within the module.

Suppose we grant, now, for the sake of argument, that Rey has succeeded in showing both that narrow content has a role to play in the characterization of psychological states and that the functional role, or characteristic processing of a sensory symbol constitutes its narrow content.[44] The question is, is there anything to this account of qualitative character that takes us significantly beyond traditional "psychofunctionalism"?[45] Is the representationalism of this account making a unique contribution to an explanation of qualitative character? I think not.

Whether or not one is treating a qualitative state's functional role as an element of content, there are still basically two alternative sources for a specification of the relevant role: conceptual analysis or empirical investigation. On "analytic functionalism," we derive the relevant functional specification from our grasp of the concept of that qualitative state. This fits well with an understanding of narrow content on which it is supposed to be *a priori* accessible to the subject entertaining the concept. But obviously one can be an analytic functionalist without treating the specification of the functional role as a characterization of content. Either way, whether or not one treats the functional role as a kind of content, the solution to the explanation of qualitative character is the same. Our concept of qualitative character is a concept of a state that plays a certain functional role, and then we find that certain neurophysiological states play that role. As far as the mind-body problem is concerned, that's all we need to say.

Of course we have predicated our entire discussion on the failure of analytic functionalism. "Psychofunctionalism," as applied to qualia, is the doctrine that qualitative character is identifiable with functional role, where the specification of the functional role is to be discovered empirically. On Rey's version, it's the characteristic processing of the relevant symbol.[46] It seems clear that the very same considerations that support the claim of an explanatory gap between physiological description and phenomenal description also support a similar claim regarding the relation between functional description and phenomenal description. We still don't know how what seems to be a distinctive, intrinsic property of my experience—its reddishness—could be the property of processing information in this characteristic manner. So, what do we gain by adding that this processing counts as a kind of content? It would be different if this content were evident to us merely from inspection of our concept of reddishness, but this isn't the claim. Rather, we empirically discover that our sensory symbol <r> undergoes processing of a certain type, and then for theoretical reasons we call that processing its narrow content. Fine. I still don't know why it should seem like *that* (ostending my reddish experience).

Notice that on the externalist version of representationalism we at least had a bid to capture what is supposed to be the distinctive, apparently intrinsic property of reddishness—namely, redness itself. When I direct my attention to the reddish character, the externalist tells me that it's real, objective red that I'm entertaining. If this position worked it would, I believe, have marked a genuine advance in removing the mystery of qualia. But on the internalist version of representationalism, where we take the very same functional role that the psychofunctionalist has been proposing all along, and then add that it constitutes the state's narrow content, I don't see how the project of explaining qualitative character has been advanced. If one found the connection between functional role and phenomenal feel arbitrary and unilluminating to begin with, the news that the functional role is a kind of content doesn't help.

Another way to put essentially the same point is this. Suppose we accept that reddishness is the narrow content, the mode of presentation, of our sensory representation of redness. It seems to me that I have a fairly substantive and determinate idea of what this mode of presentation is, as it seems to be immediately presented to me in experience. As I've said earlier, I would go so far as to say that it makes perfect sense to see the experiential quality of reddishness as the mode of presentation of redness. Now the only question is how to understand the relation between this apparently intrinsic property of my experience, which serves as the mode of presentation of what the experience represents, and the functional/causal role of the experience. That question is as pressing as ever.

It's worth noting the contrast here between the case of qualitative character and indexicals, the case Rey wants to use as a model for qualia. As we remarked in chapter 3, when it comes to representations of myself or the present moment, there really doesn't seem to be any substantive content there. If asked what I mean by "me," I have to say that it's this special way of picking myself out, but I don't really have a determinate content in mind that I can associate with this special way. In such a case it seems appropriate to identify the mode of presentation with the causal role, since there isn't anything else present to mind that fits the bill. But with the representations that constitute my color experience, the situation is quite the contrary. Reddishness has a rich, determinate content, and it doesn't seem at all captured by a description of the characteristic processing of the relevant representation.

In the end, it is evident from the positions of Rey and White, the two philosophers who explicitly endorse representational internalism, that the characterization of qualitative character as a form of narrow content is not really doing any significant work. White defends not only representational internalism, but also analytic functionalism. In fact he endorses the Chalmers-Jackson form of argument that only if our concept of qualitative character is functionally analyzable can we support the claim that it is physically realized. For this reason he argues that cases of inverted qualia are conceptually impossible. But once one has this much, one doesn't really need any more to defend materialism, though there may be other reasons to want to treat these functional roles as forms of content.

On the other hand, Rey, who explicitly endorses psychofunctionalism, admits in the end that representational internalism is not an adequate account of qualitative character. He grants explicitly that we seem, in conscious experience, to be confronted with a property that is not at all explicable in terms of functional role, whether or not we call it narrow content. This is why he marries his representational internalism to eliminativism. The point is that what we seem to be confronted with in experience is really an illusion. Thus, for Rey, the really hard work in a theory of conscious experience is being done by eliminativism, not representationalism. Given the considerations above, that makes perfect sense.[47]

4.7 Conclusion

In this chapter I have examined various reductive strategies for removing the explanatory gap and found them all wanting. Qualia appear to be intrinsic properties of experience, but, if they are, it's hard to see how to make sense of them in physical terms. All the relational strategies, on which their realization would be explicable, have failed to provide satisfying or convincing accounts. It's time, then, to consider what seems at first blush an impossible alternative: qualia are not explicable in physical terms, because they don't really exist.

5

"You've Got Me Blowin', Blowin' My Mind"
Eliminativism

5.1 Introduction

In chapter 1 I argued that a fairly strong version of materialism must be true. In particular, the only basic properties and lawful relations are those that obtain at the level of fundamental physics. All other properties and lawful relations must ultimately be realized in these basic ones. Furthermore, I argued in chapter 3 that to *explain* how all non-basic properties and lawful relations are realized in basic ones—to provide realization theories for non-basic properties and lawful relations—one had to deductively derive the instantiation of the non-basic properties and relations from descriptions of the basic ones.

On the other hand, in chapters 3 and 4 I argued that we have no reason for optimism concerning the search for a realization theory for conscious experience. There seems to be an unbridgeable explanatory gap yawning between the physical and the qualitative sides of mental life. Functionalist attempts to bridge the gap, including recent theories such as HO and representationalism, don't seem very promising. Faced with these gloomy prospects, it makes sense to consider seriously the hypothesis that what's causing all the trouble—qualitative consciousness—is just too much trouble to keep around. Hence, eliminativism starts to seem like a plausible alternative.

5.2 Qualophilia: Bold and Modest

The arguments of chapters 3 and 4 mark me as a "qualophile," and I confess, it's true. By a "qualophile" I mean someone who finds that the phenomenon of conscious, qualitative experience resists a materialist explanation.[1] However, let's distinguish two sorts of qualophile: modest and bold. The bold qualophile argues that we can tell, through *a priori* reflection on the nature of our own conscious experience, that materialism is false. We can just see that conscious experience has certain features that make it incompatible with any description couched in terms of the natural sciences. Conscious experience is just not, in this sense, a natural phenomenon.

The modest qualophile makes no strong, positive claims of this sort. Far from claiming to see so clearly into the nature of conscious experience that its non-material character is evident, the modest qualophile finds the nature of conscious experience a source of deep puzzlement. Who can tell whether its ultimate ontological status is material or immaterial merely by means of having it? Rather, the challenge conscious experience is believed to pose has a more negative characterization. The modest qualophile finds that no materialist theory seems to really explain our experience, to make intelligible how a system satisfying the materialist's description could be a subject of conscious experience. As should be clear from the presentation of my position so far, it is only the modest version of qualophilia to which I confess.

Let's distinguish two basic kinds of materialist response as well: "reductivist" and "eliminativist." The reductivist argues that conscious experience is indeed a natural, material phenomenon, and in fact can be adequately characterized by her favorite psychological or neuroscientific theory (or some combination of the two). The eliminativist, on the other hand, agrees with the qualophile that no such theory provides an account of conscious experience, but that's not because of some lack in the theory. Rather, the problem is that conscious experience doesn't really exist. Of course we talk and act as if it does, but such talk is just that, "talk." Instead of the fairly unified phenomenon we think we have in mind when referring to "conscious experience," there is a multifarious collage of psychological and neurological phenomena, none of which answers to our simple conception of there being something it's like to see color and feel pain.

In response to the bold qualophile, any materialist must be an eliminativist. After all, the bold qualophile claims that qualia—the phenomenal, qualitative characters of conscious experiences—are immaterial, outside the natural, physical order. The materialist claims there are no such phenomena; hence she is an eliminativist with respect to the posits of the bold qualophile. So if there is a difference between the two materialist responses, it must be in addressing the modest qualophile that it manifests itself. The modest qualophile claims that something is left out of the materialist's theory. The reductivist responds, no, there isn't. The eliminativist says, yes, there is, but it's not a real something after all; it's a kind of cognitive illusion.

Let's dig deeper into the question of what precisely divides bold from modest qualophilia. Both forms of the condition find their home in the first-person point of view. I think this is undeniable,[2] and it is the source of the great difficulty both in eliminating qualophilia and in defending it. At any rate, it seems clear that were we not to have access to our own experience— or were God to guarantee that we were the only ones who had conscious experience—we wouldn't find any explanatory gap in the account of others' behavior (or not from this quarter anyway). But we do have experience, and it seems that merely by having it and reflecting on it we can generate questions that seem very difficult to answer: How could neurons transferring signals amount to this? Why should selectively responding to such-and-such surface reflectance properties look like that?

Both bold and modest qualophiles take the deliverances of first-person experience seriously. Where they differ is in how rich and how determinate they take those deliverances to be. The bold qualophile believes that certain metaphysical claims can be established on the basis of what is presented in experience. For instance, it is often claimed that qualia couldn't be physical properties, or that they are simple, unstructured properties. The idea is that when it comes to the contents of our own minds we can attain a level of Cartesian clarity and distinctness sufficient to reveal their essences. Descartes claimed to demonstrate that extension was no part of the essence of a thinking thing, and the mind was indivisible by nature. These are bold, metaphysical claims, and I, as a modest qualophile, do not feel they are warranted by what is presented in experience. Of course this is precisely what divides the advocates of the conceivability argument from their opponents, as we saw in chapter 2.

Bold and modest qualophilia can be summed up this way. Both claim that there is an aspect of mental life, conscious experience, which is left out of the standard materialist theory of the mind. The bold qualophile maintains that it is left out in the sense that it constitutes a domain of phenomena outside the natural, physical order. The modest qualophile maintains, on the contrary, that it must be located within that order, but the problem is that materialist theories don't explain how that is so. Both, of course, agree on the metaphysical reality of conscious experience, and that it is a phenomenon to which we have a kind of special, first-person epistemic access. But, again, whereas the bold qualophile draws the conclusion that this access provides insight into the essential nature of conscious experience, and in an incorrigible manner, the modest qualophile only maintains that the nature of this access is as puzzling as that to which it provides access. We can draw no positive metaphysical conclusions, and it is always possible that what is presented within first-person experience embodies errors of all sorts. Still, we have this experience, we have first-person access to it, and this requires explanation.

It is interesting to note the complicated web of relations that hold among the modest qualophile, the reductivist, and the eliminativist. Although along one dimension the reductivist is clearly more friendly to the qualophile than is the eliminativist, along another, perhaps more significant dimension, it is the qualophile and the eliminativist who are closer in spirit. To defend the first part of the claim is easy. Reductivists say that of course conscious experience exists; there is something it is like to see, feel, and so on, no doubt about it. But in fact materialist theories, whether of the computational sort or the neurophysiological sort, do a pretty good job of explaining it. What hasn't been explained is waiting for completion of the various theories of perception, cognition, and emotion that are currently under development. The problem with qualophiles is that they don't know enough science; they can't see that what they're after is in fact visible on the horizon. The very phenomenon the qualophile is pointing at when she goes "But how do you explain *this*?" is just what the materialist theory has an account of.

So, it looks as if the reductivist at least agrees with the modest qualophile about the ontological question. On the other hand, the eliminativist accuses the qualophile of a cognitive illusion—of positing states and properties that literally do not exist. Where the reductivist sees ignorance, the eliminativist sees illusion. Perhaps it's unclear which is a greater cognitive vice, but it might appear that the reductivist is the friendlier, for at least she allows that the qualophile is talking about "a something" and not "a nothing."

Still, on another dimension, I think it is the eliminativist who best understands the qualophile's challenge, and, for that very reason, takes such an uncompromising ontological stand. As an example of what I have in mind, let me just note a recent debate between Lycan (1997) and Rey (1983), the former a reductivist and the latter an eliminativist. To oversimplify greatly, it comes down to this. Rey argues that consciousness couldn't be a matter of certain computational mechanisms, for those are easily realized on your favorite laptop. Lycan disagrees, arguing that your favorite laptop, when suitably programmed, just has consciousness. Rey maintains that nothing which is so easily realized on a laptop could provide an explanation of what we have in mind by conscious experience, and so in that sense is friendlier to the qualophile than Lycan. Of course, he also maintains that there isn't anything in fact going on in us that couldn't easily be realized on a laptop, so the qualophile is guilty of an illusion. What Rey gives with one hand, he takes away with the other.

This brings us quite naturally to a discussion of Dennett's (1991) response to the qualophile, since what he claims to do, in the very title of his book, *Consciousness Explained*, is precisely what the modest qualophile is requesting, and therefore he might seem to be a reductivist. Despite the title, though, Dennett's response to the qualophile is not so much to explain qualia as to eliminate them as candidates for explanation. The actual explanatory work is reserved for our belief in qualia, our temptation to ascribe these quite mysterious properties to our experience. Dennett puts it this way: "I *am* denying that there are any such properties. But . . . I agree wholeheartedly that there seem to be qualia" (Dennett 1991, 372, emphasis in original).

In fact, I think the sort of affinity with the qualophile attributed above to Rey is manifested also by Dennett in his rejection of what he calls "Cartesian materialism." That doctrine claims that conscious states are straightforwardly identical to certain brain states (or realized in certain brain states: it doesn't matter for these purposes). There's a place in the brain where it "all comes together." Some states count as conscious, others not. Dennett's arguments to the effect that there couldn't be such a brain center of consciousness, while not exhausted by this consideration, do largely rest on the insight that there is nothing in the brain center story that really explains the difference between the conscious brain states and the unconscious ones. What, after all, could there be that so fundamentally distinguishes those bits of information processing that are non-conscious from those that are conscious? Given this lack of explanatory connection, the best materialist strategy is to show that there is nothing here to be explained in the first place, that it is all a chimera. In this way the explanatory burden is lifted from the materialist's shoulders.

5.3 Five Eliminativist Strategies

On the face of it, of course, the qualophobe's denial of conscious experience seems ludicrous. After all, what could be more obvious than the fact that we have conscious sensory experiences? How could you deny that there is something it's like to see red, smell a rose, or feel pain? What possible illusion could we be suffering from in thinking these are all genuine properties of our experience?

There are moments when I'm tempted to just stop there. "What are you talking about?" I would say to the qualophobe. "I literally don't understand what it means to deny *this*" (pointing somewhere vaguely in the direction of my head). But I'm going to attempt to do better. As I see it, qualophobic strategies basically break down into five types: (1) assimilating modest and bold qualophilia; (2) accusations of theoretical irrelevance; (3) displacing the question from experience to what we say and judge about experience; (4) skeptical arguments; and finally, (5) denigrating the first-person perspective. Though I've characterized these as five different strategies, to me it's more useful to see them as stages in a single dialectic. Even calling them "stages" is misleading because as the dialectic develops, various stages are constantly revisited. So, in this section I will try to map a path through the various stages through which the qualophile-qualophobe confrontation plays itself out, by the end emerging with a clearer picture of how all the considerations interact. I will follow this overview of the five strategies with a more detailed examination of certain eliminativist arguments in the sections that follow.

As emphasized above, the bold qualophile makes claims about the nature of qualia that are very difficult to substantiate merely from the deliverances of first-person experience. A common response to qualophilia then is to point out the problems with these positive, bold claims. If there are nonphysical properties of the sort the bold qualophile posits, how do they cause behavior or causally result from physical stimuli? There are all sorts of phenomena that seem to shake our conviction that the contents of our experience are always knowable without possibility of error, yet incorrigibility is usually part of the bold qualophile's conception of experience. So, the qualophobe argues, there really couldn't be any phenomena answering to this description, and it must all be an illusion.

Now, given that the modest qualophile makes no such bold claims about the contents of conscious experience, such arguments have no force. I, as a modest qualophile, claim that, for all I know, qualia are perfectly respectable physical properties, and I don't claim that it is logically impossible that one be mistaken about the content of one's experience. Still, perhaps the qualophobe might argue that I'm the one who's cheating here. For if I look closely at what it is that I claim is left unexplained by current materialist theories, it will turn out, the qualophobe argues, that it is precisely those properties in which I claim not to believe.

To see what I mean, let's take the case of visual experience of color. I'm looking at my red diskette case, and there is a certain quality to the experience, and I wonder what it is about the information processing, or its physical realization, that could explain it. When pushed to describe just what it is that is so hard to explain, I might easily slide into talk about the uniformity, the simplicity, the ineffability of the visual field. I might say that it *seems* as if my inner, phenomenal space is painted with what Dennett calls "figment" (1991, 346), and it's the nature of figment that cries out for explanation here.

Of course if I do talk this way, I am guilty of practicing bold qualophilia. It is then appropriate for the qualophobe to point out that there can't be such a thing as figment, that the properties that seem to me so simple, homogenous, and the like are really quite complex and heterogenous. This is one way of understanding the lesson of Dennett's Jell-O box example (1991, page 376).[3] It is an example of a very simple representation of a complex state. Once we see how our visual experiences can carry quite complex information in a form that hides its complexity from us, we should not find the apparent simplicity of our color experience so puzzling. There literally isn't anything in us that answers to the description we use when characterizing our purported explanandum.

I have to admit that providing a helpful characterization of the explanandum at issue here is quite difficult. So far, all I know how to do is point at the phenomenon, using hand-wavy terms like "what it's like to see the red diskette case." But that I can't provide a satisfactory description doesn't mean either that I must accept the one provided for me by the qualophobe, or that there is nothing I'm pointing at in my hand-wavy sort of way. Adhering as I do to a fairly strict separation between matters metaphysical and matters epistemological, I don't claim to have privileged knowledge concerning the actual simplicity or complexity, homogeneity or heterogeneity, or any other aspect of the ontological nature of my visual experience. Thus, that there isn't anything fitting such descriptions doesn't automatically eliminate the object of my concern. I, as a modest qualophile, merely maintain that I am a subject of such experience, and that that I am a subject of experience, and what it's like to be one, is not explained by any materialist account I know of.

But now, the qualophobe argues, moving on to strategy (2), if you really aren't prejudging the metaphysical issue in an *a prioristic* way, then the question comes down to which theory—the qualophile's or the qualophobe's— better meets our general epistemological norms for theories. Qualia, she continues, like all mental states, are posited as part of a theory, "folk psychology." Like all theoretical entities, we have reason to believe in them only to the extent that they do explanatory work. If we can find a more elegant, parsimonious way to do the explanatory work qualia do, but without the problems they cause, then of course we should eliminate qualia from our ontology. In fact, psychological explanations can get along very well without adverting to qualia. Functional and neurophysiological processes can take us from stimuli, through the various levels of cognitive processing, all the way to behavior. What theoretical function then do qualia perform? Without sufficient reason to believe in qualia, the rational default is to eliminate them.

If qualia, or the qualitative characters of conscious experiences, entered the game only as theoretical posits, then of course they would be more trouble than they're worth. When people speak of mental states as theoretical entities, part of the explanatory machinery of folk psychology, they have in mind a pre-theoretical delineation of the data relative to which these theoretical entities are expected to do their explanatory work. The data are usually presumed to be behavioral responses to stimuli. We want to know why English speakers sort wave forms into two categories—grammatical and ungrammatical—and posit an internal representation of the grammar of English to explain this.[4] The "posit" here is the internal representation, not the sorting behavior itself.

My response to the second strategy, then, is to challenge the status of theoretical posit to which conscious experience is relegated, instead treating it as a basic datum that itself requires explanation. No one ever proposes to doubt that human beings behave in various ways that require explanation, though of course there are quarrels within psychology over the validity of particular bits of behavioral data. Any theory that denied human linguistic behavior to start with wouldn't be worthy of even superficial consideration. Sure, you can deny that the behavior is sufficiently systematic to warrant positing internally represented rules, but you can't deny that people talk to and understand each other. This isn't a logical truth, and of course Descartes's demon could be invoked to doubt it, but it's still the data you have to begin with and you can't reasonably deny.[5]

It's precisely this question of what the data are that Dennett attempts to address with his "heterophenomenological method," and with this we slide gracefully into strategy (3). He claims that the theory of consciousness ought to be constrained by everything we are tempted to say about our experience. The constraint isn't that there must turn out to be a phenomenon that satisfies our intuitive descriptions, but rather that our theory of the mind, taking what we say about our experience as data, must be capable of accounting for why we say what we say. If we are compelled to describe our experience as consisting of an internal, mental field of figment, then the correct theory ought to explain this compulsion. As mentioned above, this is the point of examples like the Jell-O box: to demonstrate how something could be one way though we are tempted to think of it quite another way.

Though I don't think it is obvious that even if we adopt the heterophenomenological method Dennett's account succeeds, I do think he has won the better part of the battle if we accept this move from the outset. As he describes it, heterophenomenology is "a method of phenomenological description that can (in principle) do justice to the most private and ineffable subjective experiences, while never abandoning the methodological scruples of science." As for the latter "scruples," they include, essentially, "insistence on the third-person point of view" (1991, 72).

Now, you might well wonder how a phenomenon like subjective experience, with its apparent privacy and ineffability, to which we seem to have access primarily from the first-person point of view, is going to be done justice from the third-person point of view. The answer is that it is the pronouncements we make *about* conscious, subjective experience that are to be done justice, and these of course are readily available to the third-person point of view. It is our statements, our verbalized and verbalizable judgments, that constitute the data concerning experience which are to constrain the construction of theory. Of course if these are your data, then conscious experiences themselves, qualia, become legitimate only as explanatory posits. Once we see how to account for the data without qualia, their legitimacy is undermined.

I maintain, however, that conscious experiences themselves, not merely our verbal judgments about them, are the primary data to which a theory must answer. Of course this means taking the first-person point of view seriously—not, as the Cartesian perspective of the bold qualophile demands, by treating it as a source of theoretical hypotheses itself, but still as a legitimate source of data. I maintain, that is, that I don't just say, or think (in the sense of verbalized judgment) that I am having an experience of a certain sort right now, but I *am* having such an experience.

Anticipating just such a response, Dennett presents the following, instructive dialogue between himself and the qualophile Otto:

> OTTO: Look, I don't just *say* that there seems to be a pinkish glowing ring; *there really does seem* to be a pinkish glowing ring! [He's here talking about the color spread phenomenon depicted on the back of Dennett's book. The crucial point is that the pinkish glowing ring is an illusion.]
>
> DENNETT: I hasten to agree . . . You really mean it when you say there seems to be a pinkish glowing ring.
>
> OTTO: Look. I don't just mean it. I don't just *think* there seems to be a pinkish glowing ring; *there really seems* to be a pinkish glowing ring!
>
> DENNETT: Now you've done it. You've fallen in a trap, along with a lot of others. You seem to think there's a difference between thinking (judging, deciding, being of the heartfelt opinion that) something seems pink to you and something *really seeming* pink to you. But there is no difference. There is no such phenomenon as really seeming—over and above the phenomenon of judging in one way or another that something is the case. (1991, 363–364, emphasis in original)

Of course, if Dennett is right that there is no difference of the sort that Otto is worried about, then there really is nothing left about which to argue. But Dennett, at least in this passage, isn't really arguing for the claim of no difference as much as he's asserting it. He's basically saying that there are these judgments concerning what's going on around us, and though we are tempted to endow some of them with the title "conscious," there is no principled difference marked by the term. Well, that is the qualophobic position. But what is supposed to show that Otto is making a mistake, "fallen into a trap," as Dennett puts it?

I think what's doing part of the work here is the unclarity over the relation between a state's qualitative, phenomenal character and its representational content; in a sense, Dennett is slipping in some representationalism to make his eliminativism go down easier. Take the case of the pink glowing ring. I am having a visual experience, and its content is of a pink glowing ring. What sort of "content" is this? In one sense the phrase "of a pink glowing ring" describes the state of affairs represented by the experience. Visual experiences are certainly a species of mental representation, and they represent what's happening in the space around us. In our case, the representation is an illusion, so the state of affairs represented doesn't really obtain. But that doesn't mean the representation doesn't obtain, and this is what Dennett means by admitting that of course it seems to Otto that there is a pink glowing ring on the book jacket. That is just as real as the sentence, "There is a pink glowing ring on the book jacket."

But the phrase "of a pink glowing ring" is doing double duty here. It describes the representational content of the experience, in the sense just presented, and when embedded in contexts like "what it's like to see . . ." it also describes the phenomenal character of the experience itself. It is this second use of the phrase that Otto is getting at when he complains "but I really do seem to see . . ." Of course, given the precise terms in which Dennett allows him to express himself here he is easily deflected, since he seems still to be talking only about the experience's representational content.[6]

As we've seen earlier, there is no doubt an intimate link between the phenomenal character and its representational content; qualia are most naturally thought of as ways of presenting the world to us. But acknowledging this intimate link—as well as the fact that it is very dimly understood—does not, as I argued in chapter 4, automatically lead to acknowledging that all there is to qualitative experience is its representational content.

My complaint against Dennett in this passage comes down to this. I claim we have access to data in our own experience that demands explanation from a theory of the mind. Dennett claims that all we have access to is our propensity to make judgments. He illustrates his point with Otto by showing how Otto's attempt to characterize what he has access to commits him to a distinction between degrees of seeming. But drawing the distinction between conscious experiences and unconscious representational states in terms of their representational status—"really seeming" versus "mere seeming"—is already to ignore the very phenomenon with which Otto, "along with a lot of others," is concerned.

But how do I know I really have this experience to which I claim access? This is the standard qualophobic retort, and now we slide into strategy (4). Just how tangled is the epistemological web here can be seen by reflecting on the fact that the very same thought experiment—the so-called "zombie"—is used by both qualophile and qualophobe. A "zombie," remember, is supposed to be a creature that is a functional duplicate of me but lacks conscious experience altogether.[7] It is the creature envisioned in the absent qualia hypothesis. The bold qualophile claims that such a creature is possible, and therefore conscious experience is not a matter of functional organization. The modest qualophile claims that such a creature is conceivable—where this is not taken to entail metaphysical possibility—so therefore functional organization does not explain conscious experience. In either case, the epistemological possibility of a zombie carries a large part of the qualophile's argumentative burden.

But then the qualophobic response is to turn the tables, using the possibility of zombiehood against the qualophile. After all, a zombie would say everything you say, think (in the non-question-begging sense of occupying states with informational content) everything you think, so how do you know you're not a zombie yourself? To which I respond, because I have these experiences, that's how I know. But, the qualophobe presses again, you *say* that, and I see how sincerely and emphatically you insist on it, but *so would your zombie twin.* Your own position commits you to the conceivability of such a convincing zombie facsimile, so, again, how do you know you're not one yourself?

I think the epistemological issues concerning zombies are quite complex, and I will delve into them in some detail in chapter 6. For now, a more superficial treatment will have to suffice. So, what I say to the challenge just posed is this. If the question is, literally, *how* I know I'm a genuine subject of experience and not a zombie, there's a two-part, quite unilluminating answer: the fact that I am a genuine subject of experience is undoubtedly responsible for my knowing that I am, but just *how* this is accomplished, just what the epistemic mechanisms are, I haven't the faintest idea. Of course the challenge "How do you know?" is meant to elicit justification, not an account of epistemic mechanisms, but then the two are fairly closely connected anyway. Let's try to sort some of this out.

I am faced with two hypotheses: (1) I am a subject of genuine conscious experience, or (2) I am a zombie. The qualophobe demands justification for belief in (1) and rejection of (2). Why should I even begin to take (2) seriously? It might be said: because it's conceivable, at least on the qualophile's view, and therefore I need a reason for ruling it out. Of course it can't be that it's the mere conceivability of (2), the fact that (2) is not logically false. Lots of statements I know to be false are not logically false. The challenge to justify believing a statement, and ruling out its negation, based on the conceivability that it's false, has bite only if we have specified in advance a relevant data base. So then the claim of conceivability is not mere conceivability on its own, mere self-consistency, but rather the much more substantial conceivability you get from consistency with all the available, relevant data.

But if this is the challenge in this case, there are two straightforward replies. First, even when faced with alternative hypotheses, each consistent with all the relevant data, we don't standardly reject claims to knowledge. Some doubts are merely skeptical doubts. Skepticism always has its foot in the door when you allege that some characterization of a state of affairs is strictly consistent with the data, even if you would normally consider it crazy to believe it actually to obtain. So of course if the qualophile argues that there is no contradiction involved in a description that includes both my functional organization and a lack of conscious experience, she immediately opens the door to a skeptical "How do you know there aren't such creatures? How do you know you're not one yourself?" But how does this differ from the hypothesis that the world was created by God five minutes ago?

The second reply addresses the challenge at an even earlier point. Who says it's really conceivable that I'm a zombie? The fact that it is logically consistent with any data I could obtain that *there could be a* zombie doesn't show that it is similarly consistent with any data I could obtain that *I* am a zombie. After all, why doesn't my conscious experience itself count as part of my data base? (And here we see stage (2) emerge again as the focus.) Of course, you can argue that appeal to this evidence is illegitimate, because it's the very hypothesis at issue. But then you could mount the same challenge with regard to any data, including what I'm inclined to say, even what I have said. The point is that we have already admitted a logical, epistemic gap between the data derivable from an account of functional organization and the data of experience itself. This should only be an embarrassment to the qualophile's claim to know (1) if there is some reason to screen off conscious, first-person experience itself as a source of data. But why do that?

Let me put this another way. How do certain skeptical possibilities begin to get a grip on our epistemic imaginations? It isn't their mere conceivability, but rather our becoming convinced that things could seem just as they do, down to the very last detail, and yet we could be radically wrong about some fundamental belief. My "notional" world could be just as it is, yet I could be a brain in a vat. Now, with respect to such epistemic possibilities, there is my first reply, that it's just skepticism, and there seem to be only two choices when faced with skepticism: give up realism or stop worrying. But still, we do see what's worrying the person who refuses to stop.

I submit that the rhetorical, intuitive power of the qualophobe's skeptical challenge derives from conjuring up a picture of how it is with me now and claiming that it could be just like this even without conscious experience. But in what sense could things be just as they are with me now, epistemically, notionally, without my having genuine conscious experience? Only if I excise the conscious experience itself from this conception of how it is with me now. But then what's left isn't a very convincing picture of what my epistemic position really is, and I don't see any reason to worry that such a creature, one just like me but without the qualia, would have a genuine skeptical problem. Such a creature, after all, isn't really very much like me at all.[8]

Of course, as has become apparent from the way the dialectic has developed, the question of justifying belief in (1) has come down to the question it was invoked to settle: whether first-person conscious experience constitutes pre-theoretic data for a theory of the mind, or is a highly theoretical, and thus epistemically vulnerable posit. Dennett's comparison at one point between belief in qualia and belief in undetectable gremlins reinforces the point (1991, 403).[9] We would have to posit such gremlins as explanatory mechanisms in order to justify belief in them, and I grant you can't do that with qualia. But I contend the situation is much closer to the one we'd be in if we saw and touched the gremlins, but still couldn't explain their presence.

Well, what if someone swore they really did see and touch the little devils? What then? People say they experience all kinds of things, and we usually discredit these reports when they don't comport with our overall theory of the world. What's more, there's a whole body of psychological data demonstrating how untrustworthy first-person reports can be, giving the lie to the Cartesian perspective of incorrigible access to our own minds. In other words, aren't qualophiles guilty of an unscientific methodology by taking the first-person perspective seriously at all?

This, more than the skeptical doubts, is where the issue is really joined, I believe, and it brings us to strategy (5). In a sense, this is where we started. Qualophilia is a first-person phenomenon—some no doubt think of it as a disorder—and its legitimacy depends on the legitimacy of that perspective. The considerations just adduced on behalf of the qualophobe certainly seem to bring the legitimacy of the first-person perspective into doubt. These considerations break down into the following three types: (i) an objection to incorrigibility, (ii) a concern for the objective character of scientific evidence, and (iii) an indictment of the qualophile's inability to provide a theory of the epistemic mechanisms of first-person access.

It can easily seem as if the qualophile's claims concerning conscious experience involve appeal to the incorrigibility of first-person access. For one thing, this has been a traditional claim of dualists, and for another, it has a certain intuitive plausibility, so why shouldn't the qualophile avail herself of the claim, since she's relying on intuitions anyway? Also, appeals to the incorrigibility of first-person access have played an important role in foundationalist epistemological theories, so it is plausible again that anyone appealing to the data revealed within this perspective does so in this traditional, foundational manner. Once this identification with the traditional foundational notion is made, then of course any attack on traditional foundationalist epistemological theories is easily seen as an attack on the legitimacy of any data at all emanating from the first-person perspective. Once the "myth of the given" is given up, what's left?

While appeals to incorrigibility, along with providing a secure foundation for all claims to knowledge, may be part of the bold qualophile's agenda, it is no part of the modest qualophile's. I agree that "the given" is a myth if by this phrase one intends a source of knowledge with no possibility of error built in. I see no reason to doubt any of the vast body of data showing just how wrong we can be about what's going on in our own minds;[10] in fact I argued above that when it comes to essences, or natures, we have no special epistemic access even in the case of our own mental states.

But does this acknowledgment of the possibility of error impugn our first-person knowledge of our own experience? Why should it? Unless one thought that one can never claim knowledge when even a possibility of error remained, the rejection of incorrigibility, and of the foundational role of the "given" in experience, doesn't entail that we must totally discount what seems to be the case from within the first-person perspective. Of course in some sense I *could* be wrong that I'm now having a certain visual experience (though in normal cases I find it quite difficult to know what this would amount to—but let's admit it anyway). I'm also convinced that there are all sorts of cases where I *am* wrong about first-person judgments I make. But what follows from this is not that I should doubt, in a substantive, and not just skeptical way, that I really have the data of experience I believe I have.

Let's turn now to the qualophobe's concern for scientific objectivity. As we all know, in the "bad old days" psychology was hobbled by an assumption that its domain was the phenomena available to introspection. Of course no systematicity in the data is possible if each theorist must look into her own soul, and nowhere else, for the data upon which to build a theory. Furthermore, some people claim to know all sorts of things in an immediate, first-person sort of way. Science demands some check on this sort of claim, a recourse to third-person, public verification. Thus psychology really has no business taking data available only from the first-person perspective seriously. Far from an explanatory burden, it should be relegated to the dust bin of mythology.

While of course I endorse the general goal of scientific objectivity, I don't think such a concern entails totally neglecting a source of data that is, as it were, "right in front of your face." It does mean, however, that we must proceed with extreme caution, and not jump to insupportable conclusions. This is one reason I endorse modest, and not bold, qualophilia. To claim to know what the nature of experience is just by having it, or to base a theory on data that are publicly inaccessible, would be to run afoul of sound scientific practice. The modest qualophile is not pushing a theory, however, but pointing to an area of inadequacy in one. All data, no matter how garnered, are fair game for that purpose.

Now this concern for objectivity does connect rather directly with the issue of skepticism, not of the first-person sort but of the third-person sort. We have reason to take the qualophile's concerns seriously to the extent that we share the data. I myself am not going to find fault with a theory that fails to explain something to which *only you* seem to have access, especially if I have a perfectly good explanation of your claiming to have access to such data even when you don't. However, to the extent that we all find ourselves in a similar predicament, to the extent that we all find something puzzling about experience that seems inadequately explained by information-processing or neurophysiological models, there is nothing unscientific about taking this epistemic state seriously. It's true that so long as we don't understand clearly what's going on we can't stop there; we have to keep digging into what the problem is, how to better articulate it. But seeing that you don't understand a phenomenon is not sufficient reason for ignoring or eliminating it.

Well, leave aside how I know I have conscious experience, if it's conceivable that someone functionally identical to me could lack experience, how do I know that my first-person data really do reflect a more general phenomenon? Maybe I'm the only one. In other words, the qualophobe turns again to strategy (4), skepticism. Fine, I have two answers to this. First, I repeat the first answer to the skepticism argument presented above. Second, I say that it doesn't really matter.

Again, we don't normally accept the principle that we must abstain from claims to knowledge whenever there's a logical possibility that we're wrong. Yes, it is conceivable that someone could talk and act just like you and yet not be conscious, even if I open their head and they have a normal human brain.[11] I also claim to know that you are conscious. I don't accept the argument that my knowledge claim must be justifiable in a way that closes the logical gap between the data and the claim, and that therefore the claim itself must either be analyzable in terms of the data or count as some sort of nonsense. I'll be convinced of an analysis when it actually does the job of analyzing what I have in mind, not when it can be justified only indirectly, by relieving skeptical pressure.[12]

But suppose you really did convince me that I can't claim to know you are conscious. So then I might conclude that materialist theories explain all there is to explain about you, at least as far as I know. Still, what about me? Perhaps you have no good reason to take my protestations seriously, but I still do. I believe each one of us is in that position, but if I'm wrong that doesn't automatically undermine my own puzzle about my own conscious experience.

The problem for the qualophile here is supposed to be this. I have conscious experience, and by way of that experience I have a conception of that experience. I point to my experience when characterizing that conception. Now, that very thing I'm pointing to, that very experience of which this is my conception, I attribute to you on the basis of your behavior and your general physical similarity to me. The data—your behavior and general physical similarity to me—do not literally entail the truth of the attribution of conscious experience to you. The possibilities are these: (a) I know you have conscious experience because it's reasonable to believe this even though no data I have literally entail it; (b) I don't really know you have conscious experience after all; (c) my conception of conscious experience—to which I point in my own case—is actually analyzable in terms of some idealized set of third-person accessible data; or (d) this conception of conscious experience to which I point in my own case is just incoherent and does not correspond to any phenomenon at all.

The qualophobe chooses (d), the reductivist (c). But both argue that (a) and (b) can't be maintained. In particular, it's supposed to be obvious that either (c) or (d) is more plausible than (b). The idea is that I can't seriously entertain the possibility that what I have in mind by conscious experience—what I the qualophile care about—is lacking in you. Therefore, what I have in mind must really be about your behavior, or functional organization, or nothing at all. But what sort of inference is this, anyway? I maintain that (b) is unsustainable as well, but for me that's a strong argument for (a). If you tell me that no, (a) is also insupportable, then I'll choose (b) over either (c) or (d). Well, you say, but (b) is crazy. I agree, but then I think that shows that the epistemological principles at work in undermining (a) must be suspect. After all, they give you (b), or, even worse, (c) or (d).

But look, responds the qualophobe, clearly exasperated at this point, your position is worse than the normal case of maintaining knowledge in the face of skepticism. If your only reason for rejecting (a) were adherence to absurdly strong epistemic scruples, then it wouldn't show (a) to be any worse off than many other, quite mundane knowledge claims. A logical space into which doubt can creep is not sufficient to defeat claims to knowledge in general. But in this case there is an added defect. Not only is there the logical space for error, but we have no theory of what's transpiring given even that there is no error. This is the third consideration mentioned above, the qualophile's inability to provide an account of the mechanisms of first-person epistemic access.

To see the force of the objection, compare the case of my knowledge of your conscious experience with my knowledge that there's a chair right in front of me. Of course I want to claim that I know the latter, and also, it seems to me, that there's always logical room for doubt. I could be a brain in a vat, after all. Still, on the assumption that I'm not a brain in a vat, I can tell a story about a mechanism that starts with the hypothesized chair and ends with my occupying a state with the informational content that it's in front of me. But I clearly can't give anything like such a story that begins with your experience and ends with my occupying a state with the informational content that you're having genuine conscious experience.

This argument constitutes a general indictment of the first-person perspective, and hence applies even to knowledge claims about my own experience. Or better, it's not really a matter of knowledge, or skeptical doubt, but just a general suspicion of a source of data about the workings of which there is no theory. Now to this charge the qualophile has to admit guilt. If information-processing models cannot explain conscious experience, they can't explain our knowledge of conscious experience. But, the qualophobe presses, to a rough approximation, information-processing models are the only models of epistemic access we have. Hence, we don't have a model of first-person epistemic access. Of course we clearly have epistemic access to our own minds. Hence, it must not be a phenomenon that matches the qualophile's conception of experience to which we have access. So, the qualophobe concludes with a flourish, there just isn't any phenomenon corresponding to the qualophile's conception of experience, and there's nothing therefore to explain beyond what information-processing models explain!

Again, the question of whether we can provide an account of the mechanisms of first-person access is a matter I will investigate more closely in the next chapter. Still, let me address the argument briefly right here. Why does it follow that if information-processing models can't explain conscious experience then they can't explain our access to conscious experience? This isn't obvious, actually. Couldn't there be a kind of phenomenon to which our epistemic access is explicable in information-processing terms even though the phenomenon itself isn't? Of course this is possible, since we can explain our access to lots of non-cognitive phenomena. So the problem isn't located in the information-processing aspect *per se*, but rather in the fact that information flow is itself explicable only in terms of causal transactions, and it's between the conceptual framework of physical causation and the conceptual framework of conscious experience that the explanatory gap is located.

Let me spell this out a bit. An account of epistemic access will explain how a subject's cognitive state, A, carries information about some other state, B. To the extent we are providing a naturalistic account of this relation, it seems that it must involve some sort of causal dependency of A on B. So, in the standard case, my belief that there's a chair in front of me carries information about the chair because the chair's being in front of me is causally responsible for the belief. Information flow, the basic notion of information-processing models, is explained in terms of, indeed reduced to, a causal relation realized ultimately by the basic causal mechanisms of the physical world.

So suppose B is a state of conscious experience. I want to understand how a cognitive state, A, carries the information that B. It seems that in order for me to understand that relation, I must first understand how B is realized in those very physical mechanisms by which the information that B is to be carried to A. But, by the qualophile's own hypothesis, this understanding is not currently available. That is, I don't understand how B is itself realized in physical mechanisms. So, it follows that I also don't understand how information concerning B can flow to A. Hence, I don't have an account of first-person epistemic access.

Now, having admitted that we do lack an account of the mechanisms of first-person epistemic access—indeed, I would go further, it is part of the very same puzzle about conscious experience that drives the qualophile's position—must I then admit that there is no such access? Of course not! I think the crucial slide in the qualophobe's argument came in the passage above, which I repeat here: "Of course we clearly have epistemic access to our own minds. Hence, it must not be a phenomenon that matches the qualophile's conception of experience to which we have access."

Whence the "hence"? Of course we do have epistemic access, so there must exist a story about how it works, but that doesn't mean that the story must be available to us. The qualophile's whole point is that we don't understand this phenomenon. To accuse her of not having a real phenomenon in mind because she can't explain one of the very features she insists can't be explained is to rule her position out of court from the outset. But why should she agree to play by rules that are clearly weighted against her in this way? (If you're tempted to reply that these rules ensure a proper respect for objectivity, that's why she should play by them, then return to our discussion above.)

Finally, it might also be that the argument from "we don't have an account of first-person epistemic access to conscious experience" to "there isn't anything here to which we have access" is really aimed at the bold qualophile. If so, as I myself argued above, I am sympathetic (though it's not clear to me, given what else the bold qualophile is willing to buy, that this increases the cost all that much). If qualia just aren't physically realized, then there couldn't be a physical mechanism underlying the information flow from qualitative state to the relevant cognitive state. But remember that the modest qualophile is willing to grant that qualia are in fact physically realized, so she need not accept the consequence that no such mechanism of information flow exists. Once we understand how brain states realize qualia, we'll also presumably understand how we have knowledge of them.

Let me briefly summarize the discussion so far. The qualophile, the qualophobe, and the reductivist maintain a complex, triangular relationship. The qualophile points to her experience and wonders, "How could *that* be a matter of neurons pushing each other around?" The reductivist says, "Well, that's just what it is." The qualophobe understands that what bothers the qualophile can't be relieved by reference to serotonin or opponent-process theory, but diagnoses the problem as obsession with a picture, a fixation on a Cartesian fantasy-theater to which literally nothing corresponds. I have tried to show that nothing in the qualophobe's bag of tricks really ought to convince the qualophile that she is guilty of such a conceptual disorder. So long as the qualophile maintains a modest demeanor, none of the five strategies surveyed in this section, either alone or in combination, reveal the qualophile's sense of puzzlement to be illegitimate, merely the result of a philosophically infantile obsession.

5.4 Eliminativist Representationalism

What emerges from our discussion of the five eliminativist strategies is the centrality of the qualophile's claim that qualia must be treated as data. I argued that various attempts to dislodge this pillar of the qualophile's position through skeptical challenges ultimately fail. But it still might seem that there is something "tendentious" about the qualophile's tenacious grasp of her first-person data. As Rey (1997) argues, in order to genuinely defeat eliminativism one needs to point to non-tendentious data. This of course the qualophile can't do, by the very nature of the case. Let me elaborate a bit.

Rey, though an eliminativist of sorts about qualia, is concerned to counter eliminativist challenges about the mental in general, particularly the propositional attitudes. He argues that it isn't sufficient merely to point to the patent absurdity of the claim that we don't have beliefs and desires, since the eliminativist knows full well that her position is counterintuitive, but finds sufficient reason for adopting it anyhow. What one wants, Rey claims, is data that are themselves not in dispute by the eliminativist: "non-tendentious" data, to use Rey's term. With respect to the propositional attitudes, Rey thinks one can readily find such data. There are various regularities, such as, to use his example, correlations between what's written on standardized tests and the pencil marks on the answer sheets, that are best explained by appeal to the beliefs and desires of the students taking the exams. What's crucial about this case is that the description of the regularity is itself neutral with respect to the existence of mental phenomena; it can be described in purely non-mental terms. Thus the regularity counts as a non-tendentious datum.

On the other hand, appeal to qualia as data is obviously tendentious with regard to the eliminativist about qualia. The eliminativist is casting doubt on the very existence of that which the qualophile takes to be her data. Of course, there's no way out for the qualophile here. The only use to which non-tendentious data can be put is to serve as the explanandum for abductive arguments that posit the phenomenon in question in the explanans. But the qualophile admits already that we don't need to posit qualia to explain any other phenomenon. Hence there is no way for her to find non-tendentious data. Part of the burden of the discussion of section 5.3 was precisely to counter the demand for non-tendentious data as illegitimate in this case.

While I stand by that argument, the tendentiousness of the qualophile's first-person data does provide a space for a certain sort of eliminativist reply. If the eliminativist could show why we are so tempted to believe in this data, even while exposing it as an illusion, then it certainly seems that she would be justified in claiming at least that she had shifted the burden of argument back onto the qualophile to better defend her appeal to first-person data. Of course we've seen one attempt to do this, with Dennett's heterophenomenological method. But we dismissed that move because it took only what we say as what needed explanation. If, however, something closer to our actual experience, short of the qualia themselves, could be shown to be explicable on the hypothesis that qualia themselves are merely an illusion, then perhaps the eliminativist move would be successful after all.

In this spirit I want to look at Rey's attempt to explain away our first-person intuitions concerning qualia. In fact, he is somewhat concessive, as I mentioned in section 5.2. On his view, we retain a certain sort of reality for that special feature of conscious experience that seems to elude functional accounts, but as a species of "intentional inexistent." Yes, in a way qualia exist, not as genuine properties of experience, but rather as the contents of certain representational states. Of course this sounds just like representationalism. In fact it is, but it differs from both externalism and internalism in saying that qualia, as representations, purport to predicate properties that don't actually exist.[13] We can think of this as a kind of fictionalism: qualia as Santa Claus.

Rey calls his view a "projectivist" account of qualitative character. The notion of projection at issue he explains using various analogies. The most interesting one is a particular explanation of the fairly bizarre psychological disorder known as Capgras syndrome. People suffering from this disorder are under the delusion that their loved ones and friends have been replaced by duplicates. One explanation for this syndrome is that normally people use their own emotional reactions to their loved ones as a kind of "emotional fingerprint" by which they recognize them. If for some reason such as nervous system damage, this standard emotional reaction should become disrupted, the afflicted person might project the difference in their own experience onto their loved ones, thus perceiving them to be different in some important way.[14] The main idea is that we project a feature of our reaction to a phenomenon onto the phenomenon itself.[15]

What sort of projection is involved in our qualitative experience? Again, we can approach the answer with an analogy, actually two, this time somewhat closer to the target phenomenon. To quote Rey (1995):

> Many of us are deeply disappointed to learn that the redness (that appears to be) in rainbows, grease spots, tomatoes and roses is no single "natural" property, but an enormously complex disjunction of such properties, unified only by the fact that they have a certain effect upon (some of) us. We are inclined to posit an objective correlate *in* things that standardly look red that corresponds to the apparent simplicity and stability of the experience in us. . . . The problem of personal identity provides a still more gripping case: we project an enduring object that corresponds (in our own case) to our personal concerns and (in the case of others) to the (more or less) standing effects they have upon us. But, as Hume and Parfit (1984) have argued, there is no "suitable" thing that corresponds to these projections, nothing that's an appropriate object of our reactions and concerns for them or for ourselves. (137)

What comes across from all the examples is this. We find in ourselves a stable reaction to what appears to be a simple, unified phenomenon, so we project or posit a single property as the correspondent of this stable reaction. It turns out, however, that no such property exists; our stable reaction is in fact a response to a heterogenous set of phenomena, none of which, nor the disjunction of which, is recognizable as the referent of our intended posit.

In the case of qualia, Rey seems to have in mind two different sources of stable reaction that are responsible for the projection. First, in our own case we find ourselves recognizing our experiences in an immediate, triggered fashion, which causes us to project as the source of that recognitional reaction a simple, intrinsic, non-functional property. Second, we find ourselves reacting differently to certain embodiments of the relevant functional system—such as other persons and higher animals—than we do to others, such as computers. This difference in our reactions, undoubtedly the product of evolution, we then project onto the objects, thus causing us to believe in the existence of some non-functional correlate. The idea is that we can't take seriously the notion that the China-head,[16] for instance, is a proper object of moral concern, and can't help but view other human beings as very much objects of such concern. We can't take seriously the notion that they are really no different, in the relevant respects, from the China-head. This powerful intuitive difference in our experienced reactions is then hypostasized into a real difference in the objects.

There are two dimensions along which to evaluate Rey's proposal. First, is projection of the sort he describes a plausible account of the source of our cognitive illusion with respect to the existence of qualitative properties? Second, is it plausible that qualia are really intentional inexistents, fictional properties? Of course these two dimensions are intimately related, but they aren't identical. The projection story itself might be plausible as an account of our mistake were it plausible that it was a mistake to believe in qualia; and even if projection isn't a convincing source, it still might be that fictionalism itself makes sense.

I remain unconvinced by his account, and my reservations involve both dimensions. But let me start with the second one. That is, could it really be that reddishness is a fictional property? Let's consider some non-controversial cases of non-veridical representations. Take Santa Claus and a hallucinated pink elephant. In both cases we can say that we are representing objects that don't exist: one in thought, the other as a percept. (Let's allow in both cases that we don't really believe the objects exist.) How can you represent an object that doesn't exist? Well, it's easy. The representations involved contain singular terms (or elements relevantly like singular terms) that don't refer. But that isn't enough. There is, after all, a difference between thinking of Santa Claus and thinking of Pegasus, between hallucinating a pink elephant and a purple tiger. The obvious move is to say that we distinguish these non-existent "objects" by the very real properties we ascribe to them. But since the properties themselves are real, these examples can't serve as a model for reddish qualia.

Here's another example of Rey's. Consider our notion of magic. It's plausible to say that "magic" refers to a way some feat is accomplished that involves no mechanism. Unlike the cases of Santa Claus and the pink elephant, it's not clear there are any real properties involved in an analysis of magic. Furthermore, it's quite reasonable to say that not only is there in fact no magic, but, by its very nature, there couldn't be. Could reddishness be like magic?

The fundamental problem I see with treating reddishness like magic derives from the very source of the explanatory gap itself: the determinacy and substantiality of our conception of qualitative content. It is the richness and determinacy of the mode of presentation of my concept of reddishness that causes the problem in the first place, since it is this factor that makes any purported identity with physical or functional properties gappy. But it is also this feature that renders the fictionalist solution implausible. I have an idea of a quite specific way in which my reddish qualia differ from my greenish qualia, and, again, this difference is not adequately captured by any mere formalistic description of, say, distance in a color-similarity space. On Rey's view the difference has to consist in the difference between the two representations. But I don't see how you can get the representational difference to do the work it has to do without there being a difference in the properties represented, which there can't be if they don't exist. In other words, how could I have the sort of substantive and determinate idea I have of the difference between reddish and greenish if there weren't any reddish and greenish in the first place?

This problem of determinacy affects both aspects of the view. First, as just mentioned, it's hard to see how ideas of two merely fictional properties could possess the determinacy of my ideas of reddish and greenish. Second, it's hard to see how the projection story can account for our ideas of this determinate difference. Remember, there are supposed to be two sorts of projections: a first-person one and a third-person one. Consider the latter first. I see how I could posit a property as the correlate of my differential reactions to human beings and computers, but it would, I assume, be of the "a something I know not what" variety, as empiricists used to claim about our ideas of substance as the substratum of properties. The reason is that I have no direct access to what it is in others that might be responsible for this difference in my reactions.

In cases where the idea involved seems to lack much substance, the projection story makes a good deal of sense. The case of magic falls into this category, since all I can say about what it is involves saying what it isn't. But when it comes to qualitative character the idea involved—though perhaps inexpressible in language—is not indeterminate in this way. On the contrary, it has a vivid, full-fledged determinacy. There seems to be a clear determinable-determinate relation that groups reddish and greenish together as distinct determinates of the determinable color experience.

When it comes to the first-person projection it might seem that there is less of a problem. After all, there is no issue here of direct access. In fact, it is precisely the directness of the access that seems to be responsible for the projection. But again, if there really is no such property as reddishness, if it's only fictional, then whatever dimension of difference exists with respect to its fellow determinates must exist within the representation itself. But what in the representation is supposed to fill the bill? We have it that my representation of fictional greenish is triggered by certain other states, themselves representational states within the sensory module, and similarly for my representations of reddish. There is of course the bare difference between them, that one is triggered by this representation and one by that one. But how does this translate into the sort of difference between reddish and greenish that is manifestly part of our experience? Projection of a difference in properties as a source for a difference in reactions still seems to buy only a difference of the "I know not what" variety; my conception of such a difference would have to be, to use the term introduced earlier, "presentationally thin."

The obvious place for Rey to turn for a source for this determinacy is to the characteristic processing discussed in chapter 4, that which determines the narrow contents of the qualia themselves on his internalist representationalist account. But there is a problem with this move, which can be put as a dilemma. Either we need the eliminativism, the fictionalism, or we don't. If characteristic processing, essentially functional role (albeit of a restricted form), captures what seems present to us in our experience of reddishness, then why bother with the fictionalism? We are pushed to the fictionalism because what seems present to us in experiences of reddish and greenish is not plausibly captured by appeal to their characteristic processing. But then if we find it hard to account for the determinacy of what seems present to us in these experiences by appeal to projections from stable reactions—if treating them as fictional properties doesn't capture this determinate qualitative content either—appeal to the characteristic processing can't help. After all, it's precisely what that characteristic processing couldn't capture that was supposed to be fictional!

Before concluding, I want to clarify how the problem of determinacy of content arises for the fictionalist view. Remember, if we're dealing with a case like Santa Claus, or pink elephants, or even round squares, there is no problem explaining how we can be representing these non-existent objects in the way we do. For in all of these cases there are genuinely existing properties—properties instantiated in this world—which provide the content. (In the round square case we have the constituent properties of roundness and squareness, together with the conjunction, or intersection operation.) What's hard to see is how to get the kind of content we have in our idea of reddishness from a representation that purports to refer to an impossible property, without any constituents of genuine properties.

Notice that it's crucial that the property be really impossible, like magic. One might have adopted the position that our ideas of qualia involve fictions, but in the following way. We attribute certain properties to our experiences that they don't have. However, the properties involved, though not in fact instantiated in our experiences—and, let's say, uninstantiated in our world—are nevertheless instantiated in some possible worlds. The eliminativism comes in as the claim that we're wrong in thinking them instantiated in our world—not in thinking they exist as properties, capable of instantiation in other worlds.

Such a view is not altogether implausible. It fits nicely into our understanding of materialism, as presented in chapter 1. After all, dualism is supposed to be logically possible; materialism is an empirical thesis. So we can imagine that there are possible worlds where properties like reddishness are basic, or realized in non-physical stuff. It's just that, according to the materialist who's an eliminativist, these properties are not instantiated at all in our world, not even through realization in physical properties.

On this view, the determinacy of content in our idea of reddishness would be accounted for by the ontological determinacy of the property itself. It's really reddishness that I'm predicating of my experience—just mistakenly, that's all. But if we adopted this view, we'd have another, correlative problem. How is it that the genuine property of reddishness can be the actual content of one of my representations, if not only is it never instantiated in my experience, but never in my entire world? While we lack at present any really adequate theory of content and so can't appeal to one to show definitively that such a situation is impossible, it is quite hard to see how any theory of content would legitimate it. It does seem you might as well claim that the qualitative property is actually instantiated in our experience, given that its genuine existence as a property already causes enough problems.

So it's clear that to make fictionalism work you need to claim not only that qualia are not actually instantiated in our experience, but also that they couldn't be. They are impossible properties in the sense that they are not instantiated in any possible world. Also, they aren't impossible by virtue of being logically impossible constructs out of actually existing properties, but impossible *simpliciter*. But then, it seems, the problem of the determinacy and the substantiality of our notion of reddishness tells against this view.

I conclude that Rey's treatment of qualia as fictional properties, projections of the impossible from perceptions of stable reactions, does not succeed in shifting the burden in favor of eliminativism. Of course, it's still always open to the eliminativist to just insist that despite what seems clear from our experience, we don't actually experience the properties we think we do. Rey is right that any data to the contrary is tendentious, in his sense. But to this charge I submit that the argument of section 5.3 provides the necessary reply.

6

"Purple Haze, All Around"
Consciousness and Cognition

6.1 Introduction

In the Introduction I said that the mind-body problem divides naturally into two problems: intentionality and consciousness. I claimed that with respect to the first problem there are reasons to be hopeful because some genuine progress toward providing a materialist realization theory has been made. On the other hand, my discussion in the last three chapters shows that with respect to conscious experience there is little reason for optimism. As we saw, it is partly recognition of this contrast between the progress made on the problem of intentionality and the apparent lack of progress on the problem of qualia that motivates representationalism, though we found fault with that view as well. While I continue to maintain that, at least with respect to unconscious cognitive states, the problem of intentionality has yielded somewhat to materialistic analysis, in this chapter I want to explore further the ways in which the problem of qualia infects our understanding of the intentional contents of conscious cognitive states. As we have seen already, subjectivity, being for the subject, is as much a mystery for our thoughts about experience as it is for experience itself.

The intimate connection between conscious thought and sensation has been a significant factor in two of the principal arguments presented already. In chapter 3 I argued that there is a fundamental difference between identities that are gappy and those that aren't. Gappy identities, I argued, involve representations that express substantive, determinate modes of presentation, quite different from the "presentationally thin" contents associated with terms like "water." My idea of reddishness, I claimed, has a substantial content that is present to me in a way that my idea of water is not, and it is hard to see how any causal account of representational content could account for this. In my argument against Rey's eliminativism, I also appealed to the substantiality and determinacy of my idea of reddishness to show that his projectivist account couldn't explain how I came by such an idea. Clearly it is not only the experience of reddishness itself that gives rise to a philosophical puzzle, but also my idea of such an experience.

I will begin my exploration of this connection between qualia and ideas of qualia by revisiting the problem of zombies. As noted in the last chapter, though the conceivability of zombies is the paradigmatic expression of the qualophilic position, it is also a source of anti-qualophilic arguments, both from functionalist reductivists and eliminativists. There are three sorts of zombie argument that interest me. First is the one we've already seen. If zombies are possible, then what justification do I have for thinking I'm not one? Two other zombie puzzles are what I'll call the "replacement argument" and the "zombie epistemology argument."[1] The replacement argument starts from the premise that functional zombie duplicates are possible, and then tries to show that we get a paradoxical consequence by considering cases of gradual change from a normal brain into a zombie "brain." The zombie epistemology argument is distinctive in that it adopts the zombie's point of view and attempts to show that zombies must be just as puzzled as we are about their experience, yet, by hypothesis, they don't have any. I'll begin with the replacement argument.

6.2 The Replacement Argument

Suppose Zjoe is functionally identical to me, but lacks qualia. Presumably, there is something about the difference between what he's made of and what I'm made of that's responsible for this. Even a dualist could say this (a property dualist, anyway). For the property dualist there is a basic law that relates my being in certain physiological states to my having certain qualitative experiences. If Zjoe lacks qualia, it must be that his internal physical states don't maintain any nomological relations with qualia the way mine do.

Now, imagine that my internal parts are replaced bit by bit with parts like those of Zjoe. If he's made of electronic circuits, then we can suppose electronic circuits of just the same sort gradually replace my neurons. Or we can suppose that radio transmitters are planted in my head with communication links to circuits of the right sort. What's crucial about the thought experiment is that the change is gradual, and that it preserves all the relevant functional relations. The question is: what would happen? What would my experience be like during the gradual process of change?[2]

Searle (1997) explicitly tackles this problem. He imagines that due to some disease, doctors are gradually replacing his neurons with electronic chips. According to him, though what precisely will happen is an empirical question, the following three scenarios seem to be the relevant possibilities:

(1) His externally detectable behavior remains unchanged, but his qualia gradually diminish, until, at the end of the replacement process, he's a zombie. He imagines that all the while that the doctors are marveling over the complete success of the replacement surgery, he is internally suffering a nightmare of fading consciousness. Since the input-output functions of the chips mimic those of the neurons they're replacing, no one on the outside will be able to tell what's going on inside.

(2) Both his externally detectable behavior and his conscious experience remain unchanged. It turns out that the chips are able to support conscious experience as well as neurons do.

(3) The reverse of (1). The chips can support conscious experience, but not the input-output functions that determine behavior. Thus the doctors think he's essentially brain-dead, though in fact he's having full-fledged conscious experiences.

For our purposes, only scenario (1) matters. Searle is careful to say that we can't determine *a priori* whether scenario (1) would occur, but it's important that we can't rule it out *a priori* either. The fact that we can coherently envision scenario (1) demonstrates, claims Searle, the "behavior independence" of conscious experience. But in fact it's not so clear at all that we can coherently envision scenario (1). The problem is that Searle is assimilating functional equivalence with behavioral equivalence.

As Searle describes scenario (1), he feels himself gradually losing his conscious experience, as if the volume is being slowly turned down, but is unable to communicate this to the doctors. They hear him say that everything is fine, so they don't have a clue what's happening to him. His depiction of this scenario reminds one of the stories about curare, the paralytic that was mistakenly thought to be an anesthetic.[3] Patients were suffering horribly but unable to move a muscle, so the doctors believed them to be unconscious. If all the replacement were supposed to preserve is behavioral equivalence, then this depiction of scenario (1) would make sense.

However, Zjoe is supposed to be functionally equivalent to me as well as behaviorally equivalent. So when Searle is gradually turning into his zombie counterpart, Zjohn, we have to suppose that functional equivalence is maintained. Functional equivalence involves a lot more than behavioral equivalence, especially with respect to what's going on inside. Not only would Searle's behavior have to match that which he would manifest were his consciousness to be maintained, but all of his internal states would have to maintain all of their causal relations as well.

In particular, consider his introspective states. Throughout the replacement process his introspective states would maintain their functional role. So suppose that state I-R is his belief state with the content "I am now having an experience of type R" (where "R" refers to a reddish experience). I-R, presumably, is normally caused by experiential states of type R. At some point in the replacement process states of type R will disappear, replaced by states of type E-R (ersatz R-experiences). But E-R will still cause I-R, since functional equivalence is maintained. Furthermore, since I-R had the content "I am having an experience of type R" before the replacement, there is no reason to refuse to attribute to it the same content after the replacement. But that means Searle would continue to believe he is having R-experiences, quite unlike the way he described the scenario. In fact, it seems as if he would be as clueless regarding his fading consciousness as the doctors. But if that's the case, what difference could consciousness make to him in the first place? Any conception of consciousness on which one could lose it without noticing does not seem to be a conception of the phenomenon we care about. Thus the zombie hypothesis seems to reduce to absurdity.

The replacement process allegedly leads to an absurdity. The source of the absurdity seems to be the fact that the process is gradual; hence Chalmers's name for the argument, "fading qualia." How could my qualia be gradually fading and yet I be unaware of it? If, on the other hand, the process were instantaneous, then presumably the sense of absurdity would diminish, or vanish altogether. If I go from being conscious to being a zombie in one fell swoop, then there's no point at which I should be noticing something happening but, by the hypothesis of functional identity, am unable to notice it. If replacement yields total and instantaneous loss of consciousness, then it's no harder to swallow than the existence of a zombie in the first place.

So one possible response to the replacement argument is to maintain that consciousness is realized in such a way that either it's completely there or it isn't there at all. In fact, one wouldn't have to maintain that there was a single consciousness cell, or something of that sort, which really would be quite implausible. It might be that there is some very complex physical configuration which, when it's completely present, so is consciousness, and, when any part of it is absent, consciousness goes completely. Thus ridding the brain of one neuron might turn one into a total zombie, but there's no one neuron that has the honor of being the consciousness neuron. Losing any one out of a whole bunch might do the trick.

Though not obviously incoherent, this reply does seem desperate. Is it really plausible that some small physical change could turn one into a zombie? We just have no reason to think that the psycho-physical link works that way. For the qualophile to insist that it must be so is to adopt an *ad hoc* position, pressed into service merely to undermine the replacement argument. It would be much more compelling to show that sense could be made of the replacement scenario even if consciousness is lost gradually.

Another possible line of reply for the qualophile is to deny the premise of functional identity, a premise that is crucial to the charge of absurdity. That I and Zjoe are functionally identical is built into the zombie hypothesis, so the qualophile can't mess with that. But it doesn't follow from the claim that I and Zjoe are functionally identical that replacement of my parts with Zjoe's parts would leave me functionally unchanged. Call the realizers of my functional states, the ones with qualitative character, "Q-states," and the realizers of Zjoe's functional states, the ones without qualitative character, "Z-states." Where Qr realizes my reddish visual experience, Zr realizes Zjoe's functional analogue of my reddish visual experience, his ersatz reddish experience. The replacement argument depends on the assumption that were my Qr to be replaced by Zr, then when I look at my red diskette case, and go into state Zr, I would be occupying a state functionally identical to the state I used to occupy, but would fail to have the conscious experience that used to accompany it. But why should we assume this? In Zjoe, Zr played a certain functional role. Why think it would play this role in me?

Again, though perhaps this line could be pursued, it really doesn't seem to get at the heart of the issue. Of course it may be that, given the natures of both conscious and non-conscious realizers, it's not possible to mix them in such a way as to preserve functional identity. But at most the sense of "possibility" at issue must be nomological. It's certainly not conceptually impossible, and it seems hard to see good reason to think it's metaphysically impossible, though one can insist that it may be nonetheless. It seems to me that the qualophile should allow both that replacement might preserve functional identity, and that the loss of consciousness might be gradual, or piecemeal. Now, can the qualophile make these concessions and still avoid the *reductio?*

Here's one way to begin to break the sense of absurdity. As the scenario is standardly described—this certainly comes across from Searle's description—I am supposed to be experiencing a fading of consciousness, as my conscious realizers are replaced by ersatz realizers. The image one gets is of one gradually losing consciousness before going to sleep. But there is no justification for this way of imagining what would happen. In fact, there is an interesting fallacy involved in this depiction of the replacement process, one akin to a fallacy that Dennett and Kinsbourne (1992) point out with respect to consciousness of time. They emphasize that one shouldn't confuse the consciousness of a time interval with the interval, or duration, of a state of consciousness. In this case, one shouldn't confuse the fading of consciousness with the consciousness of fading. Both happen (often) as one falls asleep, but only the former is involved in the replacement process.

Let me elaborate. It's supposed to be absurd that I could be experiencing a fading, or limiting of my conscious experience without being aware of it. But there's nothing in the initial description of the replacement process that should lead one to describe me as having an experience of fading, or diminishing, or even limiting of my conscious experience. What would happen—all we are justified in assuming will happen—is that my conscious experience will actually fade, or, rather, in piecemeal fashion will fail to manifest itself. But that doesn't mean there will be some overarching consciousness of this fading or limiting. There is no reason to think I should consciously feel this loss. Again, to lose a bit of consciousness is not the same thing as being conscious of losing something.

Once we recognize this distinction, it isn't so clear that we are faced with an absurd situation. As my internal parts, say the realizers of my visual experiences, are replaced by their non-conscious functional duplicate parts, certain states that used to be conscious experiences for me will cease to be conscious. So, say, when Qr is replaced by Zr, though Qg is still in place, it might be that I cease to have reddish experiences even though I continue to have greenish ones. What makes it seem absurd is the appearance of my consciously observing the loss of my reddish experiences, and yet supposedly still being cognitively unaware of it. But there's nothing in the story about losing Qr that entails consciousness of losing my reddish experience. It just goes, that's all. When I see green things, I consciously experience them, and when I see red things, I don't.

Of course such a situation does seem quite odd. If I could be consciously experiencing some colors but not others my consciousness would be fragmented in a way that seems quite hard to imagine. In particular, consider the case in which I'm looking at red and green objects simultaneously. One is driven to ask, "What on earth would *that* be like?" As long as we're careful about what that question means, it seems perfectly appropriate. But it's awfully tempting to take it to mean that there must be a way it is like to experience fragmentation of consciousness, and that sneaks in the assumption that there would be consciousness of the hole in experience caused by the substitution of Zr for Qr. Again, a hole in consciousness is not consciousness of a hole.

Though recognizing the distinction between a hole in conscious experience and experience of a hole in consciousness goes some way to alleviate the sense of incoherence in the replacement scenario, one might still legitimately wonder about explicitly introspective states. As I mentioned above, both before and after the replacement I might entertain the judgment that I am now experiencing reddishly. The assumption of functional identity seems to guarantee that even after my reddish experiences have disappeared I will still judge that I have them. This seems paradoxical.

But here again, we have to be careful about just what it is that seems paradoxical. It is very easy, as the preceding discussion about the distinction between fading consciousness and consciousness of fading showed, to sneak in some consciousness where it doesn't belong and thereby induce a sense of absurdity into the scenario. When one imagines apparent but supposedly illusory introspective awareness of having a reddish experience it could certainly seem quite absurd. After all, if you are apparently having a reddish experience, then you are having one, right? It's not like apparently seeing something red—having a reddish experience—but not really seeing something red (as in an optical illusion, or hallucination). With conscious experience the appearance is the reality. So if turning into a zombie leaves one's apparent experiences the same, there doesn't seem to be any difference between being conscious and being a zombie after all.

However, to characterize an introspective judgment to the effect that I am having a reddish experience as apparently experiencing reddishly is to endow the judgment with consciousness—not only that, but with reddish qualitative character as well. But reddish qualitative character is precisely what one would lose once Zr was substituted for Qr. Perhaps a better way to think about what would be going on when I introspectively judge that I'm having a reddish experience even though I've lost the capacity is to see it as similar to cases of anosognosia. In such cases, subjects with various sorts of lesions lose the ability to see over large portions of their visual field, or sometimes lose the ability to notice what is happening to one entire side of their body (hemineglect), yet will sincerely deny having any deficit at all.

When confronted with what would appear to be incontrovertible evidence of their deficit, such patients will confabulate wildly and maintain their denial. Similarly, after my Qr parts are replaced by Zr parts, I would cease to have any reddish experiences, yet I would sincerely deny having lost any part of my conscious experience. Of course the difference between the two cases is that my loss in our replacement scenario would not be accompanied by any functional loss, so there would be no way to provide me with evidence of my loss, and thus no need to confabulate. But I don't see that this difference matters for the issue at hand. We at least have some model for how one could sincerely judge that something was going on in one's experience even though it wasn't. Admittedly it's hard to quite imagine what that would be like, but that goes for the anosognosia cases as well, and no one claims they are impossible, or incoherent. They can't be; they actually happen.

The response, so far, to the replacement argument is this. What makes the idea of gradual, or piecemeal loss of conscious experience, together with the preservation of functional equivalence, seem so absurd, is that one is sneaking into the picture consciousness that doesn't belong. When one imagines that one doesn't notice the missing experience, one has in mind a kind of noticing that involves conscious awareness. So then it seems as if there's conscious awareness both present and absent at the same time. But that isn't what the replacement scenario involves. The sort of noticing with respect to which one wouldn't notice the missing conscious experience is non-conscious itself. It isn't that one consciously experiences having a reddish experience even though one isn't having one. The consciousness of a reddish experience is just missing.

Though I think this response does move us in the right direction, it still leaves an important issue unresolved. For what we are inclined to wonder about now is the distinction between conscious and non-conscious belief (or judgment). It seems clear that anyone who recognizes a distinction between conscious and non-conscious states has to recognize such a distinction within the realm of cognitive states. Clearly there is a difference between those beliefs (thoughts, judgments, etc.) I'm explicitly considering in my conscious, waking moments, and those that are either latent because I'm not currently considering them—they're not occurrent states—or are deeply unconscious in the way that, say, my knowledge of grammar is supposed to be unconscious and inaccessible according to the Chomskian linguist.

So, when my Qr parts are replaced by Zr parts, and I therefore no longer have reddish experiences, what happens to my conscious beliefs to the effect that I'm having reddish experiences? On the one hand, given the inability to experience reddishly anymore, it would seem that I could no longer consciously believe that I'm experiencing reddishly. On the other hand, given that the assumption of functional identity seems to entail the preservation of my previous beliefs' propositional contents, it looks as if the contents of my conscious beliefs must remain the same.[4] Since it would violate functional identity for me to cease to have these occurrent conscious beliefs just because their normal cause were absent, and since their contents would remain the same, it seems that I would continue to consciously believe that I'm having reddish experiences. But how could that be? We seem to be back to a paradox.

In order to tackle this problem, we need to address the question of just what a conscious thought or belief is. In one sense to say that a thought is conscious just means that it's occurrent. This seems to be a matter of what Block (1995) calls "access consciousness." The thought is "on-line," accessible to processes that govern behavior, especially speech. Obviously, this can't be the sense of "conscious" that distinguishes my conscious beliefs from the non-conscious beliefs of Zjoe. But is there a "phenomenal consciousness" (what Block contrasts with access consciousness) that attaches to non-sensory cognitive states?

Well, clearly there are phenomenal experiences that tend to at least accompany conscious thoughts. When I think to myself, "I'm having a reddish experience now" or "I have had reddish experiences frequently," there are two sorts of phenomenal experience that might accompany the thought: an auditory, or even visual image of the words I use to express my thought in natural language, and a reddish visual image itself. With respect to the silent soliloquy, it seems clear that the sentences I imagine myself uttering are expressions of the belief, not the belief itself. After all, I wouldn't identify the belief with an actual vocal utterance of the sentence, so why with its utterance to myself? In both cases we have avowals that express the belief.

It clearly makes more sense to identify my belief that I have reddish experiences with an actual reddish visual image; or, better, to take the visual image to partially constitute the belief. It's not that only by having such images can I think about reddish experiences; we've established already that that's not the case. Still, there does seem to be something special going on when, entertaining such an image, I think, "I'm having one of *those* now," or "*That's* what it's like when I look at my red diskette case." Such thoughts, which seem to literally incorporate the image into their contents, or modes of presentation, do seem to differ cognitively from thoughts not involving images in this way. Let's distinguish then between two sorts of conscious thoughts (or beliefs): those that are qualia-involving in an essential way, such as those we've just been discussing, and those that are qualia-involving inessentially, such as those where any phenomenal accompaniment only serves as the thought's expression. I'll call the former "phenomenally constituted" thoughts, and the latter "phenomenally accompanied" thoughts.

Let's return now to the question before us. The problem was supposed to be that we don't have a coherent description of what's going on with my conscious thought to the effect that I'm currently having a reddish experience on the replacement scenario. Given the distinction just introduced, it seems to me that the right way to characterize the situation is as follows. When my Qr states are replaced by Zr states, then not only do I lose the ability to have reddish experiences, but I also lose the ability to have phenomenally constituted thoughts to the effect that I'm having a reddish experience. There are no more reddish images available, so there can't be any thoughts that essentially involve them.

One might object that this description of what's going on violates the assumption of functional identity, since to lose the ability to occupy certain cognitive states constitutes a functional change. However, we only violate functional identity if the loss in question is not made up by the presence of appropriate functional analogues. It seems to me, again, that the right way to describe what's happened in this admittedly quite bizarre scenario is that where I once enjoyed a phenomenally constituted thought with the propositional content that I'm having a reddish experience, I now have its functional, but phenomenally non-conscious analogue: an at most phenomenally accompanied thought with the same propositional content. The phenomenal accompaniment might involve an auditory image of saying something like "I'm having one of *those* now," just as before. But because it lacks the essential connection with a reddish image, even though it shares a referential (or propositional) content, it is a very different cognitive state. I can't tell, from a metacognitive point of view, that I've lost both these sensory experiences and the relevant thoughts, but this is to be accounted for, again, on the model of cases of anosognosia.

The important point to keep in mind, as I've emphasized above, is that we verge on incoherence only if we characterize the situation in such a way that it appears that the experiential character is both there and not there at the same time. So long as we realize that a loss of qualia while retaining functional identity does not entail this incoherent consequence, even when we consider phenomenally constituted thoughts, the replacement scenario does not undermine the qualophile's position. Of course, such a scenario would be bizarre in the extreme, and it's very difficult to substantively imagine what it would be like. But, after all, it *is* a bizarre scenario, so our inability to imagine what it's like isn't at all surprising. I still maintain that we haven't entered the realm of genuine incoherence.

In the course of this discussion of the replacement argument, I've introduced the notion of a phenomenally constituted thought. That there are such thoughts has already been anticipated in my claim that the mode of presentation associated with phenomenal concepts is substantive and determinate in a special way. The problem is to understand just how the qualitative character of an experience can be involved, or constitutive, of a thought about it in the way that seems necessary. Before confronting this problem head on, I want to consider the other zombie arguments. We'll see how in response to these arguments as well we will need to appeal to this very puzzling aspect of subjectivity.

6.3 The Zombie Epistemology Argument

The zombie epistemology argument (my name) is from Katalin Balog (forthcoming). She primarily uses the argument as a response to the anti-materialist conceivability argument. However, as we will see, it has implications that go beyond metaphysical anti-materialism. If her argument works, it might undercut the line of inference from the conceivability of a zombie to the existence of an explanatory gap as well.

Let's begin with a quick review of the conceivability argument, as I reconstructed it in chapter 2. Relative to the description "X has physical properties P1 . . . Pn but no qualia," a zombie is conceptually possible. That means, roughly, that there is no *a priori* derivation from this description of a zombie to a representation that is formally inconsistent. So either zombies are metaphysically possible as well, or there is an *a posteriori* derivation from the standard description to a formally inconsistent representation. But since the crucial bridge premise in the derivation, one that connects the mental vocabulary with the physical vocabulary, is not *a priori*, there must be distinct, contingently related properties expressed by the modes of presentation of the mental and physical terms. Since they are contingently related, it's metaphysically possible for a creature to have the one property (say, the physical) without the other (the mental). Thus zombies are metaphysically possible either way.

In chapter 2 I criticized this argument on the grounds that it depended on the "distinct property model" for explaining the *a posteriori* character of some metaphysically necessary truths. Balog's objection takes the form of a *reductio*. Suppose, she says, the conceptual possibility of a zombie really did entail its metaphysical possibility. Consider the epistemological situation of a zombie. By hypothesis, my zombie twin, Zjoe, shares all of my functionally characterizable states. So when I entertain a thought, or make a judgment, Zjoe occupies states that are functionally identical to those thoughts and judgments. These states are caused by the same sorts of stimuli (together with other internal states) as are my cognitive states, and they tend to issue in the same verbal behavior that my cognitive states do. Whatever causal or nomic relations obtained between my mental representations and the external world, the very same ones would obtain between Zjoe's functional analogues of my mental representations and the external world. Unless one just stipulated that unconscious states cannot be genuine cognitive states, or that only conscious creatures can have cognitive states, it's hard to see why Zjoe wouldn't count as having thoughts and judgments.[5] So, for now at least, let's assume Zjoe has thoughts and judgments.

Once we grant Zjoe thoughts and judgments, then he is capable of making derivations and judging whether or not one representation follows *a priori* from others. Zjoe, then, is in a position to appreciate that the standard description of a zombie is conceptually possible. If there is no *a priori* derivation for me from the premise "X occupies brain state B" to the conclusion "X is experiencing R," then there won't be for Zjoe either. So if the inference from the conceptual possibility of B without R to its metaphysical possibility is valid for me, it should be valid for Zjoe as well.

At first blush there is nothing embarrassing about this conclusion for the advocate of the conceivability argument. Given that the situation of instantiating B without instantiating R is supposed to be metaphysically possible, it shouldn't matter that it's Zjoe who is considering it. After all, whether a situation is metaphysically possible is not determined by who is entertaining a description of it. In fact, since Zjoe is himself a zombie, in this case the possibility of occupying B without R is guaranteed by its actuality.

However, as Balog argues, there really is a problem here. Let S be the situation that is accurately described by the representation "X has B but not R" as employed, or entertained, by me. According to the metaphysical anti-materialist, S is metaphysically possible. Let S′ be the situation accurately described by the representation "X has B but not R" as it is employed by Zjoe. If S′ is the same situation as S, then there is no problem. But why think the two situations are the same? In particular, why think that "R," as it occurs in Zjoe's language, refers to the same property as the "R" that occurs in my language?

In fact, one can see good reasons for thinking that the two occurrences of "R" don't refer to the same property. I experience qualia, and therefore it's straightforward how it is that I am capable of entertaining a representation of a reddish quale. But Zjoe, by hypothesis, has no qualia. How, then, could his "R" establish a referential connection to the property of being reddish? There is no reddishness in his experience; on some scenarios, there are none in his entire world. It seems likely, then, that his "R" refers to some internal state of him (whether functional or physical).

If the argument above about the reference of Zjoe's "R" is right, then S′, the situation he is representing when considering "X has B but not R," is not identical to S. Let's now consider the modal properties of S′. S′ is clearly conceptually possible relative to "X has B but not R," since, as we argued above, if I am not capable of deriving a contradiction from it *a priori*, neither is Zjoe. But is it also metaphysically possible? It doesn't seem to be. Since "R" refers to a property of Zjoe, and since Zjoe is already a zombie, we can assume any physical duplicate of Zjoe will instantiate every property Zjoe instantiates. Thus, S′ is not metaphysically possible. Zombies can't have zombie twins of their own, only genuine duplicates.

Suppose Balog is right about Zjoe. That is, suppose S′ is metaphysically impossible even though for Zjoe, relative to "X has B but not R," it is conceptually possible. What does this show with regard to the anti-materialist's argument? It shows that one cannot infer from conceptual possibility, or conceivability, to metaphysical possibility. If Zjoe can't legitimately make the inference, then neither can I, it would seem. But then the anti-materialist argument must not work.

The crucial premise in Balog's argument is that Zjoe's "R" describes a property he actually instantiates. For if Zjoe was wrong in applying "R" to himself, then his own situation would demonstrate the metaphysical possibility of having B without R. I presented considerations above for thinking Zjoe's "R" did correctly describe his own states, but we should note that there is certainly room for the anti-materialist to reply. So let's briefly consider again Balog's crucial premise.

To begin with, consider the question whether Zjoe's "R" and mine can mean the same thing. For an argument that they can't mean the same thing, we can turn to the very considerations I pressed against Rey's eliminativism in chapter 5. In a sense the situations are the same, since, according to the eliminativist, we really are zombies. I argued there that the eliminativist can't say that our concept of a reddish quale is of a property that might be instantiated in a dualist world, because without any contact with such a property in this world there seems to be no plausible way for us to acquire a concept of it. Clearly if there are qualitative properties of the sort that the qualia realist supposes there to be, then the only way to acquire concepts of them, at least of the sort that we have, is by having the relevant experiences. It seemed clear that the eliminativist had to say that our concepts of qualia were of impossible properties (i.e., properties that are not instantiated in any world). Of course Rey himself takes that line.

So it looks as if the anti-materialist who wants to resist Balog's objection can't maintain that Zjoe's "R" means the same as my "R," But that doesn't mean she automatically has to admit that Zjoe's "R" truly applies to his own states. In fact, why not take the analogy with the eliminativist seriously? Since the eliminativist thinks, in essence, that we are zombies, under the cognitive illusion that we instantiate properties we couldn't possibly instantiate, the anti-materialist ought to be able to appropriate that position for her zombie twin. So, the anti-materialist will argue, while the eliminativist is just wrong about us, she's got a pretty good story to tell about Zjoe.[6]

If this could be made to work, would it block the objection? It seems that it would. For Zjoe, the situation S′ is conceptually possible relative to "X has B but not R" because he cannot derive *a priori* any contradiction from that representation. We have a counterexample to the inference from conceptual possibility to metaphysical possibility only if S′ turns out to be metaphysically impossible. However, under the eliminativist interpretation of Zjoe's "R," S′ is metaphysically possible. Indeed, Zjoe is himself an instance of S′. So Zjoe's case doesn't show the relevant inference pattern invalid.

The question remains, however, whether the eliminativist ploy can be made to work. Here's one reason for thinking not. Consider again an eliminativist position like Rey's. On his view, the concept of a reddish quale is necessarily unsatisfiable. He compares it to the concept of magic. What is it about the concept of magic that makes it necessarily unsatisfiable?[7] Supposedly, it's the fact that it lays down incompatible conditions for its satisfaction. To put it roughly, to be magic is to be a mechanism for effecting change in the physical world that defies all the mechanisms for effecting change in the physical world. No mechanism could possibly fulfill that condition. Similarly, according to Rey, to be a reddish quale is to fulfill certain conditions—say, being a simple non-physical cause of physical events—that couldn't possibly be fulfilled.

In chapter 5 I criticized Rey's argument, objecting that his purported analysis of the concept of a reddish quale did not capture what was essential, and attributed what was not essential. Whether I'm right or not in my criticism, it seems pretty clear that the anti-materialist must take my side on this. That means that there isn't an analysis of my "R" along the lines Rey suggests. For me, no inferential connection between "I'm experiencing R" and any of the descriptions suggested by Rey has *a priori* status. But given the functional equivalence between me and Zjoe, that means that none of these inferential connections has *a priori* status for Zjoe either. Any analysis of Zjoe's "R" that entailed incompatible satisfaction conditions would have to be incorrect as well. But without such an analysis, how can we justify the claim that Zjoe's "R" is necessarily unsatisfiable? The case for treating Zjoe's "R" along eliminativist lines seems unavailable to the anti-materialist.

Perhaps the anti-materialist can find some legitimate ground for the claim that Zjoe's "R" fails to apply to his own states. For the moment, however, suppose we grant Balog her crucial premise. Then, for all we've seen so far, Balog's argument fits perfectly well with my attack on the DPM in chapter 2. I gave a direct argument against the principle underlying the anti-materialist's argument, while Balog gives a *reductio* of the argument form. My argument and Balog's would seem to reinforce each other. But remember that in chapter 3 I presented a second anti-materialist argument: the "thick" conceivability argument. An important question to address is whether Balog's objection works equally well against both.

If we grant her the crucial premise, then it seems clear to me that her objection is cogent with respect to the original, thin conceivability argument of chapter 2. After all, the thin conceivability argument takes the bare conceptual possibility of having B without R as sufficient grounds for asserting its metaphysical possibility. But we have shown that for Zjoe, B without R (his R, of course) is conceptually possible but not metaphysically possible. So bare conceptual possibility isn't sufficient for metaphysical possibility.

But now, consider the thick conceivability argument of chapter 3. The conceivability premise involves the claim that having B without R is thickly conceivable, where that means that the only way to derive a contradiction from the description "X has B but not R" is through a gappy identity. Again, a gappy identity claim is one for which a request for explanation is intelligible. The question is, is having B without R (his R) only thinly conceivable for Zjoe, or is it also thickly conceivable? In other words, is the identity "R = B (or some suitable surrogate for B)" a gappy identity for Zjoe?

It certainly seems as if it would be. Zjoe, we argued, is functionally identical to me. If I'm inclined to say that a certain identity claim requires explanation, Zjoe will be similarly inclined. Again, this isn't merely behavioral equivalence. Whatever informational states in me are causally implicated in my verbal dispositions will be present in Zjoe as well, playing the same causal role with respect to his verbal dispositions. So if the Balog argument works against the thin conceivability argument, it seems as if it works against the thick one as well.

The question I want to raise now is what implication this result has for the status of the explanatory gap. As I said above, since my own position is that metaphysical anti-materialism is mistaken, or at least unwarranted, the conclusion that even thick conceivability fails to entail possibility should not cause trouble for my position. Still, a problem does lurk here.

The problem is this. Balog's argument could be used to demonstrate not only that conceivability fails to entail possibility, but also that a functionalist, or as I like to call it, an "architectural" solution to the explanatory gap must work. The idea is this. Consider Zjoe again. If Zjoe is cognitively like me, then Zjoe will of course say that he finds the identity claim "R = B" to be gappy. It makes sense for Zjoe to ask for an explanation of this identity. Now, by hypothesis, we know that Zjoe is a purely physical device whose cognitive states are functionally characterizable. Thus there must be a functional account of Zjoe's perception of an explanatory gap. But if there is a functional account of Zjoe's perception of an explanatory gap then we should be able to use that functional account to explain my perception of an explanatory gap.

By a functional, or "architectural" account of the explanatory gap, I have in mind something like the following. The reason we can't appreciate that reddishness just is a certain neurophysiological property, and that this identity does not intelligibly call for an explanation, is that our psychological architecture is such that we cannot make our first-person representation of this property commensurate with our third-person, theoretical representation. The two modes of access involve, as it were, distinct and incommensurate vocabularies. In particular, the first-person mode of access involves an immediate cognitive response with a primitive representation, so any identity claim involving that representation will appear brute and irreducible. We looked at a view of this sort in chapter 3: Brian Loar's account of phenomenal concepts as type-demonstrative recognitional concepts. The point is, if Zjoe suffers from an explanatory gap, it must be that the explanation for this is that his cognitive architecture is designed along the lines just described. But if this explains Zjoe's cognitive state with respect to the explanatory gap, why not ours as well?

In reply, I appeal to the discussion in chapter 3 in which I argued that a Loar-type account of phenomenal concepts doesn't seem to do justice to our first-person representations of qualia. The problem is that on such an account the content of our concept of reddishness is akin to a demonstrative in being "presentationally thin," and this doesn't capture the substantive and determinate idea we have of properties like being reddish. So, when I entertain the thought that R = B and then wonder how this could be so, when I ask for an explanation of this alleged identity, the correct characterization of my cognitive state must take account of this "thick," substantial conception I express with "R" (or "reddish"). Put in the terms introduced in the last section, the thought I express by saying, "How could R be B?" is a phenomenally constituted thought.

Now Zjoe, by hypothesis, is incapable of experiencing genuine reddishness. It stands to reason, then, that the mode of presentation associated with his term "R" cannot match the character of mine. Thus, whatever is going on with him when he claims to find the identity "R = B" in need of explanation is not the same as what goes on in me. For him, the Loar-type account might make perfect sense. But since our cognitive situations are not the same, it doesn't follow that the same account works for me.

One might very well object at this point that the reply just presented begs the question. The argument presented in chapter 3 against the various architectural accounts of phenomenal concepts appealed to a special feature of our conception of phenomenal character that distinguished it from other cases to which, on the architectural account, it should be similar. There are other cases, such as demonstrative and indexical concepts, or, on my view, even natural kind concepts, where a mental vocabulary difference prevents an *a priori* reduction of descriptions couched in these terms into descriptions expressed in other terms. Nevertheless, the argument goes, when all is said and done, identities like "this = my diskette case" or "water = H$_2$O" are not gappy. That is, when the full story is told in third-person terms, there is nothing further it makes sense to ask for by way of explanation. The fact that there is nothing left to explain, despite the fact that one can't analytically derive the demonstrative-laden description, or the "water" description, from the description not containing those terms, is explained by the lack of any substantive content to the concepts expressed by these terms. They really are essentially labels. On the other hand, the fact that we still recognize the intelligibility of the request for an explanation of identities like "R = B," even after the entire physical and functional story is told, is explained by the substantial content of the relevant phenomenal concepts.

But if appeal to the asymmetry between the two sorts of cases is the basis for the claim that phenomenal concepts are really different in kind, then we run into trouble again from Zjoe. After all, Zjoe will, presumably, say that he doesn't understand what one could be asking for when requesting an explanation of how water could be H$_2$O (again, after all the relevant chemistry is cited), yet will claim to understand how one could ask how R = B. But, again, the explanation for the difference between these two sorts of cases can't be a matter of there being something special about Zjoe's phenomenal concepts. Whatever we cite by way of explanation for Zjoe's noting a difference in the two sorts of cases could then be cited as an explanation of our own cognitive situation. Thus, the fact that we find identities of qualia with physical/functional states gappy doesn't show that there is anything to distinguish our phenomenal concepts from those of Zjoe.

My response is to insist again on the claim that my cognitive situation is different from Zjoe's. True, Zjoe will *say* that he perceives a difference between the case of demonstratives and the case of phenomenal concepts, just as I do. However, in his case, as opposed to mine, his saying that he perceives this difference is just that, a form of behavior. He occupies states that are functionally identical to mine, so if there is a state of mine—my contemplating my concept of reddishness—that tends to cause me to say certain things, then of course Zjoe will occupy a state that tends to cause him to say the same things. But this doesn't entail that the state he's in is *cognitively* identical to mine. I am really entertaining this substantive and determinate conception of a reddish qualitative character; my thought is really phenomenally constituted, whereas Zjoe is, as it were, merely going through the motions. What distinguishes us is precisely the fact that I am a conscious subject of experience and, by hypothesis, he isn't. Only if being such a subject of experience could be identified with the tendency to cause one to say certain things would it follow that Zjoe and I must share cognitive properties. In other words, I really do find psycho-physical identities gappy, whereas Zjoe only says he does. To really "find" it gappy, to occupy a state cognitively similar to mine, one has to be conscious.

Seen in this light, the argument for the gappiness of psycho-physical identities was never a mere appeal to what we find ourselves saying in certain circumstances. Clearly one can program in the relevant tendency to any machine. One can just stipulate that for certain internal vocabulary items there are rules that connect identities involving them and certain other vocabulary items with expressions of puzzlement, where what counts as an expression of puzzlement for such a device is also functionally articulated. There was never any doubt that all this could be programmed into a non-conscious creature. The argument for gappiness is not a matter of noting what we would *say*, but noting what we would *think*. My claim is that we really do *think* the relevant thought about gappiness, a phenomenally constituted thought, whereas Zjoe doesn't.

My reply to the zombie epistemology argument, then, comes down to this. The argument relies upon two crucial premises: (1) when Zjoe employs the representation "R," he's referring to a state of himself; (2) my cognitive/ epistemic situation is, by virtue of our functional identity, the same as Zjoe's. While I have entertained objections to the first premise, I do not now dispute it; in fact, I find it quite plausible. Rather, my disagreement is with the second premise. I want to say that my cognitive/epistemic situation is, by virtue of my being a subject of conscious experience, significantly different from that of Zjoe. The very having of conscious experiences alters my cognitive/epistemic situation in a way that makes my appreciation of the gappiness of psycho-physical identities fundamentally different from Zjoe's. Put another way, when I'm considering how *this experience* could be a matter of such-and-such neural firings, there is a mode of presentation of what I'm wondering about that is absent from any thought of Zjoe's.

Of course, even granting the coherence of the distinction between a conscious creature's cognitive situation when contemplating the gappiness of psycho-physical identities and a zombie's when occupying a functional analogue of such contemplation, one must still face the skeptical challenge: how do you know you're not really a zombie yourself? How do you know you really are thinking what you think you're thinking, with all its fullness and determinacy of content? This brings us back again to the original zombie first-person skepticism argument. That argument, remember, goes like this. If zombies are conceivable, then I could have all the beliefs and evidence I currently have and yet be a zombie myself.

There are of course various ways of meeting the skeptical challenge that don't rely on marking the fundamental distinction between conscious and non-conscious cognition that I introduced above. One might insist on the distinction between conceivability and possibility here, a distinction my sort of qualophile can appeal to. The point is this. It's not clear that the mere conceivability of a situation is sufficient to undermine my knowledge that it doesn't obtain, even if it's consistent with all my data. So long as it's metaphysically impossible one might plausibly argue that my claim to knowledge is quite secure. Another reply, mentioned in chapter 5, is that in general mere possibilities, even if we don't worry about the distinction between conceivability and possibility, don't undermine claims to knowledge. Thus it's not clear that either the mere conceivability or possibility of a zombie undermines my claim to know that I'm not one.

However, neither of these two replies really gets to the heart of the matter. After all, it isn't just that we want to find a conception of knowledge on which I count as knowing I'm not a zombie, despite my inability in some sense to rule out the possibility from within. If we come down to that sort of move, then I think the qualophile has already given in. The fact is, whether one thinks there is a fundamental distinction between conceivability and possibility or not, it is not really even conceivable to me that I might be a zombie. I *can* rule out this possibility from within. This was the point of my principal reply in chapter 5. First-person skepticism doesn't get even a foothold because my epistemic situation in some way includes my conscious experience. There is no sense in which everything could be, cognitively and epistemically speaking, just as it is but without the qualia. The qualia are essential components of how, cognitively and epistemically, it is with me. Thus we see that the replies to both the zombie epistemology argument and the first-person skeptical argument reinforce each other.

The conceivability of zombies, according to the objector, is supposed to throw doubt both on the significance of the explanatory gap and on the security of my first-person knowledge of my own experience. The argument works the same way for both doubts: zombies would think just the way you do, and yet there can't be any such problem or knowledge in their case. The qualophile's reply is to deny the cognitive similarity between subjects of conscious experience and their zombie functional duplicates. The question, however, is how to really understand this difference in cognitive and epistemic status. What I will argue in the next section is that in fact we don't have an explanation of the special cognitive status of subjectively presented, experienced contents, especially if materialism is true.

6.4 Materialism and Subjectivity

In chapter 4 we discussed the higher-order theory of consciousness (HO). HO's strength is its attempt to grapple straightforwardly with the fact that consciousness involves awareness. Whereas other functionalist theories attempt to explain what is peculiarly qualitative about sensory qualia by reference to either their physiological realizations or their representational format, HO maintains that for there to be something it's like to have an experience entails that the subject of the experience is aware of whatever it's like. To the extent that the essence of qualitative experience is there being something it's like, and this is supposed to be what distinguishes conscious from unconscious mental states, then a theory of this distinction must be a theory of awareness.

There are of course two major problems with this approach. First, by forcing a division between the quale itself—the object of conscious awareness—and the awareness of it, the phenomenon we're interested in seems to disappear. Unfelt pains and unconscious reddish experiences may make some sort of theoretical sense if one already accepts an identification of qualia with neurophysiological states, but these states really do not seem to be the sorts of states we have in mind when thinking of qualia. Second, as Karen Neander has argued, this bifurcation between higher-order and lower-order state, though apparently necessary to model the act-object relation involved in conscious awareness, leaves the locus of qualitative character totally unclear. When the higher-order state misrepresents the lower-order one, which content—higher-order or lower-order—determines the actual quality of experience? What this seems to show is that one can't divorce the quality from the awareness of the quality.

Block's (1995) response to HO, as to many other functionalist theories of consciousness, is that it is a theory of the wrong type of consciousness—namely, access consciousness. What we want, on the contrary, is a theory of phenomenal consciousness. But the problem with this distinction is that it suggests that phenomenal consciousness has nothing itself to do with access. I don't mean just that phenomenal states are themselves quite plausibly representations that afford access to external objects and their properties. No one denies that. Nor do I mean that phenomenal states can themselves be the objects of introspective awareness. Block's distinction certainly doesn't contradict that either. Rather, what the notion of phenomenal consciousness seems to leave out is precisely the insight that fuels HO: that to be phenomenal is for there to be something it's like to be in the state in question, and that means being aware of it. Qualia, phenomenal states, are bits of awareness. Access is at their core.

The inadequacy of both HO and the access/phenomenal distinction manifests the paradoxical duality of qualitative experiences: there is an awareness relation, which ought to entail that there are two states serving as the relevant relata, yet experience doesn't seem to admit of this sort of bifurcation. Let's call this the problem of "duality." That qualia have this dual nature, and that certain conscious thoughts are phenomenally constituted, are clearly intimately connected. Qualia are such as to necessitate awareness of them, and certain thoughts seem to include qualia in their modes of presentation in a cognitively special way. These are the two sides of the problem of subjectivity.

What resources does materialism allow us to construct a theory of subjectivity, a theory of the duality of qualia and the existence of phenomenally constituted thought? As we've noted already, the only basic relation that materialism provides is the causal relation, out of which the relation of information transfer can be built. So, is there a way to account for subjectivity ultimately in terms of causal relations-cum-information transfer/processing?

There seem to be two strategies worth considering for explaining subjectivity: viewing the relevant causal relation as a conceptually constitutive, or individuative relation, and implementing/realizing distinct functional roles with the same physical state. I will explore each of these alternatives in turn.

The first strategy itself might break down into two versions, a weaker and a stronger one, depending on which phenomena one is trying to capture. The weaker version is aimed at capturing only the intimacy of the connection between one's conscious thought about a quale and the quale itself—that is, explaining phenomenally constituted thought. When I consciously entertain the idea of a reddish experience, there certainly seems to be something intimate about the connection between my idea and the quale—the sense of presentation of the quale—that is lacking between my idea of an external object/property and that object/property. One way to capture this intimacy is to maintain that in this case the idea is itself partly individuated by its object. We don't count a thought as of that type without its being accompanied by the relevant qualitative experience. That a thought is phenomenally constituted, then, is explained by reference to its conceptually mandated individuation conditions.

While the appeal to a conceptually mandated constituency relation between the quale and the idea of the quale addresses the issue of the cognitive intimacy involved in conscious thought, it doesn't address the other crucial aspect of subjectivity: the fact that qualia are necessarily experiences, and therefore always objects of some sort of awareness. The stronger version of the conceptual constituency option, then, adds another conceptually mandated condition: that nothing counts as a quale unless it is represented by another state. This is HO without the consequence that there are unconscious qualia.

The basic problem with the conceptual constituency strategy is that it substitutes a purely conceptual, or nominal relation for a real one. Suppose, for instance, that one proposed to solve the mystery of the Trinity by saying the following. Yes, there are three persons, the Father, Son, and Holy Ghost, each distinct from the others in just the way that persons are normally distinct from one another. Still, the claim that God is One is true since by "God" we mean the Holy Family, the set containing Father, Son, and Holy Ghost. This would not be very convincing, since one has made this set of three count as a single entity by stipulative definition. What we wanted to know was how, given our previous notion of singularity of personhood, these three persons could be one. It's clear that the redefinition strategy gets us nowhere on this project.

Perhaps an analogy that's closer to our topic is this. As I've maintained above, skepticism about the external world gets a grip when we realize that we might be having the very same perceptual experiences even if we were wildly mistaken regarding the facts about external objects and their physical properties and relations to us. After all, the whole scene in front of us could be a giant hallucination. Now, a move that is tempting, and has been made, is to deny that in these situations we would really be having the same perceptual experiences. After all, I currently see the computer screen in front of me. I couldn't rightly be said to "see" the computer screen in front of me if it weren't there to be seen. I might "seem to see" it, but I wouldn't actually see it. "See," as we say, is a success verb, as is "know," and a host of others. So, if we describe my current perceptual state in terms of the success verbs that characterize it, then the premise that I could be in the same state even if what I think I see I don't really see is wrong. My perceptual state would be significantly different.

While all this is certainly correct as far as it goes, it doesn't help much with skepticism, since the obvious question then becomes: how do I know whether or not I'm seeing the computer screen now or merely seeming to see it? Including the object of perception within the characterization of the perceptual state is a cheat for these purposes; it's merely a verbal trick. Similarly, I want to claim, including the qualitative state within the characterization of what it is to be aware of it merely amounts to a stipulative solution. By drawing the line that defines the cognitive state's content so as to include the qualitative state as well, it seems to create the sort of intimate relation between idea and object that we are trying to capture by speaking of a phenomenally constituted thought. But drawing the line of content in this inclusive way can't obscure the fact that we're dealing with two distinct states that are only causally connected, and the nature of that relation isn't significantly different from that which obtains between a cognitive state and any non-conscious object that determines its content. The special nature of the cognitive relation in the case of conscious experiences—the quite special way that a phenomenally constituted thought includes the phenomenal property it is about—is not explained.

Notice, again, the difference I've emphasized between external world skepticism and first-person zombie skepticism. Though we may dismiss the former on various grounds depending on our theory of knowledge, the doubts upon which it is grounded clearly get a grip on us. We can understand quite well how things could appear just as they are yet we be brains in a vat, or deceived by an evil demon. Thus when one makes the stipulative move, the skeptical response seems quite to the point. How do you know you're really perceiving and not merely seeming to perceive?

On the other hand, part of what we need a theory of phenomenally constituted thought to account for is precisely the fact that no counterpart of external world skepticism seems even to get a grip when it comes to first-person zombie skepticism. We can't really make sense of everything seeming just as it is but without our being conscious, since our conscious experiences are genuinely part of how things seem to us. If someone were to say, "But how do you know they really seem that way? Maybe they only seem to seem that way," the doubt they're attempting to engender just doesn't get to first base. However, if phenomenally constituted thought were merely a matter of defining the cognitive content of a qualitative belief (a belief about a qualitative state, that is) in such a way that it counts as one only if it's actually formed by causal interaction with a qualitative state, or even at the same time as a qualitative state, the skeptical response would clearly be to the point. Sure, you seem to be having qualitative beliefs, but how do you know you are? The point is we need a model whereby the cognitive state in question actually wears its content on its sleeve, and this we don't get from the conceptual constituency strategy.

The second materialist option seems a better bet. The idea here is to capture the intimacy of the cognitive connection not by drawing a content line around two states, but rather by identifying both representation and content with the very same state. The intimacy doesn't seem to be merely a verbal trick here—not a matter of substituting a nominal for a real relation—because the identity of the state that realizes both cognitive state and its object is a very real relation. You can't get more intimate than identity!

There are two, non-exclusive ways to go about implementing this option. First, there is the straight functionalist version.[8] A quale and a cognitive state that is about the quale are distinguished from each other by their functional roles. That is, they constitute distinct functional states. However, it turns out that it is the very same physical state that realizes them both. What we have then is a single physical type whose tokens simultaneously instantiate two distinct functional types. This could happen if tokens of this physical type simultaneously satisfy the descriptions definitive of the two functional types. Thus it turns out that qualia are always the object of awareness, and awareness of them somehow includes them, because any realization of the one, say the awareness, is a realization of the other, its object.

The second way to go is to account for phenomenally constituted thought, for the way qualia are "for the subject," in terms of self-representation.[9] The idea is that a quale is a representational state that has its own occurrence as its content. When it is tokened, it says, in effect, "I am happening." As I mentioned above, these two versions of the identity option are not exclusive. The self-representation version can be taken as a way of specifying more concretely the types of functional role involved in the straight functionalist version.

Though there isn't the same sort of stipulatory character to the relation between quale and awareness of it on the identity option that there is on the conceptual constituency option, the problem with this option is still quite similar to that which besets conceptual constituency. To make this clear, let me for the moment focus only on the self-representation version of the identity option. The idea is supposed to be that when the state R is tokened, it represents that it's tokening. Under what description does it represent itself? Well, there are several alternatives to consider. Using the letters

"R" and "B" as we have throughout the book (our standard first-person representation of reddish qualitative character and the physiological property it is at least correlated with, respectively), it could be representing itself as "R," as "B," or via an indexical, like "I." Since "B" is obviously a nonstarter—there is no reason to think first-person self-representation delivers a neurophysiological description—I'll consider "R" and "I" in turn.

Suppose R's content is "R is tokening now." The question that immediately arises is, what makes the "R" in "R is tokening now" about R? In particular, as we focus on the reddish quale, how does the reddishness itself come to constitute the content? The answer to this can't be merely that the representation and its object in this case are the same thing, since that doesn't really answer the question. Representations don't normally include themselves in their content, so there must be something special in this case. It might be that there is something about the state qua representation such that it justifies interpreting it as being about reddish qualitative character, a feature that must be over and above the mere fact that it is itself an instance of reddish qualitative character. Whatever this feature is—and since we're materialists here it must be ultimately realized in a physical relation—it isn't going to be any more enlightening regarding the phenomenon of interest to us than any other physically constructible relation. That is, the relation of the representation "R" to the property R is no more intimate, no more substantive and determinate in its mode of presentation for being tokened in the same state than it is when the two relata are tokened in distinct states.

Perhaps an analogy would help. The word "word" is self-referential in the sense that it is a member of its own extension. Similarly, according to this version of the self-representation strategy, R-states are self-referential in that they too are members of their own extensions. But notice that there is nothing especially interesting about how the word "word" gets its content—in particular, nothing that depends in any way on its being a member of its own extension. "Word" happens to be about words, which it happens to be an instance of. How it gets to be about words is no different from how any other word gets to be about what it represents. Similarly, if we take the representational content of qualitative states to be self-regarding merely in the sense that by virtue of what they mean they happen to be members of their own extensions, nothing about subjectivity, about how qualia are present in thought and make the special cognitive contribution they do, will be illuminated.

The other alternative is that the representational content of a qualitative state is explicitly self-referential; it has the form "I am being tokened" (or something of the sort). To evaluate this proposal, it's instructive to compare it to the demonstrative proposal discussed back in chapter 3. On that view, when I'm thinking of a qualitative state, my thought about the state has a content expressible as something like "that is happening now." But we have already found this view inadequate. The problem was that it couldn't account for the fact that our conception of qualitative character is both substantive and determinate. When I have a reddish experience, what is present to me is not merely that I'm having some experience or other, but that it is *reddish*, as opposed, say, to greenish. The reddishness is there in my experience, available in its substantive and determinate character to my mind. The problem for the demonstrative view is that it can't capture this cognitive presence, since demonstratives are "blind" in the relevant sense; they pick out whatever it is that they point to, not by virtue of its character but by virtue of its relation to the demonstrative. Now, if this is a problem for the demonstrative view, I don't see how it helps any to transform the demonstrative into the first-person indexical. The very same thinness of content attends indexicals as attends demonstratives. The fact that the representation is pointing at itself rather than something else doesn't really make a difference with regard to this question. What's distinctive about phenomenally constituted thought—its substantiality and determinacy—is left unexplained.

My criticisms of the identity option have been aimed at the self-representation version, but they apply to the straight functionalist version as well. In fact, the straight functionalist version doesn't appear to get us as far as the self-representation version to begin with. Straight functionalism, remember, identifies the same physical state as the realization of both the quale and a cognitive awareness of the quale. Without a theory of the cognitive state's content, the mere fact that both functional states share a realization doesn't have any explanatory value. For all I know, or care, from the psychological point of view, many different psychological states are realized by the very same physical states. Why should this make a psychological difference? The only reason the identity of the two functional states' realizations should matter is if their identity were reflected psychologically. But for this to occur, it has to be that the cognitive state's content is specially constituted in some way by the very fact that its object is realized by the same state. How would an account of this special constitution go? It would seem that it has to involve the cognitive state's being self-representational. If not, it's just not clear how the identity of the realization should matter. Thus the two versions really reduce to one.

The problem with both materialist strategies for explaining subjectivity is this: all the materialist has out of which to construct the subjective relation to the contents of experience is the relation of cause and effect, or nomological covariation. But appeal to causal/nomological relations can't explain the cognitive intimacy we need for an account of conscious cognition. In fact, the problem goes even deeper than materialism. The duality problem is really a problem about how there can be anything like conscious awareness, which seems to require both unity and distinctness all at once. It is the quale, the phenomenal experience, that at once has the qualitative character that is "for me," present to my mind, and is also the awareness of itself. If we think of awareness as a relation, then we can't really understand how the reddishness, one relatum, is somehow packed into the awareness of it, the other relatum. But if we don't think of awareness as a relation, how do we think of it? What else can it be? The explanatory gap not only remains, but it widens.

6.6 Conclusion

In this chapter I've tried to do two things. First, I was concerned to defend the conceivability of zombies from two important challenges: the zombie epistemology argument and the replacement argument. Second, I explored the notion of conscious cognition, and attempted to show both that this phenomenon could be used to meet the zombie challenges and also that it was indeed beyond the explanatory grasp of materialism.

The basic response to the zombie challenges is this. Zombies are not, merely by dint of their functional identity to conscious subjects, cognitively identical to their conscious counterparts. The absence of consciousness makes a cognitive difference. The difference is that when one is consciously entertaining a thought, one's relation to the object of one's thought is different in kind from that which obtains when one is representing unconsciously. Qualitative experiences, as a species of conscious cognitive states, are themselves bits of awareness which, as experiences of a subject, are simultaneously objects of, and acts of, awareness. So when imagining a zombie who is supposedly non-veridically "aware" of having conscious experiences, one isn't imagining the sort of paradoxical situation one would be imagining if the awareness were of the conscious variety. The zombie's illusory "awareness" is of a totally different nature, and therefore nothing about our own situation with respect to our apprehension of our mental states follows from the situation of the zombie, and there is nothing paradoxical about the zombie's "thoughts" about its own situation.

It turns out that qualia simultaneously present two explanatory challenges. On the one hand, they are properties of experience that don't appear to be constructible out of (i.e., realizable in) basic physical properties. On the other hand, our very appreciation of this mystery itself generates another mystery. How is it that there can be the sort of cognitive relation to these properties that engenders the explanatory gap? Subjectivity, the fact that when qualia are instantiated they are necessarily objects for the subject in whose experience they appear, is itself a phenomenon that has no model in physical interactions and relations. While it certainly still seems as if experience, both cognitive and sensory, must be constituted by the physical processes in the brain, we are a long way from understanding how this can be so.

Coda
"Is It Tomorrow, or Just the End of Time?"

My aim in this book was to establish that, when it comes to conscious experience, we face a kind of Kantian antinomy. On the one hand, we have excellent reason for thinking that conscious experience must be reducible, in the requisite sense, to a physical phenomenon, and, on the other hand, we don't see how it could be. My argument for the materialist side of the antinomy was based primarily on the fact that mental states had both physical causes and physical effects. I argued that only if conscious experiences were realized in physical states could we make sense of their causal relevance. In the process I addressed arguments to the effect that mental properties were not in fact causally efficacious, either for reasons having to do with their being parasitical on the physical, or for straightforward epiphenomenalist reasons. I also addressed one of the primary anti-materialist arguments, the conceivability argument. I argued that one could not derive the metaphysical possibility of zombies from their conceptual possibility, and that therefore materialism was not committed to the conceptual impossibility of zombies.

On the anti-materialist side, while I do not claim to have an argument that conscious experience absolutely could not be a physical phenomenon—in fact, for the reasons mentioned above, I think it really must be—I do claim that we can't really understand how it could be. There are two, inter-related features of conscious experience that both resist explanatory reduction to the physical: subjectivity and qualitative character. When I look at the red diskette case ever by my side as I work away at the computer, I have a reddish visual sensation, a conscious experience of a certain type. I argued that though conceivability considerations do not suffice to establish metaphysical anti-materialism, they do in fact show that theories couched in physical terms fail to really explain the instantiation of properties like reddishness. In the course of establishing this claim, and responding to certain challenges, it emerged that there is a kind of conceivability at issue here—I called it "thick" conceivability—that goes beyond mere conceptual possibility. The fundamental idea was that when I think of a property like reddishness, there is a substantive and determinate content to my conception. In this respect it differs from the contents of demonstrative concepts and, I argued, natural kind concepts as well. Somehow what distinguishes reddishness from greenishness (not to mention all other qualitative properties) is present to me, included in my conception, in a way that what water is, or what "that diskette case" is, is not. It is this cognitive immediacy that gives rise to the explanatory gap.

From the foregoing argument, it appears that, in a sense, the source of the problem with providing a physical explanation of qualitative character resides in the subjectivity of conscious experience. Clearly the substantiality and determinacy of our first-person conception of reddishness is part of what it is for a reddish experience to be "for me." I explored various theories of subjectivity, the most prominent being the higher-order theory. I argued that its principal virtue was also its principal vice: by splitting experience into two states, the awareness and what it is awareness of, the essentially experiential character of a qualitative state is somehow lost. After surveying various other attempts to provide reductive theories of conscious experience, I took up the challenge of eliminativism. Perhaps the reason we can't provide an explanatory reduction of conscious experience is that it doesn't really exist. My response to eliminativism took two tacks. First, I argued that the eliminativist failed to show that the qualophile's conception of conscious experience is vulnerable to various standard reductions to absurdity. Second, I argued that, again, the substantiality and determinacy of the way qualitative experience is presented in thought could not be explained if its content were really of a non-existent phenomenon.

Finally, after revisiting various zombie puzzles which were supposed to demonstrate the absurdity in the qualophile's position, it emerged in yet another way that phenomenal consciousness makes a cognitive difference—that some thoughts are phenomenally constituted, where that involves precisely the sort of substantive and determinate presentation noted earlier. A key aspect of the subjectivity of qualitative experience is the feature of duality, whereby the very same state is both cognitive apprehension and object of cognitive apprehension. Conscious awareness, as a cognitive phenomenon, stands in need of explanation as much as, or more than, its object. I surveyed various attempts to explain subjectivity in materialist terms, and found them all inadequate.

In the Introduction I said that with respect to the feature of intentionality I thought the prospects for a materialist reduction, or naturalization, were much better than those for conscious experience. It seems clear now that part of what is distinctive about conscious experience is the mode of cognition it involves, and this clearly has implications for our understanding of intentionality. I am inclined to think, then, that there are fundamentally two different types of intentionality: conscious and unconscious. For unconscious intentionality we have an idea how to theoretically construct it out of its physical constituents, but for conscious intentionality we are in the dark.

Thomas Nagel (1974) emphasizes that what makes the problem of consciousness so hard is that we apprehend experience from a subjective point of view, and what is so apprehended cannot be simultaneously apprehended from the (more) objective point of view of physical theory. Of course this is a view with which I have great sympathy, and to which my own arguments owe a great debt. However, if I understand him correctly, it seems to me that he doesn't sufficiently appreciate that the entire idea of a point of view is itself deeply puzzling. A way to put the problem of duality is just this: how could anything like a point of view exist?

It's important to emphasize, in considering possible solutions to this puzzle, something else Nagel has pointed out. Though we are fond of presenting the puzzle of conscious experience as a matter of the conflict between materialism and our subjective, intuitive conception of our experience, it isn't really physicality that presents the problem. The point is that merely positing a new kind of property—call it a basic mental property—doesn't really shed any light on how to understand conscious awareness. This is why even non-materialist theories—or neutral monist theories like Russell's (1927)—have a problem. The point is that if nature just has a richer stock of basic properties than we thought—so that reddishness is somehow included in the base, or maybe proto-reddishness—it's not clear how subjectivity, the cognitive relation constitutive of a point of view, can be explained in terms of these properties. Yes, we can say that reddishness is instantiated in a basic way; the question how this fact becomes a fact "for me" is still pressing.

As I said above in section 1.4, I've not really attempted to address various non-standard alternatives to materialism in this book. I don't expect my brief remarks above to convince anyone who is interested in pursuing such alternatives that there is no prospect of success. Perhaps there is a way to make them work; if so, there clearly is a need for further research in that direction. For the purposes of this book, I hope to have established that, at least with respect to traditional attempts to understand the place of conscious experience in the natural world, we really do continue to face a genuine puzzle. The mind-body problem is still a problem.

Notes

Introduction

1. This is in fact a title by Dretske (1995), but the phrase is used by many others.

2. My convention is to use quotes to indicate terms in natural language, angle brackets to indicate mental representations, and upper-case letters for contents (or concepts).

3. See Dretske (1981), Fodor (1990), and Millikan (1984).

4. See Fodor and Lepore (1992) and (1993). This is a topic to which we will return.

5. Note I am using "reddish" to refer to a feature of my experience, not the surface of the diskette case. Throughout the book I will use terms like "red" and "green" to refer to features of physical surfaces, and "reddish" and "greenish" to refer to features of experiences. I don't intend thereby to beg any questions about the existence of either sort of feature. I will deal with the eliminativist argument that properties like reddishness don't exist, and the reductionist argument that reddishness is really just red, in due course.

6. I include under "physical" here functional properties as well.

7. It may seem odd to refer to the nomic relation between a symbol and its referent as a "mode of presentation," since by that term one might intend precisely that which is cognitively present to the subject. However, a mode of presentation is also that feature of a representation by which it brings the subject into contact with the object of her thought, and it is this feature that nomic relations share with traditional modes of presentation. At any rate I will continue to speak of modes of presentation in this extended sense. I am indebted to William Taschek for pointing out this oddity in my use of the term.

8. The contrast I'm after between the modes of presentation of qualitative properties and other properties (or objects) is perhaps captured in Russell's (1959) distinction between "knowledge by acquaintance" and "knowledge by description." We are acquainted with the contents of experience, but not with anything else. Since I don't want anything in my discussion to depend either on interpretations of Russell or on the epistemological purposes for which he employed this distinction, I will forbear from using this terminology.

9. By "phenomenal concepts" I mean our concepts of phenomenal properties, or qualia. Of course what I have described as distinctive is their modes of presentation, but for most purposes these can be identified with the concepts themselves.

10. Whether subjectivity infects the problem of intentionality itself depends on whether conscious contents must be different in kind from non-conscious ones. If so, then there are two problems of intentionality, and only with respect to non-conscious intentionality is the naturalistic approach described above promising. On the other hand, it might be that for both conscious and non-conscious representational states the theory of their content might be the same, but there is something added in the nature of the relation between the subject and the relevant content when it comes to conscious experience. This seems to be McGinn's (1997) view. I discuss this view briefly in chapter 4 (note 39).

Searle (1992) argues that there is no proper notion of non-conscious intentionality, so he is not at all impressed by the alleged progress in the naturalization project described above. I do not share his view, since I think the sort of non-conscious information processing posited by most of cognitive science involves genuine representation. But as this is beside the point here, I will not argue for this claim.

Chapter 1

1. See Shoemaker (1984) for an argument that property individuation depends on causal role. Kim (1993) argues that for a property to be real it must play a causal role.

2. We would have to be careful to exclude negative properties which are described using physical terminology, such as the property of not having extension. I am not going to worry about exactly how this would go.

3. I will generally use "[]" to indicate properties.

4. See Carroll (1994) for a defense of the view that laws cannot be analyzed in non-nomological terms.

5. Thus realization at least amounts to supervenience of the realized properties on the realizing properties.

6. I assume the relation of realization is transitive. Thus if mental properties are realized by neurophysiological properties, and they in turn by biochemical properties, and they in turn by basic physical properties, the mental properties count as realized by the basic physical properties.

7. See Putnam (1991) and Fodor (1974) for classic statements of this objection to the Identity Theory. Not everyone finds the objection compelling. See Hill (1991) for a dissenting opinion.

8. I hope it's obvious that I am not pretending to provide here a realistic neurophysiological account of sleep.

9. I will adopt the shorter expression "basic property" for "property realized in a basic way," except where confusion will result.

10. This principle is often called the "Causal Closure of the Physical." See Kim (1993).

11. Let me emphasize here that I'm not talking about a theory that takes us all the way to fundamental physics. Rather, I'm talking about one that takes us to neuroscience. I assume that neural properties in turn are realized in more basic biochemical properties, and then eventually it all bottoms out in fundamental physics. Realization, as mentioned in note 6, is transitive.

12. I don't mean to be ruling out connectionist theories here. They are formal theories, too, in the sense relevant to this discussion.

13. I take this to be a version of what Yablo (1990) has in mind by his version

(4) of dualism, the claim, "I could have existed with my thought properties alone" (152).

14. For arguments along these lines see Crane and Mellor (1990) and Chomsky (1988). For general discussion of this topic, see Poland (1994) and (forthcoming), Melnyk (1997), Montero (1999), and Smart (1978).

15. See Poland (1994) for extended discussion of this problem, together with his own solution. In Poland (forthcoming) he expresses dissatisfaction with this solution.

16. I heard him express this sentiment in a lecture while visiting at MIT in the late 1970s. I don't know if it appears in print.

17. Montero (1999) points to a similar position.

18. Fodor spoke only of intentionality, of course, but that was his only concern in that discussion.

19. This is how Chalmers (1996) formulates it.

20. Of course the basic law in question would not relate light hitting the retina with the reddish qualitative experience. Rather, the light hitting the retina would cause nerve impulses to reach higher levels in the brain, all according to standard physical laws. Somewhere in the brain would be a configuration that satisfies the antecedent of the relevant psycho-physical basic law, and which thereby causes the reddish experience.

21. In particular, see Chalmers (1996).

22. The following is not intended as a reconstruction of Chalmers's argument, though some of the points are clearly similar to ones he makes. For his detailed replies to anti-epiphenomenalist arguments, see Chalmers (1996, 150-160 and 192-203).

23. Chalmers argues that there is something else, namely satisfying the relevant "primary intension" (Chalmers 1996, 201). So my use of the phrase "the largest star in the universe" need not be causally connected to the largest star in the universe to pick it out; it need merely describe it. My short response is that reference by satisfaction only works once one already has some referring terms in play and that not all terms can work this way. Satisfaction cannot ultimately ground reference. This is a point I will return to in the next chapter.

Of course primary intensions need not be explicitly formulated. They are just functions that can serve as one component of the contents of expressions. While not wanting to get into a long discussion about contents and intensions here, let me just say this. There has to be something about an expression by virtue of which it has the primary intension it has—that is, the function from possible contexts to referents that it has. It could be that the expression is analytically equivalent to a description that determines the function. If so, then my remarks above about satisfaction apply. If it isn't that, then I don't really know what else it could be if not some feature about the causal role of the expression in question. But how could a property that is causally inert, like a quale, become an element in the range of the primary intension of an expression whose primary intension is determined by its causal role?

24. Note that in his discussion of reference, though he begins by worrying about what we say as well as about what we think, Chalmers formulates his reply in terms of concepts, not terms or expressions. Perhaps we have mental states that are connected to experiences in especially intimate ways, as I conceded above. This may be a matter of a special mental causation, or some other peculiarly mental relation. My point here is that appeal to such a special mental

relation between concept and content in the case of qualia can't explain how physical tokens, like utterances and inscriptions, get their contents.

25. See Rosenberg (1997), Strawson (forthcoming), and Lockwood (1989). An earlier version of the idea is Russell's "neutral monism" (see Russell 1927). Chalmers (1996) expresses interest in the view but stops short of explicitly endorsing it.

26. I say "plausible," but that doesn't mean necessarily "true." I don't want to take a stand on the question whether relational properties or dispositions can be basic. The position that they can't be, however, is certainly plausible.

27. Kim puts the matter in terms of supervenience rather than realization, but as noted in note 5, realization entails supervenience.

28. Notice I don't mean the token individual that instantiates the property; that is not the sense of token instance at issue. Rather, it's this redness or painfulness itself, not the diskette case or person that has it. The classic source for the theory of tropes is Williams (1953).

29. Advocates of this view are David Robb (1997) and Georges Rey (in conversation).

30. Of course these will be *ceteris paribus* laws, but that doesn't mean they aren't laws. For an interesting discussion of the nature of *ceteris paribus* laws, see Pietroski and Rey (1995).

31. I will not add the word "lawful" in what follows, but it should be understood. The point is that I am not a Humean about causation and laws; for me, as noted above, lawfulness is primitive.

32. I am indebted to Louise Antony for this argument, which appears in our joint paper, Antony and Levine (1997).

33. L. Antony (1998) presents an intriguing variation on the position presented here in which it is allowed that mental properties are identical with their correlated disjunctive properties, but it doesn't undermine the case for causal relevance.

34. For more on this topic, see L. Antony (1991), (1995), and (1998), Antony and Levine (1997), Block (1997), and Fodor (1997).

35. Two points: First, I may differ from Baker, in that I think even highly warranted upper-level generalizations may be defeated by new findings about the micro-level. Second, interestingly, at one point (at least) Baker seems to recognize the distinction between the metaphysics and epistemology of explanation, only to subsequently ignore it. Here is the crucial passage:

> In general, we should distinguish between having an adequate causal explanation and knowing the physical conditions that in fact obtain when the explanatory properties are instantiated. Knowing physical conditions for the instantiation of explanatory properties may be irrelevant to assessing the putative explanation . . . knowing the physics of television broadcast transmission may be irrelevant to understanding the influence of television on children who watch it . . . [though it] may be just what you need if you want to sabotage Saturday morning cartoons. . . . But we should not conclude that the adequacy of an intentional explanation depends on any particular relation between the intentional properties and physical properties. (1995, 136)

The first sentence nicely captures my point. In fact, I agree with everything Baker says here, so long as "adequate causal explanation" and "depends on any particular relation" are read epistemologically. The emphasis on "assessing" putative explanations indicates she intends an epistemological reading. But if by "having an adequate causal explanation" one means that the properties in the explanans are in fact causally relevant to the production of the explanandum, then it may just be that having an adequate causal explanation metaphysically depends on there being the right relation between the intentional properties and the physical properties.

36. For the purposes of this discussion I am ignoring my own qualms about the claim that qualia are physically realized. The obstacles to providing a realization theory for qualia are quite removed from the sorts of considerations on which Baker and Burge base their antagonism to materialism, or the naturalization project. My main disagreement with them is that, according to me, if, for whatever reason, we find ourselves unable to explain how a mental property could be physically realized, and yet believe it to be causally efficacious, that is a serious problem; they claim it isn't a problem.

37. I also owe this example to Louise Antony, and it too appears in our joint paper, Antony and Levine (1997).

Chapter 2

1. Smart doesn't endorse the argument but presents it as an objection to materialism. He does say, however, that it is the most troubling of the objections he considers in that article and the one he is least confident of having successfully deflected. He attributes the objection to Max Black. Also, Jackson no longer defends dualism, though he still defends the inference from conceivability to possibility that the conceivability argument is based on. See Braddon-Mitchell and Jackson (1996).

2. The material in this section is a reformulation of a similar attempt in Levine (1998a). In general, I have benefited from reading and speaking with David Chalmers and Stephen Yablo about these topics, and though they may not agree with the way I've set things up here, their influence is reflected.

3. Situations are fact-like entities, just without the connotation that they obtain. Situations that do obtain are facts.

4. That is, we will judge it to be metaphysically possible so long as we do not know that this very same situation is conceptually impossible relative to another representation, R'.

5. I do not mean necessarily that I must be aware of the logical form explicitly and make the judgment that it is contradictory. What I have in mind is that my conviction that the statement is necessarily false reflects my sensitivity to its logical form. The situation with modal intuitions is akin, I think, to the situation with grammatical intuitions. My competence with grammar, and consequent sensitivity to grammatical form, enables me to make various grammatical judgments without my being aware precisely how I do it.

On another issue, one might wonder which representational system's logical form determines my modal judgments. My inclination is to base *a priori* (when it's a matter of logical form at all) on the logical forms of mental representations, but nothing concerning my argument will depend on this. We can assume that the logical forms of natural language representations are what is at issue for those who eschew commitments to a language of thought.

6. What I'm calling here "brute" necessity and what Sidelle (1989) calls

"real" necessity amount to the same thing, I believe. What's more, our reasons for rejecting brute/real necessity are quite similar, though I've only recently come to appreciate this fact. Though I stand by my rejection of brute necessity, it isn't crucial to what follows that the reader agree with me about this. I am concerned to rebut the conceivability argument, and since rejecting brute necessity is a major concession to the argument's advocates, I am not begging any questions here.

7. I am indebted to John Carroll and Randy Carter for pressing this objection.

8. Sidelle (1989) defends keeping (1) and (2) at the expense of (3), though he puts it differently of course.

9. Or, as I prefer to think of it, relative to Z, the situation described by Z is conceptually possible. But I'll use the shorter formulation for the most part. Also, though I think the relevant representations for considerations of conceivability are mental representations, for ease of exposition I'll assume throughout this chapter that the terms and statements at issue are those of English.

10. The reader familiar with Chalmers's (1996) argument, to which I will turn below, may find this remark suspiciously similar to his attack on what he calls "strong metaphysical necessity." I will explicitly address the relation between my notion of brute metaphysical necessity and his notion of strong metaphysical necessity in section 2.6.

11. Unless, of course, one can already logically derive the higher-level description from the lower-level one, so one doesn't need a redescription at the higher-level to accomplish that. But we're working on the assumption that such a derivation is not possible when working with standard mental descriptions like "reddish experience."

12. Why couldn't it be a physical property after all, just not the one serving as the mode of presentation of "Br"? The problem is that whatever physical property you pick, the claim that the sensation has that property is going to be *a posteriori,* so the same challenge will apply all over again. The only way to block this slide would be to reject the conceivability premise, CP, which we've accepted now at least for the sake of argument.

13. Kripke doesn't use the term "conceptually possible" but rather "epistemically possible." For the purposes of the conceivability argument I think these come to the same thing. The point is that so long as I can't rule out a situation's possibility on conceptual grounds, it's going to seem possible to me, which is one way of saying that it's epistemically possible.

14. Yablo (1999) calls this model "textbook Kripkeanism" and criticizes it. I believe my own criticism of the model, to be developed below, is compatible with his, though I put the matter differently.

15. See also Jackson (1993). For a presentation of 2D semantics, see Davies and Humberstone (1980).

16. Of course one can reject this assumption, but this amounts to rejecting CP, and we've agreed to go along with it for now.

17. See Hill and McLaughlin (1999), Loar (1997), and Melnyk (forthcoming).

18. See Block and Stalnaker (1999), Byrne (1999), and Levine (1998a). I include myself as an NE-type, but I differ from the others in a crucial respect. This will become clear as we proceed.

19. However, in contrast to both other NE-types and E-types, I think that there is a significant difference between phenomenal concepts and ordinary concepts, but the difference is such as to strengthen the anti-materialist's case rather

than weaken it. That is, I think we have more reason to apply the DPM to the psycho-physical case than we do to the standard cases of *a posteriori* identities. Development of this aspect of my position must wait for later discussion, after I have introduced the idea of the explanatory gap. In this chapter, I will confine myself to the argument that the DPM is not in fact needed even for the standard cases.

20. I'm not saying that we have to interpret the statement itself as really meta-linguistic, so that it's equivalent to the statement " 'Marilyn' doesn't refer to the same person as 'Norma.' " The statement is clearly about the person, not the names. It's just that we can use the properties of being named by those names as the relevant modes of presentation.

21. Of course the ability to determine the referent given a context may be only ideal, and not in practice feasible. The question is whether in the limit of rational reflection the referent could be determined.

22. As per the discussion in section 2.2, the non-ascriptivist need not eschew all claims to *a priori* knowledge based on semantic constraints. For instance, while it may not be *a priori* that cats are animals, it may be *a priori* that if they are animals they couldn't cease to be animals and still exist. That is, that "animal" is a privileged sortal may be *a priori*. This still constitutes a significant difference from the ascriptivist. I will ignore this complication in what follows, except where relevant.

23. This model is best applied in the realm of mental representations and in conjunction with a language of thought model. However, I don't believe anything controversial about the LOT model need intrude here. Certainly advocates of the conceivability argument have in mind that our concepts are mental entities of some sort. Anyway, as I've already mentioned, I'll continue to speak both of mental representations and terms of natural language for ease of exposition, but it should be understood that it is mainly mental items to which these considerations apply.

24. See Dretske (1981) and Fodor (1990).

25. See Introduction, note 7.

26. This is akin to Putnam's (1975) notion of the class of "one-criterion" words.

27. Otherwise, one can't. But this seems right. If one really is an atomist about "bachelor," then it isn't *a priori* that no bachelor is married.

28. I don't mean to pin this particular example on the ascriptivist. The point is that some such judgment will be *a priori*.

29. One must imagine, of course, that the dummy term "REF" is replaced by a full-blown description of the reference relation, whatever external relation that turns out to be.

30. In particular, as discussed earlier, *de re* necessities like Aristotle's being a human being might involve this sort of brute necessity. I am inclined to think not, but I don't have a settled opinion on the matter. Again, see Sidelle (1989) for extensive discussion of this question.

31. This explains why, as Chalmers admits, many of those whom he characterized as believers in SMN (myself included) did not recognize themselves in the description. In his technical sense, yes, we do endorse SMN (though maybe we don't even endorse this, as argued above). However, we don't endorse *brute* metaphysical necessity, to which he assimilates SMN.

32. Remember, though, that I did present an argument above that even on

this level SMN may not exist. But my point here is that it's not a problem even if it does.

One might wonder why I don't just say that there is no such thing as primary intension, since it has no real semantic role to play. It elucidates neither epistemic nor metaphysical modalities. I have two replies. First, whether it plays a philosophically interesting role or not, it seems to me that you can't deny that the function exists; there is a function from terms, possible worlds, and the REF relation to extensions. Also, as per the discussion in 2.2, I do allow that there may be certain minimal *a priori* commitments associated with very basic notions like which sortals function to individuate objects. So there may be slightly more to primary intensions than my discussion here suggests. Again, what's crucial is that there is still no problem with admitting SMN.

33. One can find versions of this argument in Bealer (1987) and Sidelle (1989).

34. Chalmers has objected (in personal communication) that the case of animals is irrelevant, since their inability to make the relevant epistemic connections results from their cognitive limitations, and this has no bearing on whether or not those connections are *a priori*. I agree. I don't intend the example of animals, or children, or cognitively impaired human adults to demonstrate that some inference is not in fact *a priori*. My point is only that the ability to make certain *a priori* inferences is demonstrably not a necessary condition for concept possession if these subjects count as possessing concepts.

35. One final point on this argument. It might be thought that the comparison to syntax actually supports the other side. After all, what the linguist infers from the capacity to sort sentences into the grammatical and ungrammatical (or, better, acceptable and unacceptable) is the existence of an underlying competence that consists in a representation of the rules that determine these judgments. So it looks as if one does infer from the capacity to form such stable intuitive judgments to the existence of explicitly represented rules, at least unconsciously.

There are two replies to this objection. First, not everyone who takes linguistics seriously feels that the rules of grammar must be explicitly represented. There is a raging controversy over this, and the question is quite subtle one (see Stabler 1983). However, I don't want to rely on this reply since I am inclined toward the side that takes grammar to be explicitly represented.

So the more important point is this. If there is a good inference to an explicitly represented grammar that underlies grammaticality judgments, it isn't merely based on the existence of the capacity to make such judgments. It's a matter of inference to the best explanation. There is no analysis of what it is to have a grammatical capacity that entails the existence of an explicitly represented grammar. But the DPM advocate is arguing from an analysis of what it is to possess a concept to the claim that one must have *a priori* knowledge of how extension is determined by context. It is this inference that is being rejected. Whether implicit, or unconscious knowledge of the causal theory of reference is in fact the best explanation of our ability to render judgments in the Twin Earth case is an open question. But having that knowledge is not constitutive of having the concepts the causal theory is a theory of.

36. Note it doesn't help to argue as follows. But look, if confirmation theory is empirical, then certainly its truth must be metaphysically determined by all the physical facts (at least for the materialist). Well, suppose we've included all

the physical facts in the description of the scenario. The confirmation theory then is given. But this begs the very question at issue. The non-ascriptivist denies that from the fact that facts of type A metaphysically determine facts of type B it follows that we can derive a description of the B facts from a description of the A facts. So just knowing all the physical facts doesn't allow me to infer *a priori* what either the correct confirmation or correct reference theory is.

37. That is, I'm not imagining a situation where some paradigmatic sample of water is H_2O and much of the stuff in lakes and oceans is XYZ. While it's plausible that in such a case we would decide that there are two kinds of water, as we have decided that there are two kinds of jade, I can see how the case might be filled out in such a way that we wouldn't say that, but rather that only H_2O is water.

38. I've heard Block use this example in various presentations.

39. This of course presumes that explanations involve deductions, a claim I will defend in chapter 3.

40. See Papineau (1995), where a similar argument is made.

41. See note 15 for references to E-type responses. Let me enter a qualification here, though. It's not clear to me that the authors above (all of them, or any of them) really do subscribe to the DPM for most cases, and really do endorse the claim that ZH is conceptually impossible. But the main thrust of their argument is that something special is going on in the case of qualia.

42. For all these concepts, of course, there might be indexical elements added to the role descriptions, but that doesn't affect the argument.

Chapter 3

1. Described in Salmon (1989, 47). Salmon says that he is not aware that this example is published anywhere by Bromberger.

2. The term "explanatory gap" was introduced in Levine (1983), and developed further in Levine (1991) and (1993a).

3. Again, let me mention that Jackson no longer endorses anti-materialism. See Braddon-Mitchell and Jackson (1996).

4. The allusion here is to Block's (1980) example, in which the entire nation of China is enlisted to realize the functional description of a human being by passing notes to each other and the like.

5. Of course, if you already buy thesis M, or some form of supervenience, it won't make sense under that description. That is, you won't think it makes sense that something could instantiate the very same physical states as yourself and yet have no qualia, or very different qualia. (I leave issues arising from externalist theories aside for now.) But that's because you both accept thesis M and know that you have qualia. But suppose you had no idea what your physiology was like, and were given a detailed description of one just like yours, but without the crucial information that it was just like yours. It seems clear you wouldn't be able to determine merely from that description whether or not it had qualia, or of what types. At least, that is what accepting the conceivability premise entails.

6. Papineau (1995) argues along these lines.

7. Of course some would prefer to have "B" here refer to functional, as opposed to neurophysiological properties (an issue we will get to shortly). Nothing of substance here will turn on this.

8. A similar point can be found in Raffman (1995).

9. Unless, of course, one wants to invoke again the concept/property distinction for the properties involved in the two modes of presentation, maintaining that the two modes differ in the concepts they use to articulate the satisfaction conditions, but actually describe the same properties. This just pushes the question back to the identity claims involving those properties, so no real progress is made.

10. Sydney Shoemaker (1984), chapters 9 and 15, attempts to show how a functionalist theory could deal with this problem. I argue (1989) that his solution doesn't work.

11. See section 2.3 for the full argument.

12. I'm assuming this for simplicity. Of course one straightforward account of a gappy identity is that what we're seeking to explain is how the very same entity could share the distinct properties that are attributed to it through the distinct, ascriptive modes of presentation expressed by the terms flanking the identity sign. But our question is what to do when that move is unavailable, when we've come to the end of the line of appeals to properties ascribed in the mode of presentation.

Chapter 4

1. Or dispositional properties. I'm treating dispositional properties as if they were relational, since for the purposes at issue here we needn't distinguish between them. However, they aren't really the same thing. I thank Tim Crane for bringing this to my attention.

2. See Churchland (1985) and Flanagan (1992) for arguments along these lines. Though I don't claim to really understand what Searle's (1992) position is on this question, it seems to me that the arguments that follow also address his attempt to establish that there is no problem in identifying consciousness with a "higher-order" property of the brain.

3. Hardin (1988, 134–142) proposes (by way of a speculative example) that aspects of color experience like the "warm/cool" distinction might be useful in supplying the requisite structure. For my critique and Hardin's reply, see Levine (1991) and Hardin (1991).

4. For a presentation of the functionalist position, along with the objections that follow, see Block and Fodor (1972) and Block (1980).

5. M. Antony (1994) and Maudlin (1989) mount convincing arguments along these lines.

6. In a presentation at the Australian National University in July 1999, David Hilbert specifically addressed the question of what the color experience of dichromats is like, and argues that their blue would not be the same as ours, since, on his view, the similarity space within which a color experience is located is constitutive of its identity. I remain unconvinced.

7. Shoemaker proposes an interesting in-between theory on which the property of having some qualitative character or other is a functional property, but the particular type of qualitative character is determined by the identity of the physical realization. See Shoemaker (1984), chapters 9, 14, and 15, and (1996). For a critique of his position, see Levine (1989) and (1998).

8. Ned Block (1995) criticizes arguments of this sort. My objections here are

slightly different from his, though I'm sympathetic to his critique as well. I discuss the relation between our views in Levine (1995).

9. See Hilbert (1987) for a defense of this view and Hardin (1988) for objections to it. Even if this works, however, there are serious problems with the view that qualitative character is determined by the external property represented. I will explore these problems in section 4.5.

10. This is a very simplified version of the position Shoemaker outlines in (1996).

11. I will take up this issue in much greater detail in chapter 5, where I discuss eliminativism.

12. In fact, in Levine (1993b) I argue against recent attempts to revive the notion of analytic or conceptual truth.

13. Prominent advocates of HO are Armstrong (1981) and (1997), Lycan (1996), and Rosenthal (1986) and (1997).

14. Lycan defends IP, Rosenthal HOT.

15. This example is from Armstrong (1997).

16. Actually this is more of an objection to IP than HOT, given the plausibility of denying that any states within the visual processing system would count as thoughts.

17. Lycan (1996) seems to take a line like this.

18. This point is emphasized in Rey (1983), and explicitly addressed by Lycan (1996).

19. Notice that according to this reasoning there is no basis to deny qualitative character to the intensity gradient detector. Here too we have a state which can be classified by its location in a similarity space. Presumably Rosenthal doesn't find this consequence embarrassing, since any property can be the object of conscious awareness in principle.

20. Actually, a "representational externalist" position, to be discussed below, would serve his purposes as well. It's no accident that another HO advocate, Lycan, adopts representational externalism. However, as I will argue below, that position too suffers from what I see as insurmountable difficulties.

21. On the same page Rosenthal goes on to argue that we do often speak of pains that are felt "intermittently," which indicates that "common sense countenances the existence of nonconscious pains." However, I think either one of two things is going on when we say this: (1) we might have been feeling it all along, but because of distractions the pain is not at the focus of attention, and what's intermittent is its location at the focus of attention; or (2) we are using "pain" ambiguously to refer both to the feeling itself and to its physical cause, so what's intermittent is the feeling, though the cause is there all along. It might be, that is, that we individuate pains partly by reference to their causes.

22. See also Byrne (1997) for a similar objection.

23. Yet another option, pointed out to me by Georges Rey, is to remove the meta-representation from the scanning state altogether, letting it consist simply of the relevant perceptual representation's occupying a certain position in the scanner. While this move appears to answer the Neander objection, I don't consider it a version of HO, since that theory essentially involves meta-representation of some sort. One way to put it is this. Without any meta-representation, what makes the scanner a *scanner*, something with cognitive significance? Why isn't it enough to just shine a light on the relevant area of the brain? The answer

is obviously that occupying certain positions has functional significance, but then this really comes down to giving one of the non-HO functionalist answers to what makes a state conscious, which will be addressed below.

24. Interestingly, Rosenthal explicitly addresses the problem of misrepresentation. He says:

> Strictly speaking, having a HOT cannot of course result in a mental state's being conscious if that mental state does not even exist. . . . Still, a case in which one has a HOT along with the mental state it is about might well be *subjectively indistinguishable* from a case in which the HOT occurs but not the mental state. If so, then folk psychology would count both as cases of conscious states. (1997, 744, emphasis added)

But doesn't this give the game away? After all, if whether or not the object state is there makes no difference to the subjective experience, then conscious experience is not in the end a matter of a relation between two (non-conscious) states.

25. To the extent Dennett (1991) has a positive theory, this seems to be what it comes down to.

26. See Hardcastle (1995), where she identifies consciousness with the contents of the SE (or semantic episodic) memory system.

27. This is a very simplified description of a position defended by Van Gulick (1988).

28. Tye (1995) and Rey (1996) defend versions of these conditions.

29. Advocates of this view are Dretske (1995), Harman (1990), Lycan (1996), Rey (1996), Tye (1995), and White (1994).

30. Dretske, Harman, Lycan, and Tye are externalists. White is an internalist. Rey's position is a combination of internalism and eliminativism.

31. To avoid misunderstanding: the point isn't that my noticing or not is criterial for there being a change in my qualia. Rather, my not noticing a qualitative change, in the absence of evidence that the mechanisms by which such internal noticing takes place have been damaged (or the like), is overwhelming evidence that nothing has changed qualitatively.

32. This is also Tye's (1995) principal response to the objection.

33. To the extent I understand Lycan's (1996) argument for dubbing the internalist's notion of qualia "strange qualia," it bears a striking resemblance to this argument of Dretske's.

34. I presented a version of this argument in Levine (1997). I'm indebted to Louise Antony for coming up with the main idea behind it.

35. This repairs what I think is a defect in the version of the argument in Levine (1997), where I used red and green instead of red and special red. The essential point is the same.

36. See Burge (1988), and this is certainly how Dretske would handle it.

37. In fact, this is another way of putting Dretske's self-knowledge argument above.

38. Of course they must exhibit the proper format as well, but this too is multiply realizable.

39. Notice, as I pointed out in my discussion of HO, that if externalism can be made to work it at least partially supports the idea that non-conscious qualia exist. That is, if a state's being reddish is its representing red, then we can certainly see how such a state could exist non-consciously. On the other hand, one might go the other way as well. If reddishness is inherently experiential, then

externalist representationalism, by making room for the possibility of unconscious representations of red, is thereby rendered even more implausible.

An interesting position on this score is that of McGinn (1997). He argues that subjectivity is indeed mysterious, so that we really don't understand the kind of intentionality involved in conscious experience. That is, just how certain contents can be for a subject in the way conscious experience is, is a mystery. However, he thinks we can give a naturalistic account of what determines the identities of these subjective contents—what makes it reddish rather than greenish—and for this he proposes an externalist account. So the general idea is that qualia are what it's like for a mind to consciously perceive certain objective properties. We don't understand the relation of conscious perception, but we do understand what the objects of conscious perception are. I find the idea attractive, but it runs up against the anti-externalist arguments presented in section 4.5. Reddishness is not, according to these arguments, what you automatically get when consciously perceiving red, because it's possible to have greenish experiences when consciously perceiving red. Thus not only the relation of conscious perception but the contents as well elude naturalization.

40. Another problem, one mentioned in chapter 2, has to do with the ontological status of objective redness itself. It's quite controversial to treat it as an intrinsic property, or as an objective property at all, even a relational one. Tye (1995) explicitly recognizes that his view commits him to the objectivist side of the objectivist/subjectivist debate about color, and that this is a controversial thesis. For more on this debate about color, see Hilbert (1987), Hardin (1988), and Thompson, Palacios, and Varela (1992).

41. Perhaps there are ways to make sense of this, but it still doesn't seem the most plausible account.

42. Including Rey himself. See Rey (1993).

43. For extensive defense of this position, see Fodor (1983).

44. For my doubts about the first claim, see Levine (1993b).

45. The distinction between "analytic functionalism" and "psychofunctionalism" was pointed out in Block (1980), though he called the former "Functionalism" (using the upper case "F" to distinguish it from the generic doctrine, functionalism).

46. Though Rey holds that the relevant functional role is discovered empirically, given that it constitutes a kind of content it still is implicated in certain *a priori* inferences. This is an example of what he thinks of as a kind of empirical *a priori*; for more detail see Rey (1993).

47. One final comment on the alleged distinctive contribution of representationalism to a theory of qualia. Rey has argued in conversation that if we don't treat qualia as representational contents, then we don't really have an explanation of how "they can be anything to me." If they are just physiological features, or even processing features that play no role in determining content, then what really makes them part of the mind? How are they "taken up" by the mind?

I can see two ways to interpret this consideration. (As far as I can tell, Rey had both in mind.) On the first, the problem is to give a principle for determining which of the brain's states (either physiological or functional) are properly considered mental, since clearly not just any state of the brain is a mental state. On this view, if we follow Brentano's lead and make intentionality the "mark of the mental," then qualia will only pass muster as mental if they count as intentional. However, I don't find this consideration all that compelling. Clearly conscious experience is mental if anything is, and any criterion by which it is excluded is just arbitrary. Furthermore, even if we accept this reasoning, it's still the case that the claim that qualia are a kind of content is doing no genuine work in bridging the explanatory gap.

On the second reading, the problem is more directly relevant to the puzzle of consciousness itself. How are qualia supposed to be subjectively accessible in the way they are if they aren't themselves mental contents? On this view it is easier to understand how intentional contents can be "taken up" into the mind, be "for the subject," than states that are non-intentional in character. While I of course agree, as I've made clear, that our cognitive relation to qualia is at the core of the problem of consciousness, I don't see how making them intentional contents, whether narrow or wide, really helps. The problem is to understand how their substantive and determinate characters are "taken up," how they can be of cognitive significance in the way they are. How does it help our understanding of this mysterious relation if the object so "taken up" is itself an intentional content? What's interesting to see, however, is how every theory finds itself confronting this question one way or another, just what you'd expect from the core of the problem.

Chapter 5

1. The term "qualophile" comes from Dennett (1991).

2. Though some do deny it. Rey, in conversation, maintains that it's really the third-person point of view that drives his worries about consciousness. That is, though he believes that there is no principled metaphysical distinction between people and computers, he finds it impossible to see a person as a computer. I'm certainly acquainted with this form of the disease (i.e., qualophilia) but still feel that the principal form is the first-person version. I'm inclined to think that differences in one's responses to various proposals about consciousness might be predicted from a diagnosis of which form of qualophilia one has, but I won't pursue that here.

3. The example comes from an account of the Rosenberg spy case. According to one account, a means for verifying fellow spies was to tear a Jell-O box top in half, thereby creating a jagged edge with a random pattern that would be very difficult to copy. The only way of matching that pattern would be to have the other half.

4. I don't mean to take a stand here on the controversy over whether grammars are internally represented or not (see Stabler 1983). The point is only that if you believe in internally represented grammars, then this is how that belief is standardly justified.

5. For other arguments along these lines see Flanagan (1992) and Chalmers (1996).

6. My complaint against Dennett here bears a strong resemblance to my complaint against Dretske's objection to the internalist in section 4.5.

7. Actually, as we defined it in chapter 2, a zombie is a creature *physically*, not just functionally, identical to me, but without consciousness. However, to get the qualophobe's skeptical argument going functional identity is sufficient.

8. This way of looking at the skeptical argument was first put to me by Bob Hambourger in conversation years ago.

9. Actually at that point Dennett is responding to epiphenomenalism, which

is not at issue here. Still, my bet is that he would not object to citing the comparison in this context as well.

10. Nisbett and Wilson (1977) is the *locus classicus*.

11. I want to enter two caveats at this point. First, it's important to emphasize that I mean conceivability, or epistemological possibility here, and not metaphysical possibility. If our conscious experience is in fact realized in our brain, then it isn't possible to have such a brain (in good working order, of course) without conscious experience.

Second, even the epistemic possibility of someone physically like me being a zombie may be questionable. The point is that once I establish that I am conscious, that I have a brain, and that, on philosophical grounds like those adduced above, supervenience is true, then sufficient physical similarity to myself might rule out the conceivability of zombiehood in someone else. (See discussion on page 43, para. 3.) Of course, what would count as sufficient physical similarity, in the absence of an explanatory theory that determined the degree of similarity necessary? At any rate, I choose not to rely on this move to remove the skeptical doubt, since I don't think it addresses the crucial point at issue.

12. This is really more a point against the reductivist than against the eliminativist. Both of them employ skeptical arguments against the qualophile. I will return to this issue in the next section.

13. This is the alternative to treating qualia as either narrow or wide contents mentioned earlier. Notice that it shares with externalism the crucial feature of finding a place for the intuition that qualia are intrinsic. Where the externalist locates the intrinsic property in the external world, the eliminativist locates it in the realm of fantasy. With regard to Rey's position, it's really a combination of internalism and eliminativism.

14. Rey credits Eleanor Saunders, a clinical psychologist, with proposing this explanation.

15. Of course this is the classic Humean move. For instance, we find after repeated exposure to B-events following A-events that exposure to an A-event is accompanied by expectation of a B-event, and this tendency on our part is then projected onto the phenomena in the form of positing a genuine necessary connection between them.

16. See note 7, chapter 3.

Chapter 6

1. For the former see Chalmers (1996) and Kirk (1994), and for the latter see Balog (forthcoming).

2. Chalmers (1996) calls this the "fading qualia" argument. What's distinctive about Chalmers's version of the argument is that he endorses it as a way of demonstrating the nomological impossibility of functional-duplicate zombies, though not their metaphysical or conceptual impossibility. He believes that the basic laws that relate qualia to the physical world obtain at the level of functional organization, not physical realization. I criticize his use of this argument in Levine (1998b).

3. I don't have a source for the story, and, what's more, I've been told recently that it isn't true. Anyway, true or not, it makes a good analogy.

4. I have been assuming throughout this discussion that even on a causal account of content, sudden changes of etiology do not cause changes in content. I

realize one could doubt this assumption, but since holding onto it only makes my position more difficult, I don't think I need worry about begging any questions here.

5. Of course some, notably Searle (1992), do argue for just such a restriction. I do not find Searle's restriction of intentionality to conscious and "potentially conscious" states plausible, but for now it matters only that Chalmers, one of the principal advocates of the conceivability argument, doesn't himself take this way out.

6. If you're inclined to ask at this point, but then how does the anti-materialist know that she isn't really a zombie herself, go back to the discussion of first-person skepticism in chapter 5. The point is that the current argument is not about how we can tell we aren't zombies. Balog's argument is focused on the epistemic situation of a genuine zombie—which, according to the anti-materialist, is metaphysically possible. It's not about how we tell we aren't one.

7. Note, I'm not actually endorsing the claim that magic necessarily doesn't exist, though I think the case for this claim is strong. I'm just interested in how the case is made, for purposes of the analogy with qualitative character.

8. Shoemaker (1996) suggests this position for serious consideration, though he doesn't explicitly endorse it.

9. Barry Loewer has suggested this idea in conversation. I'm not sure that my elaboration of the idea properly captures what he had in mind. A similar idea, if I interpret him correctly, is in Leeds (1993).

References

Antony, L. (1991). "The Causal Relevance of the Mental: More on the Mattering of Minds." *Mind and Language* 6.4.

———. (1995). "Law and Order in Psychology." In *AI, Connectionism, and Philosophical Psychology.* Vol. 9 of *Philosophical Perspectives,* ed. James Tomberlin. Oxford: Blackwell.

———. (1998). "Multiple Realizability, Projectibility, and the Autonomy of the Mental." *Philosophical Topics* 26.1–2.

Antony, L., and Levine, J. (1997). "Reduction With Autonomy." In *Mind, Causation, and the World.* Vol. 11 of *Philosophical Perspectives*, ed. James Tomberlin. Oxford: Blackwell, 83–105.

Antony, M. (1994). "Against Functionalist Theories of Consciousness." *Mind and Language* 9: 105–123.

Armstrong, D.M. (1981). *The Nature of Mind.* Ithaca, N.Y.: Cornell University Press.

———. (1997). "What Is Consciousness?" In *The Nature of Consciousness: Philosophical Debates*, ed. N. Block, O. Flanagan, and G. Güzeldere. Cambridge: MIT Press, 721–728.

Baker, L.R. (1995). *Explaining Attitudes: A Practical Approach to the Mind.* Cambridge: Cambridge University Press.

Balog, K. (forthcoming). "Conceivability, Possibility, and the Mind-Body Problem." *The Philosophical Review.*

Bealer, G. (1987). "The Philosophical Limits of Scientific Essentialism." In *Metaphysics.* Vol. 1 of *Philosophical Perspectives,* ed. James Tomberlin. Atascadero, Calif.: Ridgeview Publishing, 289–365.

Block, N. (1980). "Troubles with Functionalism." In *Readings in Philosophy of Psychology*, vol. 1, ed. N. Block. Cambridge: Harvard University Press, 268–305.

———. (1990). "Inverted Earth." In *Action Theory and Philosophy of Mind.* Vol. 4 of *Philosophical Perspectives,* ed. James Tomberlin. Atascadero, Calif.: Ridgeview Publishing, 53–80.

———. (1995). "On a Confusion About a Function of Consciousness." *Behavioral and Brain Sciences* 18.2.

———. (1997). "Anti-Reductionism Slaps Back." In *Mind, Causation, and the World.* Vol. 11 of *Philosophical Perspectives,* ed. James Tomberlin. Oxford: Blackwell, 107–132.

Block, N., and Fodor, J.A. (1972). "What Psychological States Are Not." *The Philosophical Review* 81: 159–181.

Block, N., and Stalnaker, R. (1999). "Conceptual Analysis, Dualism, and the Explanatory Gap." *The Philosophical Review* 108.1: 1–46.

Boghossian, P. (1989). "Content and Self-Knowledge." *Philosophical Topics* 17.1.

Braddon-Mitchell, D., and Jackson, F. (1996). *The Philosophy of Mind and Cognition.* Oxford: Blackwell.

Brentano, F. (1973). *Psychology From an Empirical Standpoint,* trans. A.C. Rancurello, D.B. Terrell, and L.L. McAlister. London: Routledge & Kegan Paul.

Burge, T. (1988). "Individualism and Self-Knowledge." *Journal of Philosophy* 85.

———. (1993). "Mind-Body Causation and Explanatory Practice." In *Mental Causation,* ed. J. Heil and A. Mele. Oxford: Oxford University Press.

Byrne, A. (1997). "Some Like It HOT." *Philosophical Studies* 86: 103–129.

———. (1999). "Cosmic Hermeneutics." In *Epistemology, 1999.* Vol. 13 of *Philosophical Perspectives,* ed. James Tomberlin. Oxford: Blackwell, 347–384.

Carroll, J. (1994). *Laws of Nature.* Cambridge: Cambridge University Press.

Chalmers, D. (1996). *The Conscious Mind.* Oxford: Oxford University Press.

———. (1999). "Materialism and the Metaphysics of Modality." *Philosophy and Phenomenological Research* 59.2: 473–496.

Chomsky, N. (1988). *Language and Problems of Knowledge.* Cambridge: MIT Press.

Churchland, P. (1985). "Reduction, Qualia, and the Direct Introspection of Brain States." *Journal of Philosophy* 82: 8–28.

Clark, A. (1993). *Sensory Qualities.* Oxford: Oxford University Press.

Crane, T., and Mellor, H. (1990). "There Is No Question of Physicalism." *Mind* 90: 185–206.

Crick, F., and Koch, C. (1990). "Towards a Neurobiological Theory of Consciousness." *Seminars in the Neurosciences* 2: 263–275.

Cummins, R. (1983). *The Nature of Psychological Explanation.* Cambridge: Bradford Books/MIT Press.

Davies, M., and Humberstone, I. (1980). "Two Notions of Necessity." *Philosophical Studies* 38: 1–30.

Dennett, D.C. (1978). "Where Am I?" In *Brainstorms.* Cambridge: Bradford Books/MIT Press.

———. (1991). *Consciousness Explained.* Boston: Little, Brown.

Dennett, D.C., and Kinsbourne, M. (1992). "Time and the Observer." *Behavioral and Brain Sciences* 15: 183–247.

Dretske, F. (1981). *Knowledge and the Flow of Information.* Cambridge: Bradford Books/MIT Press.

———. (1995). *Naturalizing the Mind.* Cambridge: Bradford Books/MIT Press.

Feinberg, G. (1966). "Physics and the Thales Problem." *Journal of Philosophy* 63: 5–17.

Flanagan, O. (1992). *Consciousness Reconsidered.* Cambridge: Bradford Books/MIT Press.

Fodor, J.A. (1974). "Special Sciences." *Synthese* 28: 97–115.

———. (1983). *The Modularity of Mind.* Cambridge: Bradford Books/MIT Press.

———. (1987). "Frames, Fridgeons, Sleeping Dogs and the Music of the Spheres." In *The Robot's Dilemma: the Frame Problem in Artificial Intelligence,* ed. Z. Pylyshyn. Norwood, N.J.: Ablex.

———. (1990). *A Theory of Content and Other Essays.* Cambridge: Bradford Books/MIT Press.

————. (1997). "Special Sciences: Still Autonomous After All These Years." In *Mind, Causation, and the World*. Vol. 11 of *Philosophical Perspectives*, ed. James Tomberlin. Oxford: Blackwell, 149–164.

Fodor, J., and Lepore, E. (1992). *Holism: A Shopper's Guide*. Oxford: Blackwell.

————, eds. (1993). *Holism: A Consumer Update*. Special issue of *Grazer Philosophische Studien* 46.

Friedman, M. (1974). "Explanation and Scientific Understanding." *Journal of Philosophy* 71: 5–19.

Hardcastle, V. (1995). *Locating Consciousness*. Amsterdam: John Benjamins Publishing.

Hardin, C.L. (1988). *Color for Philosophers: Unweaving the Rainbow*. Indianapolis: Hackett Publishing.

————. (1991). "Reply to Levine." *Philosophical Psychology* 4.1: 41–50.

Harman, G. (1990). "The Intrinsic Quality of Experience." In *Action Theory and Philosophy of Mind*. Vol. 4 of *Philosophical Perspectives*, ed. James Tomberlin. Atascadero, Calif.: Ridgeview Publishing, 31–52.

Hempel, C.G. (1965). *Aspects of Scientific Explanation*. New York: Free Press.

————. (1980). "Comments on Goodman's *Ways of Worldmaking*." *Synthese* 45: 193–199.

Hilbert, D.R. (1987). *Color and Color Perception: A Study in Anthropocentric Realism*. Stanford University: Center for the Study of Language and Information.

Hill, C.S. (1991). *Sensations: A Defense of Type Materialism*. Cambridge: Cambridge University Press.

Hill, C.S., and McLaughlin, B.P. (1999). "There Are Fewer Things in Reality Than Are Dreamt of in Chalmers's Philosophy." *Philosophy and Phenomenological Research* 59: 445–454.

Jackson, F. (1982). "Epiphenomenal Qualia." *Philosophical Quarterly* 32: 127–136.

————. (1993). "Armchair Metaphysics." In *Philosophy In Mind*, ed. J. O'Leary-Hawthorne and M. Michael. Dordrecht: Kluwer.

Kaplan, D. (1979). "DTHAT." In *Contemporary Perspectives in the Philosophy of Language*, ed. P. French, T. Uehling Jr., and H. Wettstein. Minneapolis: University of Minnesota Press.

Kim, J. (1993). "Non-Reductivism and Mental Causation." In *Mental Causation*, ed. J. Heil and A. Mele. Oxford: Clarendon Press.

————. (1998). *Mind in a Physical World: An Essay on the Mind-Body Problem and Mental Causation*. Cambridge: MIT Press.

Kirk, R. (1994). *Raw Feeling*. Oxford: Oxford University Press.

Kitcher, P. (1989). "Explanatory Unification and the Causal Structure of the World." In *Minnesota Studies in the Philosophy of Science, XIII: Scientific Explanation*, ed. P. Kitcher and W.C. Salmon. Minneapolis: University of Minnesota Press.

Kripke, S. (1980). *Naming and Necessity*. Cambridge: Harvard University Press.

Leeds, S. (1993). "Qualia, Awareness, and Sellars." *Nous* 27: 303–330.

Levine, J. (1983). "Materialism and Qualia: The Explanatory Gap." *Pacific Philosophical Quarterly* 64: 354–361.

————. (1989). "Absent and Inverted Qualia Revisited." *Mind and Language* 3.4: 271–287.

————. (1991). "Cool Red." *Philosophical Psychology* 4.1: 27–40.

————. (1993a). "On Leaving Out What It's Like." In *Consciousness: Psychological and Philosophical Essays*, ed. M. Davies and G. Humphreys. Oxford: Blackwell, 121–136.

————. (1993b). "Intentional Chemistry." In *Holism: A Consumer Update*, ed. J. Fodor and E. Lepore. Special issue of *Grazer Philosophische Studien* 46: 103–134.

————. (1994). "Out of the Closet: A Qualophile Confronts Qualophobia." *Philosophical Topics* 22.1–2: 107–126.

————. (1995). "Phenomenal Access: A Moving Target." *Behavioral and Brain Sciences* 18.2.

————. (1997). "Are Qualia Just Representations? A Critical Notice of Michael Tye's *Ten Problems of Consciousness*." *Mind and Language* 12.1: 101–113.

————. (1998a). "Conceivability and the Metaphysics of Mind." *Nous* 32: 449–480.

————. (1998b). Review of David Chalmers, *The Conscious Mind*. *Mind* 107.

————. (1998). "Philosophy as Massage: Seeking Cognitive Relief for Conscious Tension." *Philosophical Topics* 26.1–2: 159–178.

Lewis, D. (1983). "New Work for a Theory of Universals." *Australasian Journal of Philosophy* 61: 343–377.

Loar, B. (1997). "Phenomenal States." In *The Nature of Consciousness: Philosophical Debates*, ed. N. Block, O. Flanagan, and G. Güzeldere. Cambridge: MIT Press.

Lockwood, M. (1989). *Mind, Brain, and the Quantum*. Oxford: Blackwell.

Lycan, W.G. (1996). *Consciousness and Experience*. Cambridge: Bradford Books/MIT Press.

————. (1997). "Consciousness as Internal Monitoring." In *The Nature of Consciousness: Philosophical Debates*, ed. N. Block, O. Flanagan, and G. Güzeldere. Cambridge: MIT Press.

Maudlin, T. (1989). "Computation and Consciousness." *Journal of Philosophy* 86.8.

McGinn, C. (1991). *The Problem of Consciousness*. Oxford: Blackwell.

————. (1997). "Consciousness and Content." In *The Nature of Consciousness: Philosophical Debates*, ed. N. Block, O. Flanagan, and G. Güzeldere. Cambridge: MIT Press, 295–307.

Melnyk, A. (1997). "How to Keep the 'Physical' in Physicalism." *Journal of Philosophy* 94.12: 622–637.

————. (forthcoming). "Physicalism Unfalsified: Chalmers's Inconclusive Conceivability Argument." In *Physicalism and Its Discontents*, ed. C. Gillet and B. Loewer. Cambridge: Cambridge University Press.

Millikan, R. (1984). *Language, Thought, and Other Biological Categories*. Cambridge: Bradford Books/MIT Press.

Montero, B. (1999). "The Body Problem." *Nous* 33: 183–200.

Nagel, T. (1974). "What Is It Like to Be a Bat?" *The Philosophical Review* 82: 435–450.

Neander, K. (1998). "The Division of Phenomenal Labor: A Problem for Representational Theories of Consciousness." In *Language, Mind, and Ontology*. Vol. 12 of *Philosophical Perspectives*, ed. James Tomberlin. Oxford: Blackwell, 411–434.

Nisbett, R.E., and Wilson, T.D. (1977). "Telling More Than We Can Know: Verbal Reports on Mental Processes." *Psychological Review* 84: 231–259.

Papineau, D. (1995). "The Anti-pathetic Fallacy and the Boundaries of Consciousness." In *Conscious Experience*, ed. T. Metzinger. Paderborn: Ferdinand Schöningh/Imprint Academic.

Parfit, D. (1984). *Reasons and Persons*. Oxford: Oxford University Press.

Perry, J. (1979). "The Problem of the Essential Indexical." *Nous* 13: 3–21.

Pietroski, P., and Rey, G. (1995). "When Other Things Aren't Equal: Saving *Ceteris Paribus* Laws from Vacuity." *British Journal for the Philosophy of Science* 46: 81–110.

Poland, J. (1994). *Physicalism: The Philosophical Foundations*. Oxford: Clarendon Press.

———. (forthcoming). "Chomsky's Challenge to Physicalism." In *Chomsky and His Critics,* ed. L. Antony and N. Hornstein. Oxford: Blackwell.

Putnam, H. (1975). "The Analytic and the Synthetic." In *Mind, Language, and Reality: Philosophical Papers, Vol. II*. Cambridge: Cambridge University Press.

———. (1991). "The Nature of Mental States." In *The Nature of Mind*, ed. D.M. Rosenthal. New York: Oxford University Press.

Raffman, D. (1995). "On the Persistence of Phenomenology." In *Conscious Experience*, ed. T. Metzinger. Paderborn: Ferdinand Schöningh/Imprint Academic.

Railton, P. (1981). "Probability, Explanation, and Information." *Synthese* 48: 201–223.

Rey, G. (1983). "A Reason for Doubting the Existence of Consciousness." In *Consciousness and Self-Regulation, Vol. 3*, ed. R. Davidson, G.E. Schwartz, and D. Shapiro. New York: Plenum Press.

———. (1993). "The Unavailability of What We Mean I: A Reply to Quine." In *Holism: A Consumer Update*, ed. J. Fodor and E. Lepore. Special issue of *Grazer Philosophische Studien* 46: 61–110.

———. (1995). "Toward a Projectivist Account of Conscious Experience." In *Conscious Experience,* ed. T. Metzinger. Paderborn: Ferdinand Schöningh/ Imprint Academic.

———. (1997). *Contemporary Philosophy of Mind: A Contentiously Classical Approach*. Oxford: Blackwell.

———. (1998). "A Narrow Representationalist Account of Qualitative Experience." In *Language, Mind, and Ontology*. Vol. 12 of *Philosophical Perspectives,* ed. James Tomberlin. Oxford: Blackwell, 435–457.

Robb, D. (1997). "The Properties of Mental Causation." *Philosophical Quarterly* 47: 178–194.

Rosenberg, G. (1997). *A Place for Consciousness: Probing the Deep Structure of the Natural World.* Ph.D. dissertation, University of Georgia.

Rosenthal, D. (1986). "Two Concepts of Consciousness." *Philosophical Studies* 49: 329–359.

———. (1997). "A Theory of Consciousness." In *The Nature of Consciousness: Philosophical Debates*, ed. N. Block, O. Flanagan, and G. Güzeldere. Cambridge: MIT Press, 729–753.

Russell, B. (1927). *The Analysis of Matter.* London: Kegan Paul.

———. (1959). *The Problems of Philosophy.* Oxford: Oxford University Press.

Ryle, G. (1949). *The Concept of Mind.* London: Hutchinson.

Salmon, W.C. (1989). "Four Decades of Scientific Explanation." In *Minnesota Studies in the Philosophy of Science, XIII: Scientific Explanation*, ed. P. Kitcher and W.C. Salmon. Minneapolis: University of Minnesota Press.

Searle, J. (1992). *The Rediscovery of the Mind.* Cambridge: Bradford Books/MIT Press.

———. (1997). "Breaking the Hold: Silicon Brains, Conscious Robots, and Other Minds." In *The Nature of Consciousness,* ed. N. Block, O. Flanagan, and G. Güzeldere. Cambridge: MIT Press, 493–502.

Shoemaker, S. (1981). "Some Varieties of Functionalism." *Philosophical Topics* 12.1: 83–118.

———. (1984). *Identity, Cause, and Mind.* Cambridge: Cambridge University Press.

———. (1996). *The First-Person Perspective and Other Essays.* Cambridge and New York: Cambridge University Press.

Sidelle, A. (1989). *Necessity, Essence, and Individuation: A Defense of Conventionalism.* Ithaca, N.Y.: Cornell University Press.

Smart, J.J.C. (1959). "Sensations and Brain Processes." *The Philosophical Review* 68: 141–156.

———. (1978). "The Content of Physicalism." *Philosophical Quarterly* 28: 339–341.

Stabler, E.P. (1983). "How Are Grammars Represented?" *Behavioral and Brain Sciences* 6: 391–421.

Strawson, G. (forthcoming). "Realistic Monism." In *Chomsky and His Critics,* ed. L. Antony and N. Hornstein. Oxford: Blackwell.

Thompson, E., Palacios, A. and Varela, F.J. (1992). "Ways of Coloring." *Behavioral and Brain Sciences* 15.1: 1–26.

Tye, M. (1995). *Ten Problems of Consciousness: A Representational Theory of the Phenomenal Mind.* Cambridge: Bradford Books/MIT Press.

Van Gulick, R. (1988). "A Functionalist Plea for Self-Consciousness." *The Philosophical Review* 97: 149–188.

———. (1993). "Understanding the Phenomenal Mind: Are We All Just Armadillos?" In *Consciousness: Psychological and Philosophical Essays*, ed. M. Davies and G. Humphreys. Oxford: Blackwell, 138–154.

White, S. (1994). "Notional Content." *Philosophical Topics* 22.1–2: 471–504.

Williams, D. (1953). "On the Elements of Being." *Review of Metaphysics* 7: 3–18.

Yablo, S. (1990). "The Real Distinction between Mind and Body." *Canadian Journal of Philosophy: Supplementary Volume* 16: 149–201.

———. (1999). "Concepts and Consciousness." *Philosophy and Phenomenological Research* 59: 455–463.

Index